Box 353550
Seattle, Washington 98195-3550

ELECTRONIC
STYLES

ELECTRONIC STYLES

A Handbook for Citing Electronic Information

Second Edition

XIA LI

and

NANCY B. CRANE

Information Today, Inc.
Medford, N.J.
1996

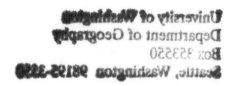
Copyright©1996 by: Information Today, Inc.
                                       143 Old Marlton Pike
                                       Medford, NJ 08055

Printed in the United States of America.

Li, Xia, 1964–
    Electronic styles : a handbook for citing electronic information /
  by Xia Li and Nancy B. Crane.
        p.   cm.
    Rev. ed. of Electronic style. c1993.
    Includes bibliographical references.
    ISBN 1-57387-027-7 (pbk.)
    1. Citation of electronic information sources. I. Crane, Nancy.
II. Li, Xia, 1964– Electronic style. III. Title.
PN171.F56L5   1996
808'. 027—dc20   96-25799
                                                           CIP

Price: $19.99
Book Editor: Diane Zelley
Cover Design: Bette Tumasz

Contents

Chapter Five. U. S. Government Documents, Legal Sources, and International Documents

PART TWO: MLA EMBELLISHED STYLE

Chapter Eleven. Discussion Lists, USENET Newsgroups, and Personal Mail

Chapter Thirteen. Other Sources   181

Chapter Fourteen. Parenthetical Documentation, Endnotes, and Footnotes

Preface

This much revised version of the 1993 edition of *Electronic Style: A Guide to Citing Electronic Information* has been undertaken sooner than we ever intended, due in large part to the explosive growth of resources available electronically. Most significant in this burgeoning area has been the introduction of the World Wide Web (WWW), Web or homepages, and "Web browsers" such as Lynx, Mosaic, and Netscape, which make the vast resources on the WWW easily accessible to large numbers of people.

The publication of the 1993 edition of *Electronic Style* preceded public notice of the WWW by just a few months. As a result, it lacks citation patterns showing how to manage Uniform Resource Locators (URLs) which are much in use at this time. While principles presented in the 1993 edition can be applied to the citation of these materials, colleagues and users of the book have entreated us to move forward with this revised work and to address the issue of how to manage these newer resources.

At the time the 1993 work was being planned and drafted (1992 and early 1993), there was no standard established for citation of electronic sources. There was a work by Karen Patrias, published by the National Library of Medicine in 1991, which gave guidance in these matters. That guide did not address citation patterns for some of the electronic resources in common use in late 1992 and early 1993 which are retrieved by following FTP, Telnet, and Gopher protocols. In addition, the guide was aimed at medical professionals, a different audience than we had in mind for our work. At that time, too, the major standards setting agency, the International Organization for Standardization, was in the very early stages of preparing standards for bibliographic citation of electronic sources.[1] Style manuals in wide use at that time, the *Publication Manual of the American Psychological Association* (3rd ed., 1983), *MLA Handbook for Writers of Research Papers* (3rd ed., 1988), *The Chicago Manual of Style* (Chicago, 13th ed., 1982), and Turabian's *A Manual for Writers of Term Papers, Theses, and Dissertations* (1987) did not address the issue of citing electronic resources.

The lack of an all-purpose guide in these matters convinced us to move forward with the project. It was decided early in the process of preparing the 1993 edition that we would select a standard citation form already in wide use and adapt it to include the elements that are needed to describe electronic sources. As we said in the Preface of that work:

> [T]he citation style recommended by the American Psychological Association (APA) was chosen because: (1) the style is used widely; (2) the date, often of paramount importance in electronic sources, is given as the second element in a citation; and (3) there is great wisdom in the simple method of in-text references recommended in the APA style (Li & Crane, 1993, p. x).

The earlier work, providing examples in the APA style, was well-received by many. However, individuals committed to MLA style have apparently not found it as easy as we had hoped to adapt the principles found in *Electronic Style* for use with the MLA style of presentation. We have had repeated requests for a parallel version of *Electronic Style* for MLA users. This new work addresses this plea by presenting citations using both of these widely used styles—APA and MLA. However, in the meantime, the new editions of the *Publication Manual* (1994) and *MLA Handbook* (1995) give examples of how to manage citation of electronic materials on pp. 218–222 and pp. 151–167, respectively. *Electronic Styles* takes into account the guidance these sources provide but greatly expands on the numbers of examples and the types of resources portrayed. We are at variance, at times, with approaches that these above-mentioned works recommend. Therefore, the styles presented here are slightly modified when it is necessary. Such modifications are detailed in Chapters One and Eight. These introductory chapters to the APA and MLA parts of the book lay out the principles for citing material in the respective styles, as well as elaborating what is new in *Electronic Styles*.

This book has been arranged so that there are two distinct parts devoted to the two different styles. The numbering systems correspond exactly, however, so that it is easy to compare a reference from one style to that of the other. For example, the reference numbered <A100> refers to the same material that <M100> does; the first presents APA style of citation, the second presents MLA style.[2] The individual works listed in each section are not lifted wholesale from the earlier edition. Most of the citations (more than 95%) are new material, and virtually all, except several of the electronic mail (E-mail) messages, were accessed in mid-1995.

We must repeat the disclaimer stated in the 1993 edition. *Electronic Styles* is

> . . . a guide to the citation of electronic sources, and only that. It does not supply information on the mechanics of using an electronic mail system, retrieving a document from a remote site over the Internet, or searching a particular online system. Once retrieved from such a source,

however, this work provides guidance in properly citing the information (Li & Crane, 1993, p. ix).

The intended audiences of *Electronic Styles*, as with the previous edition, are still librarians, scholars, and students. In time, we expect other groups to take notice—individuals whose stock-in-trade includes communicating using electronic media or who rely on information retrieved electronically.

Collecting information for this new guide has made the efforts expended in the earlier one pale by comparison. We have been much aided, however, by the easy access to the Internet afforded by the University of Vermont's Sage system, an information gateway to a wide array of locally networked and remote sources of electronic information. Sage was developed through the collaborative efforts of the University's Bailey/Howe Reference Department and Systems Office and by the work of two individuals in particular, Lyman Ross and Paul Philbin. Access to the WWW has been expedited by the University's Office of Computing and Information Technology, and for this, too, we are most appreciative. WWW resources have certainly energized our work as reference librarians and have greatly expanded the paths to information for our users.

There have been numbers of colleagues and friends who have aided our work on *Electronic Styles*. Special thanks are in order for colleagues William L. Dunlop, fellow librarian, and Robert S. Griffin, professor of education, for encouragement, editorial assistance, and advice throughout the preparation of this edition. Other colleagues in Bailey/Howe Library have been greatly supportive, including Jake Barickman, Linda Brew, Milton Crouch, Martha Day, Laurie Kutner, Birdie MacLennan, Patricia Mardeusz, Janet Reit, Lynn Richardson, Craig Robertson, Wichada Sukantarat, and the Dean of the University of Vermont's Libraries, Rebecca Martin.

Others at the University of Vermont have played key roles as we formulated the plan for this book. They are Wolfgang Mieder, professor of German; Neil R. Stout, professor of history; and Paul Eshholtz, professor of English. Discussions with them encouraged us to proceed with a section presenting MLA embellished style.

We have learned from our colleagues at several conferences where we were invited to speak about citing electronic sources. Our special thanks go to librarians and educators at the Fall 1994 Conference of the Vermont Council of Teachers of English, Vermont Council on Reading, and Vermont Educational Media Association; the 1995 Computers in Libraries (CIL) Conference; and a SUNY OCLC Mini-Conference held in New York City in April 1995. The questions posed and encouragement given by attendees at these meetings did much to hasten the preparation of this work.

We have benefited greatly from conversations held electronically—with Tom Boe at Learning in Motion in Santa Cruz, California, and Terry Passaro, librarian at the Encyclopedia Britannica in Chicago, who helped advance our thinking on management of references from the WWW; and with Jane Thacker at the National Library of Canada, and Secretary of ISO/TC46/SC9, who apprised us of the work of the group charged with drafting standards for electronic documents by the International Organization for Standardization. Finally, we have listened in on conversations on LISTSERVs (e.g., PACS-L and ETEXTCTR), which assisted us as we collected and formulated citations for this book. Participants on these lists are very much our partners in this work and to them we also extend our appreciation.

Xia Li and Nancy B. Crane
University of Vermont
June 1996

NOTES

1. At the writing of this Preface, a draft edition of the standards (*International Organization for Standardization. Technical Committee 46. Subcommittee 9. ISO/DIS 690-2: Information and Documentation—Bibliographic References—Electronic Documents or Parts Thereof*) has just been released. This new book, *Electronic Styles*, addresses many of the issues raised in the draft standards.

2. We have also presented a small number of examples using the legal citation methods set forth in *The Bluebook: A Uniform System of Citation* (15th ed., 1991) in Chapters Five and Twelve, because both APA and MLA recommend using this approach when citing legal materials.

Part One

APA Embellished Style

CHAPTER ONE

Organization and Use of APA Embellished Style

Chapters Two through Seven of this handbook follow the principles contained in the *Publication Manual of the American Psychological Association* (4th ed., 1994), with some modification in order to better cite electronic as opposed to print sources. These chapters provide two basic forms for each type of information being cited. What distinguishes the two forms is that in the first the author is known and in the second the author is not. Both forms recommend the elements to be included and their order. Explanatory notes follow each pair. Sample citations based on existing electronic sources are then provided. While this guide applies to extant sources, these basic forms can be readily adapted to materials yet to be devised.

The primary objective in making reference to any item, whether in print or electronic format, is to give information sufficient to locating it and no more than that. The elements necessary to do this vary somewhat between these two formats. Although Chapters Two through Seven adhere closely to the APA style of citation, they present new elements unique to the management of electronic information—for example, type of medium, "available" statement, and access date—while discarding some usually found in descriptions of print sources, such as place of publication and publisher. Those in need of a review of the APA style will want to refer to the Reference List in the *Publication Manual of the American Psychological Association* (1994, pp. 174–234).

In the 4th edition of the *Publication Manual*, APA adds a section on citing electronic media (1994, pp. 218–222) and adopts many of the conventions used in the 1993 edition of *Electronic Style*. The following list summarizes the key features of elements in the order in which they typically appear in the citations of electronic sources. Unless otherwise indicated, these are the elements and features proposed by APA and recommended in the 1993 edition of *Electronic Style*. In this handbook, there are several revised and new elements.

3

AUTHOR(S)

Author is the first element of a citation. When an author is not available, the title becomes the first.

- **Personal Author(s)**

  Give the last name first, followed, if available, by the first initials of the first and middle names. When there are several authors, list them in the order given in the source, inverted as above, with the last author's name preceded by an ampersand (&). For example: Bowers, K. L., LaQuey, T., Reynolds, J., Roubicek, K., Stahl, M., & Yuan, A.

- **Corporate Author(s)**

  Spell out the corporate name or names in full, and use it or them as the first element of a citation.

- **Editor(s)**

  When citing an edited work, treat the editor or editors in the same manner as an author, with the abbreviation "Ed." or "Eds." in parentheses after the last editor's name.

DATE

This work, *Electronic Styles*, generally recommends citing the date when the electronic form of a publication was created. The date is the second element and enclosed in parentheses.

- **Books, Journals, and Audiovisual Materials**

  Only the year of publication is needed, unless volume and issue information are missing. Then it is useful to include the month of publication.

- **Magazine, Newsletter, or Newspaper Articles**

  Give the year, month, and day if they are available.

- **Entire Databases, Services, and Sites**

  This edition adds several new sections on citing entire databases, services, and sites—for example, a WWW homepage or an FTP site. Sites are treated as nonserial in nature, so provide the date when the site was last updated.

- **No Date**

  If there is no information on when the electronic version of a work was created, write "No date," or "n.d."

TITLE(S)

The title follows the date when an author or editor is available. If an author or editor is not associated with the reference, or is unavailable, the title becomes the first element of a citation.

- **Book Title(s)**

  The first words of a book title and its subtitle are capitalized, as are proper nouns. All other words begin with lowercase letters. Titles are given in italics or underlined, followed immediately by the edition information, if available, enclosed in parentheses.

- **Article or Chapter Title(s)**

  When an article or chapter is cited, the first word of the article or chapter title is capitalized, as is the first word of its subtitle. The rest of the words are not capitalized unless they are proper nouns.

- **Annual, Journal, Magazine, Newsletter, and Newspaper Title(s)**

  Capitalize all words in a title other than articles, prepositions, and conjunctions. Titles are given in italics or underlined.

- **Entire Service(s), Database(s), and Site(s)**

  Treat these titles in the same manner as book titles. Information about a database or software version is enclosed in parentheses and follows immediately after the title.

TYPE OF MEDIUM

The 1993 edition of *Electronic Style* introduced type of medium as an element, placed directly after the publication title and enclosed in brackets. Publication titles are complete sources—e.g., *Public Access Computer List Review* [Online]—in contrast to article or chapter titles. The common types of medium statement until now have been online, CD-ROM, E-mail, and diskette. However, with more and more databases mounted on the Local Area Networks, it has become difficult for end users to detect the type of database they are searching. This handbook introduces "electronic" as a generic medium to distinguish the cited electronic references from print ones.

VOLUME AND PAGING

Provide volume numbers when citing articles from journals, magazines, and newsletters. The volume is either in italics or underlined. Whenever possible, give a page range after the volume information. If this inclusive paging information is lacking, apply the following rules:

1. When the initial page is known, (a) in parentheses, indicate the article length after the initial page, e.g., 10(12 pp.), 10(80 paragraphs), 10(24 screens), 10(300 lines), or 10(3,000 words); or (b) use the notation "ff" for "and following pages."

2. When the initial page is not available, indicate the article length (the number of paragraphs, screens, lines, or words). No parentheses are needed.

PUBLICATION INFORMATION

Since the 1993 edition of *Electronic Style*, publication information has generally been replaced by an optional element—producer—the entity which contributes to the content of the database. This information is useful when evaluating commercial and CD-ROM databases and should be given before the "available" statement. Since producer information is usually embedded in an Internet address of a service as part of the domain statement, it is not necessary to repeat it when citing sources retrieved on the Internet.

AVAILABLE

An "available" statement was introduced in *Electronic Style* in 1993. It replaces place of publication and publisher. This handbook eliminates the generic terms contained in the "available" statement as recommended in the previous edition and replaces them with forward slashes to separate each segment. What follows is the format of the "available" statement for commercial and CD-ROM databases:

Available: Supplier/Database identifier or number/Accession or record number.
Example: Available: Dialog/Magazine Database/47/13401091.

The format for sources retrieved on the Internet is as follows:

Available protocol: Internet address of service (i.e., domain)/search path/file.
Example: Available FTP: etext.virginia.edu/pub/texts/AnoOctC.

The common protocols for organizing and searching information on the Internet include E-mail, FTP, Gopher, HTTP, and Telnet, and should be provided right after "available" except when presenting a Uniform Resource Locator (URL). The protocol used is an essential element in a URL, and it is therefore redundant to repeat it in this context. Refer to publications in the Reference List at the end of Part One of this handbook for examples of references showing Internet protocols. Domain names are the Internet addresses for the services and, in the case of the WWW resources, these are found in the URLs. The search path indicating the steps taken to reach the target file should also be included in the "available" statement. Give the file name exactly as it appears.

ACCESS DATES

This handbook suggests that the access date should be included in a citation. *ISO/DIS 690-2, The MLA Handbook,* and *The Complete Guide to Citing Government Information Resources* have also recommended the inclusion of the access date in citations (International Organization, 1995; Gibaldi, 1995; Garner, Smith, Cheney & Sheehy, 1993). The access date validates the existence of a cited file at a given time. It also indicates, although indirectly, the possible version of a database when that becomes difficult to determine. The access date element is always the last element of a citation and enclosed in brackets.

PUNCTUATION

The APA convention is to finish each element with a period. With electronic information, however, punctuation in the context of the "available" statement can present problems. Because a stray period or comma can be mistaken for part of the "available" statement, every effort should be made to use punctuation sparingly in the "available" statement. The exceptions to this rule are that forward slashes (/) are added to separate steps in a search path, and a colon (:) is used after the "available" statement. For example in the following reference, except for the first colon, the punctuation in the "available" statement needs to be included in order to ensure obtaining the item from the supplier:

> Armour, I. D. (1995). World affairs: Special reports: Bosnia and Herzegovina. In *Britannica Online: Book of the Year* (1994) [Online]. Available: http://www. eb.com:180/cgi-bin/g?DocF=boy/94/H03245.html [1995, June 14].

UPPERCASE AND LOWERCASE LETTERS

In the "available" statement, include uppercase and lowercase letters in the path or message exactly as found in the source or reference to the source. Some computer systems are extremely sensitive to the format of letters; if they are not supplied, the communication will fail.

ABBREVIATIONS

It is the convention to present the abbreviations of protocols, users' log-in names, and discussion list names in uppercase letters (e.g., HTTP, RRECOME, and PACS-L).

NOTES

Notes providing additional bibliographic information should be enclosed in brackets immediately after the explained elements.

Section II of Chapter Five on legal sources follows the advice of the APA *Publication Manual* which states that "references to legal materials . . . will be more useful to the reader if they provide the information in the conventional format of legal citations" (1994, p. 223). Section II adheres to *The Bluebook: A Uniform System of Citation* (1991), the standard guide in the legal field. Consequently, citations in that section are very different from those in the rest of this guide.

Chapter Seven briefly presents the author-date system of in-text citation recommended by APA. Comparable to footnotes or endnotes in function, text citations direct readers to the sources of a quote or other information in a reference list at the end of an article, chapter, or book. A more detailed discussion of this method can be found in the Reference Citations in Text section (1994, pp. 168–174) in APA's *Publication Manual.*

This handbook has tried to be as faithful as possible to this excellent method of making reference to information, a style in use by thousands of people. The differences between the MLA style, shown in the Chapters Eight through Fourteen, and APA style are rather substantial, but both styles adapt well to the inclusion of information unique to electronic sources.

Finally, the International Organization for Standardization has labored for some time to make recommendations on the documentation of electronic sources in their new draft standards *ISO/DIS 690-2: Information and Documentation—Bibliographic References—Electronic Documents or Parts Thereof.* We have studied this work with care to assure that the information presented in the following pages conforms as much as possible with these draft standards.

CHAPTER TWO

Full-Text Databases: Individual Works, Books, Monographs, or Full-Length Works

I. CITE AN ENTIRE WORK

A. CD-ROM and Commercial Online Databases

Basic Forms

Author/editor. (Year). *Title* (edition), [Type of medium]. Producer (optional). Available: Supplier/Database identifier or number [Access date].

Title (edition), [Type of medium]. (Year). Producer (optional). Available: Supplier/Database identifier or number [Access date].

- If author is not available, title becomes the first element of the reference, and the work is alphabetized in the reference list by the first significant word in the title.
- If the second Basic Form is used, Type of medium statement that defines the format of this title should precede the date.
- When evaluating a database, it is useful to have information on the producer who contributes to the content of the database. If the information is readily available, supply it before the "available" statement.
- The "available" statement, when the citation is for a whole database, should generally contain only the name of the information supplier and the database identifier or number.
- If the cited work is a database, it is redundant to repeat the database name in the "available" statement.

9

<A1> *Academic American encyclopedia* [Online]. (1995). Grolier (producer). Available: Dow Jones News Retrieval Service/ENCYC [1995, May 27].
  • Indicate the responsibility of the producer in parentheses.

<A2> *The agrochemicals handbook* [Online]. (1994, January). Royal Chemical Society (producer). Available: CompuServe Knowledge Index/CHEM3 [1995, May 16].
  • When a work is under regular revision, use the date, including the month, of the last revision if that can be determined. Note that the name of the month is not abbreviated.

<A3> *The Foundation Directory* [Online]. (1995). Foundation Center (producer). Available: Dialog/26 [1995, May 27].
  • Annuals should be treated as periodicals with words capitalized accordingly.

<A4> *Hoover's handbook of world business* [Online]. (1995). Available: Mead Nexis/COMPNY/HVRWLD [1995, May 23].
  • This statement shows the characteristic path: Library: COMPANY and File: HVRWLD from this information supplier.

<A5> *Art gallery forum* [Database composed mainly of graphical images], [Online]. (No date). Available: CompuServe/ARTGALLERY [1995, June 1].
  • Explanatory note is enclosed in brackets after the title.
  • Give "No date" if the publication date is not available.

<A6> *Grolier prehistoric computer file: A multimedia who's who of prehistoric life* (Macintosh version 1.0.0), [CD-ROM]. (1994). Available: Grolier [1995, May 30].
  • Information about the database version is treated as edition information and is enclosed in parentheses after the title.

<A7> *Oxford English dictionary computer file: On compact disc* (2nd ed.), [CD-ROM]. (1992). Available: Oxford UP [1995, May 27].
  • An edition statement is included in parentheses directly after the title.

<A8> Sternberg, M. L. A. (1994). *The American sign language dictionary on CD-ROM* (Windows version), [CD-ROM]. Available: HarperCollins [1995, May 27].

B. Electronic Mail (E-mail)

1. Archived Works

Basic Forms

Author/editor. (Year). *Title* (edition), [Type of medium]. Available E-mail: LIST SERV/Get [Access date].

Title (edition), [Type of medium]. (Year). Available E-mail: LISTSERV/Get [Access date].

> • If author or editor is not available, use the second basic form.
> • Provide edition information if the work is not the first edition.
> • In the "available" statement, give the LISTSERV network address and, in the "Get" message, the file name with its extension.

<A9> Gaylord, H. (1989). *ISO* [Online]. Available E-mail: LISTSERV@ BROWNVM.BROWN.EDU/Get ISO STANDRDS [1995, June 5].

<A10> Hurlbut, J. D. (1992). *From functional feast to frivolous funhouse: Two ideals of play in the Burgundian Court* [Paper given at the 5th Annual Indiana University Symposium on Medieval Studies: Work and Play in the Middle Age], [Online]. Available E-mail: LISTSERV@IUBMV. UCS.INDIANA.EDU/Get HURLBUT PAPER [1995, May 15].

> • Supplementary bibliographic information appears after the title of work in brackets.

<A11> Pope, S. T. (1995). *Sound anthology* [Online]. Available E-mail: LIST SERV@AMERICAN.EDU/Get EMUSIC-L LOG9505E [1995, June 1].

<A12> Smith, R. (1994). *The legend of Mark Twain* [Online]. Available E-mail: LISTSERV@YORKVM1.bitnet/Get LEGEND MT [1995, May 15].

2. Real-Time Works

See Chapter Four, Section I. Discussion Lists, A. Cite a Message (page 53 forward).

C. FTP

Basic Forms

Author/editor. (Year). *Title* (edition), [Type of medium]. Available FTP: address path/file [Access date].

Title (edition), [Type of medium]. (Year). Available FTP: address/path/file [Access date].

> • If author or editor is not available, use the second basic form.
> • In an FTP "available" statement, the address will be the first segment and file the last. The path, usually several segments, lies between.

<A13> Byrds. (No date). *The Byrds' greatest hits* [Lyrics], [Online]. Available FTP: vacs.uwp.edu/pub/music/lyrics/b/byrds/greatest.hits [1995, June 3].

> • The author is, in this case, a musical group, rather than a personal author.
> • The item bears no date, so that is noted in the place of a specific publication date.
> • Descriptive note [Lyrics] follows the title of the song in brackets.

<A14> *Octovian (Cambridge): A machine-readable version* [From version edited by Frances McSparran for the Early English Text Society, no. 289; London and New York: Oxford University Press, 1986], [Online]. (1993). Available FTP: etext.virginia.edu/pub/texts/AnoOctC [1995, May 12].

> • The date in this reference refers to the date when the electronic edition of the work is created.

<A15> *Oxford text archive snapshot* [Online]. (1990?). Available FTP: hnsource. cc.ukans.edu/pub/history/Europe/Modern/Britain/oxtext.bib [1995, June 1].

> • The question mark indicates that the date was approximated.

<A16> Robinson, M. (1993). *Sappho and Phaon in a series of legitimate sonnets, with thoughts on poetical subjects, and anecdotes of the Grecian poetess* [Electronic text of an edition first published London: S. Gosnell, 1796], [Online]. Available FTP: etext.virginia.edu/pub/britpo/sappho/ RobSapp [1995, May 12].

> • The date in this reference refers to the date when the electronic edition of the work was created.

<A17> Savetz, K. M. (1994, December 19). *The unofficial Internet book list: The most extensive bibliography of books about the Internet* (Version 0.9), [Online]. Available: ftp://infolib.murdoch.edu.au/pub/bib/savetz.bib [1995, May 12].

> • This is an example of an FTP address reached through a World Wide Web (WWW) site. It is not necessary to repeat the protocol FTP after "available" because it is an essential element of the URL.

<A18> *TWU women's collection* [Online]. (1992, December 22). Available FTP: una.hh.lib.umich.edu/newstuff/diversity/abouttwu [1995, May 15].

D. Gopher

Basic Forms

Author/editor. (Year). *Title* (edition), [Type of medium]. Available Gopher: Gopher site/path/file [Access date].

Title (edition), [Type of medium]. (Year). Available Gopher: Gopher site/path/file [Access date].

- If author or editor is not available, use the second basic form.
- Provide the date when the electronic form was created.
- In the "available" statement, provide the Gopher site, search path, and file name.
- It is not necessary to repeat the protocol (Gopher) on the WWW after the "available" statement since it is stated in the URL.

<A19> Barrie, J. M. (1991). *Peter Pan* (A Millennium Fulcrum edition), [Online]. Available Gopher: gopher.tc.umc.edu/Libraries/Electronic Books/Peter Pan [1995, June 1].

<A20> Descartes, R. (No date). *Discourse on the method of conducting the reason, and seeking truth in the sciences* [Online]. Available Gopher: english-server.hss.cmu.edu/Philosophy/Descartes-on Method [1995, June 12].

<A21> *The Japanese surrender documents—WWII* [Online]. (1991). Available Gopher: gopher.tc.umn.edu/Libraries/Electronic Books/Japanese Surrender [1995, May 25].

<A22> Shelley, M. W. *Frankenstein* [Online]. (1993). Available: gopher:// gopher.etext.org/Gutenberg/etext93/frandk10.txt [1995, June 2].

E. HTTP

Basic Forms

Author/editor. (Year). *Title* (edition), [Type of medium]. Available: URL [Access date].

Title (edition), [Type of medium]. (Year). Available HTTP: URL [Access date].

- If author or editor is not available, use the second basic form.

> • The URL includes the protocol, WWW site, search path, and file name.
> • It is not necessary to repeat the protocol (HTTP) on the WWW after the "available" statement since it is stated in the URL.

<A23> American Institute for Conservation. (1994). *Code of ethics & guidelines for practice* (revised draft), [Online]. Available: http://palimpsest. stanford.edu/byorg/aic/aicethics/ethdraf2.html [1995, June 13].

> • This is a reference with a corporate author.

<A24> *Educating America for the 21st century: Developing a strategic plan for educational leadership for Columbia University—1993–2000* (Initial workshop draft), [Online]. (1994). Available: http://www.ilt.columbia. edu/CONF/EdPlan.html [1995, May 16].

<A25> Lehman, M. A. & Brown, R. H. (1994). *Intellectual property and the national information infrastructure* [Online]. Available: http://www. uspto.gov/nii/ipwg.html [1995, May 15].

<A26> Prizker, T. J. (No date). *An early fragment from central Nepal* [Online]. Available: http://www.ingress.com/~astanart/pritzker/pritzker.html [1995, June 8].

> • Write "No date" when the electronic publication date is not available.

F. Telnet

Basic Forms

Author/editor. (Year). *Title* (edition), [Type of medium]. Available Telnet: Telnet site/**login**:/**password**:/path/file [Access date].

Title (edition), [Type of medium]. (Year). Available Telnet: Telnet site/**login**:/**pass word**:/path/file [Access date].

> • If author or editor is not available, use the second basic form.
> • If log-in information and password are required in order to establish the Telnet session, provide those in the "available" statement with indications of the nature of that information.

<A27> Bowles, P. (1994). *The Paul Bowles Moroccan music collection* [Online]. Available Telnet: marvel.loc.gov/Research and Reference/Dance Heritage Coalition Network/Dance Research Resources/Library of Congress Dance Resources [1995, May 15].

<A28> *Depression primer* [Online]. (1994). Available Telnet: cap.gwu.edu/**login**: gwis/**password**: guest/Health Center/Information by Topic/Depression [1995, May 14].

<A29> *Educating America for the 21st century: Developing a strategic plan for educational leadership for Columbia University—1993–2000* (Initial workshop draft), [Online]. (1994). Available Telnet: columbianet.colum bia.edu/**login**: guest/Handbooks, Reports/Educating America For the 21st Century [1995, May 16].

<A30> Shakespeare, W. (No date). *A midsummer night's dream* (Arthur Bullen's Stratford Town Edition), [Online]. Available Telnet: library.dartmouth. edu/shakespeare plays/a midsummer night's dream [1995, June 2].

> • If the date for the creation of an electronic form is not available, write "No date" in parentheses after author.

G. USENET

See Chapter Four, Section II. USENET, A. Individual Works (page 57 forward).

H. Wide-Area Information Server (WAIS)

Basic Forms

Author/editor. (Year). *Title* (edition), [Type of medium]. Available WAIS: WAIS site/**login**:/**user identifier**:/**terminal type**:/search path/file [Access date].

Title (edition), [Type of medium]. (Year). Available WAIS: WAIS site/**login**:/**user identifier**:/**terminal type**:/search path/file [Access date].

> • If author or editor is not available, use the second basic form.

<A31> Carroll, L. (No date). *The walrus and the carpenter* [Online]. Available WAIS: quake.think.com/**login**: wais/**user identifier**: user@address/**term**: vt100/404: * [microworld.media.mit] poetry/**keywords**: walrus/001: (Poetry) The Walrus and the Carpenter Lew [1995, September 9].

<A32> *Our environmental resource base* [Document presented in Hypertext Markup Language], [Online]. (No date). Available WAIS: quake. think.com/**login**:wais/**user identifier**: user@address/**term**: vt100/227: * [atlenv.ns.doe.CA] Environment Canada/**keywords**: rivers/017: (Environment_Can) http://atlenv.bed.ns.doe.ca/soe/chapt1_2. [1995, September 9].

> • The note following the title, in brackets, describes the form of the document more fully.

• The period at the end of the "available" statement is part of the file name.

II. CITE PART OF A WORK

A. CD-ROM and Commercial Online Databases

Basic Forms

Author/editor. (Year). Title. In *Source* (edition), [Type of medium]. Available: Supplier/Database identifier or number/item or accession number [Access date].

Title. (Year). In *Source* (edition), [Type of medium]. Available: Supplier/Database identifier or number/item or accession number [Access date].

• If no author or editor is available, title becomes the first element of the reference, and the work is alphabetized in the reference list by the first significant word in the title.
• Type of medium statement, defining the format of this title, should precede the date.
• The "available" statement should generally contain the name of the information supplier, the database identifier or number, and an item or accession number.

<A33> Belloc, H. (1979). The early morning. In *Quotations database* [A poem from *The Oxford dictionary of quotations*, 3rd ed.], [Online]. Available: CompuServe Knowledge Index/REFR1/00000814 [1995, June 5].

• This is a reference to a poem from a compilation of quotations. The example shows a note, given in brackets, to help the reader identify the source of the information. In this case, the online source bears a different title than the print source.

<A34> Bosnia and Hercegovina. (1995). In *Academic American encyclopedia* [Online]. Available: Dow Jones News Retrieval Service/ENCYC [1995, June 5].

• This is an article from an encyclopedia with no author given.
• The database does not assign item numbers to specific articles, so this citation lacks that information.

<A35> [College's own in-depth description: University of Vermont]. (1995). In *Peterson's College Database* [Online]. Available: Dow Jones News Retrieval Service/COLLEGE [1995, June 5].

• If a title is lacking, supply a title and use brackets to indicate that the information was supplied.

<A36> International Trade Administration. (1995). IV. Political environment. In *Ecuador: Country Commercial Guides* [CD-ROM]. Available: National Trade Data Bank-The Export Connection (R)/Country Commercial Guides/IT CCG ECUADOR04 [1995, June 7].

• This is an example of a corporate author.

<A37> Kuru. (1994). In *Mosby's medical, nursing, and allied health dictionary* (4th ed.), [Electronic]. Available: InfoTrac/Health Reference Center/ Kuru/Dictionary definition [1995, June 7].

• Sometimes it is not possible to tell whether one is accessing an online source or a networked CD-ROM. If this is the case, use "Electronic" in the type of medium statement.

• This database does not give accession numbers for the items found in a search. The "available" statement, in this case, shows the search path in lieu of an accession number.

<A38> Louis Comfort Tiffany Foundation. (1995). In *The Foundation Directory* [Online]. Available: Dialog/26/00004187 [1995, June 5].

<A39> Nestle Ltd. (1995). In *Hoover's handbook of world business* [Online]. Available: Mead Nexis/COMPNY/HVRWLD [1995, May 23].

B. E-mail

1. Archived Works

Basic Forms

Author/editor. (Year). Title. In *Source* (edition), [Type of medium]. Available E-mail: LISTSERV/Get [Access date].

Title. (Year). In *Source* (edition), [Type of medium]. Available E-mail: LISTSERV/ Get [Access date].

• If author or editor is not available, use the second basic form.
• Provide edition information if the work is not the first edition.
• In the "available" statement, give the LISTSERV network address and the file name with its extension in the "Get" message.

<A40> Bailey, C. W. (1992, July). Electronic serials and related topics. In *Directory of electronic journals and newsletters* (2nd ed.), [Online].

Available E-mail: LISTSERV@UOTTAWA.BITNET/Get EJOURNL1
DIRECTRY [1995, June 8].
• Indicate the edition if the publication is not the first edition.

<A41> Gaylord, H. (1989, June 2). Four fundamental options in building up multi-
character sets. In *ISO* [Online]. Available E-mail: LISTSERV@BROWN
VM.BITNET/Get ISO STANDRDS [1995, June 8].

<A42> Russell, B. (1995, May 16). Parisian fairground theatre. In *PERFORM
LOG9505* [Online]. Available E-mail: LISTSERV@IUBVM.UCS.INDI
ANA.EDU/Get PERFORM LOG9505 [1995, June 8].

<A43> Twain, M. (1993, May). The balloon ascension. In *Tom Sawyer abroad*
[Online]. Available E-mail: LISTSERV@YORKVM1.BITNET/Get
TSA TEXT [1995, May 15].
• Provide the date when the electronic version is created.

2. Real-Time Works

See Chapter Four, Section I. Discussion Lists, A. Cite a Message (page 53 forward).

C. FTP

Basic Forms

Author/editor. (Year). Title. In *Source* (edition), [Type of medium]. Available FTP:
address/search path/file [Access date].

Title. (Year). In *Source* (edition), [Type of medium]. Available FTP: address/
search path/file [Access date].

• In an FTP "available" statement, the address will be the first segment and file the last. The search path, usually several segments,
lies between.

<A44> Byrds. (No date). So you want to be a rock 'n' roll star. [Lyrics] In *The
Byrds' greatest hits*. [Online]. Available FTP: vacs.uwp.edu/ pub/
music/lyrics/b/byrds/greatest.hits [1995, June 3].
• The authors are, in this case, a musical group.
• The item bears no date, so that is noted in the place of a specific
publication date.
• Descriptive note follows the title of the song and is placed in
brackets.

<A45> Holst, I. (1992). Language reform 1907–1958. In *How the Norwegian
Parliament banned the national language* [Online]. Available FTP:

nic.funet.fi/pub/culture/text/ingar-holst/murder-of-norw-language [1995, June 11].

<A46> Robinson, M. (1993). Preface. In *Sappho and Phaon in a series of legitimate sonnets, with thoughts on poetical subjects, and anecdotes of the Grecian poetess* [Electronic text of an edition first published London: S. Gosnell, 1796], [Online]. Available FTP: etext.virginia.edu/pub/britpo/sappho/RobSapp [1995, May 12].

- The date in this reference indicates when the electronic information was created.
- If the preface, introduction, foreword, or afterword is by someone other than the writer of the main work, cite in the following manner: Smith, J. (1993). Preface. In M. Robinson, *Sappho and Phaon. . .*

<A47> Title 1: Common provisions. (1992). In *Treaty on European Union (Maastricht Treaty)*, [Online]. Available FTP: src.doc.ic.ac.uk/politics/EEC/Maastricht/title1 [1995, June 5].

- Names of treaties are proper nouns so words are capitalized.

D. Gopher

Basic Forms

Author/editor. (Year). Title. In *Source* (edition), [Type of medium]. Available Gopher: Gopher site/search path/file [Access date].

Title. (Year). In *Source* (edition), [Type of medium]. Available Gopher: Gopher site/search path/file [Access date].

- If author or editor is not available, use the second basic form.
- Provide the date when the electronic form was created.
- In the "available" statement, provide Gopher site, search path, and file name.

<A48> Bacon, F. (No date). Of truth. In *The essays* [Online]. Available Gopher: english-server.hss.cmu.edu/Philosophy/Bacon-The Essays [1995, June 13].

- Write "No date" if the creation date for the electronic form is not given.

<A49> Carroll, L. (1991). Chapter XI: Who stole the tarts? In *Alice's adventures in wonderland* (The Millennium Fulcrum edition 2.7a), [Online]. Available Gopher: gopher.tc.umc.edu/Libraries/Electronic Books/Alice's Adventures in Wonderland/Chapter XI [1995, June 12].

<A50> Embassy of India. (1994). Demographic background. In *India 1993 Annual* [Online]. Available Gopher: india.bgsu.edu/India-ANU/Land, people and population [1995, June 13].

> • This is a reference with a corporate author.
>
> • Annuals are treated as periodicals; titles are capitalized accordingly.

<A51> Will caffeine enhance athletic performance? (No date). In *Caffeine: Caffeine effects on academics and athletics* [Online]. Available Gopher: hemp. uwec.edu/drugs/Caffeine/Caffeine's Effects on Academics and Athletics [1995, June 13].

> • Write "No date" when the creation date for the electronic form is not given.

E. HTTP

Basic Forms

Author/editor. (Year). Title. In *Source* (edition), [Type of medium]. Available: URL [Access date].

Title. (Year). In *Source* (edition), [Type of medium]. Available: URL [Access date].

> • If author or editor is not given, use the second basic form.
>
> • In the "available" statement, the URL includes the protocol, the WWW site, search path, and file name.
>
> • It is not necessary to repeat the protocol (HTTP) on the WWW after the "available" statement since it is stated in the URL.

<A52> Armour, I. D. (1995). World affairs: Special reports: Bosnia and Herzegovina. In *Britannica Online: Book of the Year (1994)* [Online]. Available: http://www.eb.com:180/cgi-bin/g?DocF=boy/94/H03245. html [1995, June 14].

> • Annuals are treated as periodicals; titles are capitalized accordingly.

<A53> American Institute for Conservation. (1994). Code of ethics. In *Code of ethics and guidelines for practice* (revised draft), [Online]. Available: http://palimpsest.stanford.edu/byorg/aic/aicethics/ethdraf2.html [1995, June 13].

> • This is a reference with a corporate author.

<A54> Aristotle. (1995). Part I. In *Poetics* (S. H. Butcher, Trans), [Original work written circa 350 B.C.], [Online]. Available: http://the-tech.mit.edu/ Classics/Aristotle/poetics.txt.Part_1.html [1995, June 13].

• If a translation of the original work is used as the source, cite the translation.
• Supplementary bibliographic information appears in brackets after the title of source.

<A55> Daniel, R. T. (1995). The history of Western music. In *Britannica online: Macropaedia* [Online]. Available: http://www.eb.com:180/cgi-bin/g: DocF=macro/5004/45/0.html [1995, June 14].

<A56> J.P. Morgan & Co. (No date). Data series naming standards. In *Structure of the riskmetrics data files* [Online]. Available: http://www.jpmorgan.com/ RiskMetrics/About.html [1995, June 13].
• This is a reference for a corporate author.
• Write "No date" when the creation date of the electronic form is not given.

<A57> Muir, J. (1995). Yosemite. In *Britannica online: Britannica classics* [Online]. Available: http://www.eb.com:180/cgi-bin/g?DocF-classic/ C00014.html [1995, June 14].

F. Telnet

Basic Forms

Author/editor. (Year). Title. In *Source* (edition), [Type of medium]. Available Telnet: Telnet site/**login**:/**password**:/search path/file [Access date].

Title. (Year). In *Source* (edition), [Type of medium]. Available Telnet: Telnet site/**login**:/**password**:/search path/file [Access date].

• If author or editor is not available, use the second basic form.
• If log-in and password are required in order to establish the Telnet session, provide those in the "available" statement.

<A58> Dickens, C. (No date). Chirp the first. In *The Cricket on the hearth* [Online]. Available Telnet: marvel.loc.gov/**login**: marvel/Research and Reference/Electronic Publications/Texts and Books/Online Book Initiative (OBI)/The Online Books/Charles Dickens/cricket.on.hearth.txt [1995, June 16].
• If the creation date of the electronic work is not available, write "No date" in parentheses after the author element.

<A59> Norway. (1994). In *The World Factbook 1994* [Online]. Available Telnet: LIBRARY.DARTMOUTH.EDU/World Factbook/Norway [1995, June 16].

• Annuals are treated as periodicals; titles are capitalized accordingly.

<A60> Shakespeare, W. (No date). Act I, Scene II. In *Hamlet* (Arthur Bullen's Stratford Town Edition), [Online]. Available Telnet: LIBRARY.DART MOUTH.EDU/Shakespeare plays/Hamlet [1995, June 15].

> • If the creation date of the electronic work is not available, write "No date" in parentheses after author.

<A61> Synagogue. (1992). In *Oxford English dictionary* (2nd ed.), [Online]. Available Telnet: UWIN.U.WASHINGTON.EDU/I/REF/OED/syna gogue [1995, June 16].

G. USENET

See Chapter Four, Section II. USENET (page 57 forward).

H. WAIS

Basic Forms

Author/editor. (Year). Title. In *Source* (edition), [Type of medium]. Available WAIS: WAIS site/**login**:/**user identifier**:/**terminal type**:/ search path/file [Access date].

Title. (Year). In *Source* (edition), [Type of medium]. Available WAIS: WAIS site/**login**:/**user identifier**:/search path/file [Access date].

> • If author or editor is not available, use the second basic form.

<A62> Lesotho. (1993). In *World Factbook 1993* [Online]. Available WAIS: quake.think.com/**login**: wais/**User identifier**: user@address/**term**: vt100/547:* [gopher.uwo.ca] world-factbook93/**keywords**: lesotho/001: (world-factbook9) Lesotho Geography Location: South [1995, September 9].
> • Annuals are treated as periodicals; titles are capitalized accordingly.

<A63> Water. [No date]. In *Our environmental resource base* [Online]. Available WAIS: quake.think.com/**login**:wais/**user identifier**: user@address/**term**: vt100/227: * [atlenv.ns.doe.CA] Environment Canada/**keywords**: rivers/017: (Environment_Can) http://atlenv.bed.ns.doe.ca/soe/chapt1_2. [1995, September 9].
> • The period at the end of the "available" statement is part of the file name.
> • The address, path, and file take the user only to the document level—not to the part of the chapter being cited.
> • The WAIS path includes an URL in the last element.

CHAPTER THREE

Full-Text Databases: Periodicals

I. CITE PART OF A WORK

A. Journal Articles

1. CD-ROM and Commercial Online Databases

Basic Forms

Author. (Year). Title. *Journal* [Type of medium], *volume*(issue), paging if given, or other indicator of length. Available: Supplier/Database name/Identifier or number if available/item or accession number [Access date].

Title. (Year). *Journal* [Type of medium], *volume*(issue), paging if given, or other indicator of length. Available: Supplier/Database name/Identifier or number if available/item or accession number [Access date].

> • When author is not available, use the second basic form.
> • Type of medium statement follows directly after the journal title, without punctuation.
> • Give page range whenever possible. If that is not available, apply these rules:

1. When the initial page is known, (a) in parentheses, indicate the article length after the initial page, e.g., 10(12 pp.), 10(80 paragraphs), 10(24 screens), 10(300 lines) or 10(3,000 words); or (b) use the notation "ff" for "and following pages."

2. When the initial page is not available, indicate the article length (the number of paragraphs, screens, lines, or words). No parentheses are needed.

<A64>   Achenbach, T. M. (1995). Diagnosis, assessment, and comorbidity in psychosocial treatment research: Psychosocial treatment research [Special issue]. *Journal of Abnormal Child Psychology* [Online], *23*(1), 45ff. Available: Mead Nexis/NEWS/ASAPII [1995, June 12].

　　　　　• Mead Nexis references do not have item or accession numbers for individual stories, so this information will be lacking from citations.

　　　　　• The page on which the article starts is given; the page on which the article ends in not known so the "ff" is used to indicate "and following pages."

<A65>   Beaton, J. M. (1994). [Review of the book *Sahul in review: Pleistocene archaeology in Australia, New Guinea and Island Melanesia*]. *Antiquity* [Online], *68*(261), 893(3 pp.). Available: Information Access/Expanded Academic ASAP/A16352317 [1995, June 12].

　　　　　• Example of a book review. For reviews of other media, change the statement in brackets accordingly. For example, [Review of the film *Once were warriors*].

　　　　　• This shows the article's initial page (p. 893) and the actual length statement in parentheses. The notation pp. tells the reader that length is given in number of pages.

<A66>   Bosselman, F. (1994). Four land ethics: Order, reform, responsibility, opportunity. *Environmental Law* [Online], *24*, 1439(39,389 words). Available: Mead Lexis/LAWREV/ENVLAW [1995, June 12].

　　　　　• No issue number is given in the source, so the citation shows the information that is available.

　　　　　• The page on which the article starts is given; the page on which the article ends in not known so one could use "ff" to indicate "and following pages."

　　　　　• The descriptive information on length, number of words, is given in the article and is therefore retained.

<A67>   Brookfield, H., & Padoch, C. (1994). Appreciating agrodiversity: A look at dynamism and diversity of indigenous farming practices. *Environment* [Online], *36*(5), 6(15 pp.). Available: Dialog/Magazine Index/ 47/ 15490130 [1995, June 13].

　　　　　• This example gives the format for citing more than one author.

<A68>   Clark, J. K. (1993). Complications in academia: Sexual harassment and
         the law. *Siecus Report* [CD-ROM], *21*(6), 6-10. Available: 1994
         SIRS/SIRS 1993 School/Volume 4/Article 93A [1995, June 13].

<A69>   Heartney, E. (1995). Contemporary oracles. (Report from Greece). *Art
         in America* [Online], *83*(5), 61(3 pp.). Available: Information Access/
         Expanded Academic ASAP/A16878539 [1995, June 12].

<A70>   Merlan, F. (1994). Narratives of survival in the post-colonial North.
         Oceania [Online], *65*(2), 151(24 pp.). Available: Information Access/
         Expanded Academic ASAP/A16998760 [1995, June 12].

<A71a>   Monti, D., Cicchetti, G., Goodkind, T., & Ganci, M. T. (1994). SPT: A
         new methodology for instruction. (Structured presentation technolo-
         gy). *T H E Journal* [CD-ROM], *22*(1), 66(3 pp.). Available: Infor-
         mation Access/Computer Select/16232996 [1995, June 13].
            • This is an example of multiple authors, all of whom should be
              listed.

<A71b>   Monti, D., Cicchetti, G., Goodkind, T., & Ganci, M. T. (1994). SPT: A
         new methodology for instruction. (Structured presentation technolo-
         gy). *T H E Journal* [Electronic], *22*(1), 66(3 pp.). Available: Infor-
         mation Access/Computer Select/16232996 [1995, June 13].
            • Sometimes it is not possible to tell whether one is accessing an
              online source or a networked CD-ROM. If this is the case, use
              "Electronic" in the type of medium statement.

<A72>   Shostak, A. B. (1993, November). The nature of work in the twenty-first
         century: Certain uncertainties. *Business Horizons* [Online], 30ff.
         Available: Dow Jones News Retrieval Service/TextM/Business
         Library [1995, June 12].
            • This item lacks a volume and issue number. In this case, it is
              helpful to include the month of publication in the date statement.

<A73>   Shweder, R. A. (1993). "Why do men barbecue?" and other postmodern
         ironies of growing up in the decade of ethnicity. *Daedalus* [Online],
         122(1), 279(30 pp). Available: Dialog/Magazine Database/47/
         13401091 [1995, June 13].
            • The quotation marks were given around the initial part of the
              title and are therefore retained.

<A74>   Sikula, A., Sr., & Costa, A. D. (1994). Are women more ethical than
         men? *Journal of Business Ethics* [Online], *13*(11), 859-871.
         Available: Dialog/ABI Inform/15/95-78695 [1995, June 12].
            • The example above shows Sr. in an author's name.

2. E-mail

a. Archived Works

Basic Forms

Author. (Year). Title. *Journal* [Type of medium], *volume*(issue), paging if given, or other indicator of length. Available E-mail: LISTSERV/Get [Access date].

Title. (Year). *Journal* [Type of medium], *volume*(issue), paging if given, or other indicator of length. Available E-mail: LISTSERV/Get [Access date].

> • When author is not available, use the second basic form.
> • Paging is seldom given in this format, so an issue number becomes an important, identifying element and should be included when available.
> • For information on management of paging, see the detailed guidelines in Section I.A.1., Basic Forms of this chapter (page 23).
> • In the "available" statement, give the LISTSERV network address and the file name with its extension in the "Get" message.

<A75>   Brent, D. A. (1994). Information technology and the breakdown of "places" of knowledge. *EJournal* [Online], *4*(4), 462 lines. Available E-mail: LISTSERV@uacsc2.albany.edu/Get EJRNL V4N4 [1995, June 29].

> • The beginning and ending page information is not available; therefore, only the article length is provided in this reference.
> • Names of discussion lists and the word LISTSERV are presented in uppercase letters.

<A76>   Carriveau, K. L., Jr. (1995). [Review of the book *Environmental hazards: Marine pollution*]. *Electronic Green Journal* [Online], *2*(1), 3 paragraphs. Available E-mail: LISTSERV@uidaho.edu/Get egj log03 [1995, June 21].

> • Example above shows Jr. in an author's name.
> • This is a reference for a book review; brackets indicate that title is supplied. For reviews of other media, change the statement in brackets accordingly. For example, [Review of the film *The postman*].

<A77>   Hawks, C. P. (1995). OhioLINK: Implementing integrated library services across institutional boundaries. *The Public-Access Computer Systems Review* [Online], *6*(2), 5-26. Available E-mail: LISTSERV @uhupvm1.bitnet/Get pacs-review v6n295 [1995, June 29].

<A78> Huo, Y. H., & Kwansa, F. (1994). Effect of operating and financial leverage on firm's risk. *Journal of the International Academy of Hospitality Research* [Online], (8), 2-17. Available E-mail: LISTSERV@ VTVM1.CC.VT.EDU/Get JIAHR8 TEXT [1995, June 19].
  • This is a reference with no volume number.

<A79> Olaniran, B. A. (1993). Individual differences and computer mediated communication: The role of perception/Les Differences individuelles et la communication informatisee: Le role de la perception. *The Electronic Journal of Communication/La Revue Electronique de Communication* [Online], *3*(2), 12 paragraphs. Available E-mail: LISTSERV @Vm.Its.Rpi.Edu/Get Olaniran V3N293 [1995, June 28].
  • Provide all the languages in which the article title is presented.

b. Real-Time Works

Basic Forms

Author. (Year). Title. *Journal* [Type of medium], *volume*(issue), paging if given, or other indicator of length. Available E-mail: DISCUSSION GROUP@address [Access date].

Title. (Year). *Journal* [Type of medium], *volume*(issue), paging if given, or other indicator of length. Available E-mail: DISCUSSION GROUP@address [Access date].

  • When an author is not available, use the second basic form.
  • Paging is seldom given in this format, so an issue becomes an important, identifying element and should be included when available.
  • For information on management of paging, see the detailed guidelines in Section I.A.1., Basic Forms of this chapter (page 23).
  • In the "available" statement, identify the discussion group/LISTSERV and capitalize the name as it is a proper noun.

<A80> Arens, W. (1993). [Review of the book *Reproduction & succession: Studies in anthropology, law and society*]. *Law and Politics Book Review* [Online], *3*(5), 1 paragraph. Available E-mail: PSRT-L@mizzou1.missouri.edu [1993, May 5].
  • This is a reference to a book review; brackets indicate title is supplied. For reviews of other media, change the statement in brackets accordingly, for example, [Review of the film *The postman*].

<A81>   Herring, S. C. (1993). Gender and democracy in computer-mediated communication/Sexe et democratie dans la communication informatisee. *The Electronic Journal of Communication/La Revue Electronique de Communication* [Online], *3*(2), 8 paragraphs. Available E-mail: EJCREC@Vm.Its.Rpi.Edu [1993, April 15].

   • Provide all the languages in which the article title is presented.

<A82>   Israel, G. D., & Ilvento, T. W. (1995). Everybody wins: Involving youth in community needs assessment. *Journal of Extension* [Online], *33*(2), 10 paragraphs. Available E-mail: JOE@joe.uwex.edu [1995, April 15].

<A83>   Wilson, T. C. (1995). Culture clash on the infobahn: Paradise lost? *Telecommunications Electronic Reviews (TER)* [Online], *2*(2), 5 paragraphs. Available E-mail: LITA-L@uicvm.uic.edu [1995, June 21].

3. FTP

Basic Forms

Author. (Year). Title. *Journal* [Type of medium], *volume*(issue), paging if given, or other indication of length. Available FTP: address/path/file [Access date].

Title. (Year). *Journal* [Type of medium], *volume*(issue), paging if given, or other indication of length. Available FTP: address/path/file [Access date].

   • When author is not available, use the second basic form.
   • For information on management of paging, see the detailed guidelines in Section I.A.1., Basic Forms of this chapter (page 23).
   • It is not unusual for important information to be lacking from material obtained at FTP sites. Try to give information which will help retrieve the item from the electronic site.

<A84>   Attfield, R. (1995, Spring). Preferences, health, interests, and value. *The Electronic Journal of Analytic Philosophy* [Online], 1-20. Available FTP: tarski.phil.indiana.edu/ejap/1995.spring/attfield.1995.spring.txt [1995, June 15].

   • Since this reference has neither volume nor issue numbers, alternative issue information "Spring" is added in date statement.

<A85>   Derrida, J. (1994). Of the humanities and the philosophical discipline: The right to philosophy from the cosmopolitical point of view: The example of an international institution. (T. Dutoit, Trans.). *Surfaces*

[Online], *4*(310), 34 paragraphs. Available FTP: harfang.cc.umontre al.ca/Surfaces/Articles/Ascii/vol4/A_Derrida (ang).ascii [1995, June 15].

  • Include other contributor(s) with indication of role. This work has a translator.

<A86>   Massing, W. (1995). Metaphysical windmills in robotland [Review of the book *What robots can and can't be*]. *Psycoloquy* [Online], *6*(16), 27 paragraphs. Available FTP: princeton.edu/pub/harnad/Psycoloquy/ 1995.volume.6/psycoloquy.95.6.16.robot-consciousness.11.massing [1995, June 30].

  • This reference is an example of a book review. If the review has its own title, provide that first, followed by the supplementary note on the reviewed title enclosed in brackets.

<A87>   Sengers, P. (1995). [Abstract of Madness and automation: On institu-tionalization, *Postmodern Culture*, *5*(Contents 3)], [Online]. Avail-able FTP: ftp.ncsu.edu/pub/ncsu/pmc/pmc-list/contents.595 [1995, June 15].

  • In this example, the contents of the journal, which was retrieved separately, includes abstracts. The paging or length statement is not relevant in this instance.

4. Gopher

Basic Forms

Author. (Year). Title. *Journal* [Type of medium], *volume*(issue), paging if given, or other indicator of length. Available Gopher: gopher site/search path/file [Access date].

Title. (Year). *Journal* [Type of medium], *volume*(issue), paging if given, or other indicator of length. Available Gopher: gopher site/search path/file [Access date].

  • When an author is available, use the second basic form.
  • Paging is seldom given in this format, so an issue number becomes an important, identifying element and should be included when available.
  • For information on management of paging, see the detailed guidelines in Section I.A.1., under Basic Forms of this chapter (page 23).

- In the "available" statement, give the Gopher site, search path, and file name.
- It is not necessary to repeat the protocol (Gopher) on the WWW after the "available" statement since it is stated in the URL.

<A88>   Carriveau, K. L., Jr. (1995). [Review of the book *Environmental hazards: Marine pollution*]. *Electronic Green Journal* [Online], *2*(1), 3 paragraphs. Available: gopher://gopher.uidaho.edu/11/UI_gopher/ library/egj03/carriv01.html [1995, June 21].
- Example above shows Jr. in an author's name.
- This is a reference for a book review; brackets indicate title is supplied.
- If the information is retrieved via a Gopher on the World Wide Web (WWW), indicate the Uniform Resource Locator (URL) in the "available" statement.

<A89a>   Fitch, R. H., & Denenberg, V. H. (1995). A role for ovarian hormones in sexual differentiation of the brain. *Psycoloquy* [Online], *6*(5), 56 paragraphs. Available: gopher.Princeton.EDU/pub/harnad/Psycoloquy/ psyc.95.6.05.sex-brain.1.fitch [1995, June 29].

<A89b>   Fitch, R. H., & Denenberg, V. H. (1995). A role for ovarian hormones in sexual differentiation of the brain. *Psycoloquy* [Online], *6*(5), 56 paragraphs. Available: gopher://gopher.Princeton.EDU:70/ 1ftp%3Aprinceton.edu@/pub/harnad/Psycoloquy/psyc.95.6.05.sex-brain.1.fitch [1995, June 29].
- If the information is retrieved via a Gopher on the WWW, indicate the URL in the "available" statement.

<A90a>   Israel, G. D., & Ilvento, T. W. (1995). Everybody wins: Involving youth in community needs assessment. *Journal of Extension* [Online], *33*(2), 10 paragraphs. Available Gopher: sageunix.uvm.edu/ ElectronicJournals/Journal of Extension, April 1995 Volume 33 [1995, April 21].

<A90b>   Israel, G. D., & Ilvento, T. W. (1995). Everybody wins: Involving youth in community needs assessment. *Journal of Extension* [Online], *33*(2), 10 paragraphs. Available: gopher://sageunix.uvm.edu:70/00/ joe/1995april/a1 [1995, April 15].
- If the information is retrieved via a Gopher on the WWW, indicate the URL in the "available" statement.

<A91>   Wilson, T. C. (1995). Culture clash on the infobahn: Paradise lost? *Telecommunications Electronic Reviews (TER)* [Online]. *2*(2), 5 paragraphs. Available Gopher: info.lib.uh.edu/Looking for Articles/

Electronic Journals/LITA/Telecommunications Electronic Reviews/ Volume 2 [1995, June 21].

5. HTTP

Basic Forms

Author. (Year). Title. *Journal* [Type of medium], *volume*(issue), paging if given, or other indicator of length. Available: URL [Access date].

Title. (Year). *Journal* [Type of medium], *volume*(issue), paging if given, or other indicator of length. Available: URL [Access date].

- When an author is not available, use the second basic form.
- Paging is seldom given in this format, so an issue number becomes an important, identifying element and should be included when available.
- For information on management of paging, see the detailed guidelines in Section I.A.1., under Basic Forms of this chapter (page 23).
- When providing the URL, indicate the WWW site, search path, and file name.
- It is not necessary to repeat the protocol (HTTP) on the WWW after the "available" statement since it is stated in the URL.

<A92>   Carriveau, K. L., Jr. (1995). [Review of the book *Environmental hazards: Marine pollution*]. *Electronic Green Journal* [Online], *2*(1), 3 paragraphs. Available: http://drseuss.lib.uidaho.edu:70/docs/egj03/carriv01.html [1995, June 21].
- Example above shows Jr. in an author's name.
- This is a reference for a book review; brackets indicate title is supplied.

<A93>   Inada, K. (1995). A Buddhist response to the nature of human rights. *Journal of Buddhist Ethics* [Online], *2*, 9 paragraphs. Available: http://www.cac.psu.edu/jbe/twocont.html [1995, June 21].
- No issue number is given in this example.

<A94>   Weidman, J. C. (1995). Diversifying finance of higher education systems in the Third World: The cases of Kenya and Mongolia. *Education Policy and Analysis* [Online], *3*(5), 800 lines. Available: http://info.asu.edu/asu-cwis/epaa/v3n5.html [1995, June 21].
- This is a reference where article length is given in terms of number of lines.

<A95>   Wilson, T. C. (1995). Culture clash on the infobahn: Paradise lost? *Telecommunications Electronic Reviews (TER)* [Online], *2*(2), 5 paragraphs. Available: http://chehalis.lib.washington.edu/ter/ter-2-2.html [1995, June 21].

6. Telnet

Basic Forms

Author. (Year). Title. *Journal* [Type of medium], *volume*(issue), paging if given, or other indication of length. Available Telnet: Telnet site**/login**:**/password**:/search path/file [Access date].

Title. (Year). *Journal* [Type of medium], *volume*(issue), paging if given, or other indication of length. Available Telnet: Telnet site**/login**:**/password**:/search path/file [Access date].

> • When an author is not available, use the second basic form.
> • Paging is seldom given in this format, so an issue number becomes an important, identifying element and should be included when available.
> • For information on management of paging, see the detailed guidelines in Section I.A.1., under Basic Forms of this chapter (page 23).
> • If log-in information and password are required in order to establish the Telnet session, include information in the "available" statement.

<A96>   Chaya, H. J. (1994). Analysis of Alaskan archeological obsidian artifacts [Paper presented at the Archaeometry Research Graduate Group Annual Symposium February 1994, University at Buffalo Anthropology Department]. *Journal of World Anthropology* [Online], *1*(2), 24 paragraphs. Available Telnet: library.unc.edu**/login**: LIBRARY/ Electronic Journals/UNC-CH Internet Library/Journal of World Anthropology/JWA-Volume 1 Number 2/Analysis of Alaskan. . . [1995, June 30].

> • Supplementary bibliographic information appears, in brackets, after the element explained.

<A97>   Gowing, A. M. (1995). [Review of the book *Caesar and the crisis of the Roman aristocracy*]. *Bryn Mawr Classical Review* [Online], *95*(2), 8 paragraphs. Available Telnet: ccat.sas.upenn.edu/Electronic Journals and Publications/Bryn Mawr Classical Review/95.2.10. Ruebel, Caesar and the Crisis of the Roman Aristocracy [1995, June 30].

• This is a reference to a book review; brackets indicate title is supplied.

<A98>   Mann, P. (1995). Stupid undergrounds. *Postmodern Culture* [Online], 5(3), 49 paragraphs. Available Telnet: dewey.lib.ncsu.edu/Electronic Texts/Scholarly Journals/Postmodern Culture/v5 [1995, June 30].

<A99>   Reynolds, D. J. (1993). Evaluating dial-up Internet access options. *Meck-Journal* [Online], 3(4), 17 paragraphs. Available Telnet: nicol.jvnc. net/**login**: nicol/MeckJournal/Volume III, Issue 4 [1995, June 22].

B. Magazine Articles

1. CD-ROM and Commercial Online Databases

Basic Forms

Author. (Year, month day). Title. *Magazine* [Type of medium], *volume number* (if given), inclusive paging (if given), or other indication of length. Available: Supplier/Database name/Identifier or number if available/item or accession number [Access date].

Title. (Year, month day). *Magazine* [Type of medium], *volume number* (if given), inclusive paging (if given), or other indication of length. Available: Supplier/Database name/Identifier or number if available/item or accession number [Access date].

• Give the date: *year, month* for monthly publications, and *year, month day* for weekly publications.
• Type of medium statement follows directly after the magazine title, without punctuation.
• Give page range whenever possible. If that is not available, apply these rules:

1. When the initial page is known, (a) in parentheses, indicate the article length after the initial page, e.g., 10(12 pp.), 10(80 paragraphs), 10(24 screens), 10(300 lines), 10(3,000 words); or (b) use the notation "ff" for "and following pages."

2. When the initial page is not available indicate the article length (the number of paragraphs, screens, lines, or words). No parentheses are needed.

<A100>   Buhler, P. (1993, July 1). Understanding cultural diversity and its benefits. (Managing in the 90s). *Supervision* [Online], 17ff. Available:

Dow Jones News Retrieval Service/TextM/Business Library [1995, June 12].

- This example lacks volume number and inclusive paging. It also is taken from a database that does not give item or accession numbers. In such a case, one can only cite the information given.

<A101>   Daly, D. (1995, January). The perils of collecting: Amazon exploration. *Audubon* [Online], *97*, 78ff. Available: Mead Nexis/NEWS/MAGS [1995, June 20].

<A102>   Geipel, J. (1993, August). Brazil's unforked tongue. (Portuguese dialects). *History Today* [Online], *43*, 11(4 pp.). Available: Dialog/ Magazine Database/47/14235390 [1995, June 13].

- Parenthetical phrase is part of the title.

<A103>   Goodstein, C. (1991, September). Healers from the deep. *American Health*, [CD-ROM], 60-64. Available: 1994 SIRS/SIRS 1992 Life Science/Article 08A [1995, June 13].

- This source gives no volume number, so the date of issue and page numbers become more crucial.

<A104>   Half price hotels in '95: Deals coast to coast [Includes related articles]. (1995, March). *Consumer Reports Travel Letter* [Online], *11*, 52ff. Available: Mead Nexis/NEWS/ASAPII [1995, June 12].

- This is an example of an article lacking an author. Title becomes the first element in the entry, and the date element follows.
- Explanatory note following title is given in brackets.

<A105>   Heywood, M. (1995, April 17). The importance of being Ern. (Ern Malley, Australian hoax poet). *National Review* [Online], *47*, 66(3 pp.). Available: Information Access/Expanded Academic ASAP/ A16823474 [1995, June 30].

- Parenthetical phrase is part of the title.

<A106a> Mageau, T. (1994, November-December). Listening to multimedia: The (in)sane person's guide to multimedia in education [Includes glossary and related article on networking multimedia]. *Electronic Learning* [CD-ROM], *14*, 28(8 pp.). Available: Information Access/ Computer Select/16289501 [1995, June 13].

- Supplied note following title is given in brackets.

<A106b> Mageau, T. (1994, November-December). Listening to multimedia: The (in)sane person's guide to multimedia in education [Includes glossary

and related article on networking multimedia]. *Electronic Learning* [Electronic], *14*, 28(8 pp.). Available: Information Access/ Computer Select/16289501 [1995, June 13].

- Supplied note following title is given in brackets.
- Sometimes it is not possible to tell whether one is accessing an online source or a networked CD-ROM. If this is the case, use "Electronic" in the type of medium statement.

<A107> Portz-Shovlin, E. (1995, April). Our annual guide to summer running camps: Directory. *Runner's World* [Online], *30*, 77ff. Available: Mead Nexis/NEWS/ASAPII [1995, June 12].

<A108> Reid, H. (1994, November). Forest rovers of the Amazon. *UNESCO Courier* [Online], 25ff. Available: Mead Nexis/NEWS/UNESCO [1995, June 20].

<A109> Valve replacement in the elderly. (Mitral valve). (1992, October 15). *Patient Care* [CD-ROM], 26(1 p.). Available: Information Access/ InfoTrac/Health Reference Center/July '91–July '94 [1995, May 11].

- This example has no identifying accession number in the citation.

2. E-mail

a. Archived Works

Basic Forms

Author. (Year, month day). Title. *Magazine* [Type of medium], *volume number* (if given), inclusive paging (if given), or other indication of length. Available E-mail: LISTSERV/Get [Access date].

Title. (Year, month day). *Magazine* [Type of medium], *volume number* (if given), inclusive paging (if given), or other indication of length. Available E-mail: LISTSERV/Get [Access date].

- When author is not available, use the second basic form.
- Give the date: *year, month* for monthly publications, and *year, month day* for weekly publications.
- Type of medium statement follows directly after the magazine title, without punctuation.
- For information on management of paging, see the detailed guidelines in Section I.B.1., under Basic Forms of this chapter (page 33).

- In the "available" statement, provide the LISTSERV network address and the file name with its extension in the "Get" message.

<A110>   Owens, J. (1995, May 13). A lighter burden. *DargonZine* [Online], *8*, 22 paragraphs. Available E-mail: LISTSERV@brownvm.bitnet/Get dargon v8n2 [1995, June 17].

<A111>   Snell, J. (1993, December). Different circumstances. *Quanta* [Online], *5*, 6 paragraphs. Available E-mail: LISTSERV@andrew.cmu.edu/Get quanta 1293 [1994, December 20].

<A112>   Viviano, F. (1995, May/June). The new Mafia order. *Mother Jones Magazine* [Online], 72 paragraphs. Available E-mail: LISTSERV@mojones.com/Get mojones MJ95 [1995, June 17].
- Reference has no volume and issue numbers.

b. Real-Time Works

Basic Forms

Author. (Year, month day). Title. *Magazine* [Type of medium], *volume number* (if given), inclusive paging (if given), or other indication of length. Available E-mail: DISCUSSION GROUP@address [Access date].

Title. (Year, month day). *Magazine* [Type of medium], *volume number* (if given), inclusive paging (if given), or other indication of length. Available E-mail: DISCUSSION GROUP@address [Access date].

- When author is not given, use the second basic form.
- Give the date: *year, month* for monthly publications, and *year, month day* for weekly publications.
- Type of medium statement follows directly after the magazine title, without punctuation.
- For information on management of paging, see the detailed guidelines in Section I.B.1., under Basic Forms of this chapter (page 33).
- In the "available" statement, indicate the discussion group/LISTSERV and capitalize the name as it is a proper noun.

<A113>   Owens, J. (1995, May 13). A lighter burden. *DargonZine* [Online], *8*, 22 paragraphs. Available E-mail: DARGON-L@brownvm.bitnet [1995, May 13].

<A114> Snell, J. (1993, December). Different circumstances. *Quanta* [Online], *5*, 6 paragraphs. Available E-mail: QUANTA@andrew.cmu.edu [1993, December 20].

<A115> Viviano, F. (1995, May/June). The new Mafia order. *Mother Jones Magazine* [Online], 72 paragraphs. Available E-mail: MOTHER JONES-LIST@mojones.com [1995, June 17].
   • Reference does not have volume number.

3. FTP

Basic Forms

Author. (Year, month day). Title. *Magazine* [Type of medium], *volume number*(if given), inclusive paging (if given), or other indication of length. Available FTP: site/search path/file [Access date].

Title. (Year, month day). *Magazine* [Type of medium], *volume number* (if given), inclusive paging (if given), or other indication of length. Available FTP: site/search path/file [Access date].

   • When author is not available, use the second basic form.
   • Give the date: *year, month* for monthly publications, and *year, month day* for weekly publications.
   • Type of medium statement follows directly after the magazine title, without punctuation.
   • For information on management of paging, see the detailed guidelines in Section I.B.1., under Basic Forms of this chapter (page 33).
   • It is not necessary to repeat the protocol (FTP) on the WWW after the "available" statement since it is stated in the URL.

<A116> Atwood, M. (1994, December). [Margaret Atwood, Interview with Robert Sward]. *The Blue Penny Quarterly*, [Online], *1*, 143–152. Available FTP: ftp.etext.org/pub/Zines/BluePennyQuarterly/BPQ_ 3.txt [1995, July 10].
   • This is an example of an interview. If the interview is untitled (as in this case), the material in brackets replaces the title. The brackets indicate that this is a description of the content, rather than an actual title.

<A117> Bealer, D. (1995, February). Brighton Bealer memoirs. *Random Access Humor* [Online], 3ff. Available FTP: ftp.clark.net/pub/rah/rah9502.txt [1995, July 10].
   • This reference lacks the volume information.

<A118>   Holohan, E. (1995, January). As time goes by. *My Town* [Online], *1*,
        1–2. Available FTP: quake.think.com/pub/scholastic/My Town
        (ASCII) [1995, June 11].

<A119a> Schrader, E. (1995, January–February). A giant spraying sound: Since
        NAFTA, Mexican growers are spraying more toxic pesticides on
        fruits, vegetables—and workers. *Mother Jones Magazine* [Online],
        20, 34(6 pp.). Available: ftp:mojones.com/pub/Mother_Jones_Text/
        JF95/MotherJones_JF95:_A_Giant_Spraying_Sound [1995, July 1].

<A119b> Schrader, E. (1995, January–February). A giant spraying sound: Since
        NAFTA, Mexican growers are spraying more toxic pesticides on
        fruits, vegetables—and workers. *Mother Jones Magazine* [Online], *20*,
        34(6 pp.). Available: ftp//:mojones.com/pub/Mother_Jones_Text/
        JF95/MotherJones_JF95:_A_Giant_Spraying_Sound [1995, July 1].

> • This is a reference to an article obtained from an FTP site via the
> WWW. The "available" statement has a slightly different format.

4. Gopher

Basic Forms

Author. (Year, month day). Title. *Magazine* [Type of medium], *volume number* (if
given), inclusive paging (if given), or other indicator of length. Available
Gopher: Gopher site/search path/file [Access date].

Title. (Year, month day). *Magazine* [Type of medium], *volume number* (if given),
inclusive paging (if given), or other indicator of length. Available Gopher:
Gopher site/search path/file [Access date].

> • When author is not available, use the second basic form.
> • Give the date: *year, month* for monthly publications, and *year,
> month day* for weekly publications.
> • Type of medium statement follows directly after the magazine
> title, without punctuation.
> • For information on management of paging, see the detailed
> guidelines in Section I.B.1., under Basic Forms of this chapter
> (page 33).
> • When providing the "available" statement, indicate the Gopher
> site, search path, and file name.
> • It is not necessary to repeat the protocol (Gopher) on the WWW
> after the "available" statement since it is stated in the URL.

<A120>   Holst, K. (1994, May 14). The school of life. *Twilight World* [Online],
         2, 53 paragraphs. Available Gopher: gopher.etext.org/Zines/Twilight_
         World/twilight.world-2.3.gz [1995, July 16].

<A121>   Owens, J. (1995, May 13). A lighter burden. *DargonZine* [Online], *8*,
         22 paragraphs. Available: gopher://gopher.cic.net/ElectronicSerials/
         DargonZine/dargon v8n2 [1995, July 17].
         • If the item is retrieved on the WWW, indicate the URL.

<A122>   Schrader, E. (1995, January/February). A giant spraying sound. *Mother
         Jones Magazine* [Online], 42 paragraphs. Available: gopher://mojones.
         mojones.com.:70/00/JF95/MotherJones_JF95%3A_Giant_Spraying_
         Sound [1995, May 30].
         • Note this reference does not have volume and issue numbers.

<A123>   Snell, J. (1993, December). Different circumstances. *Quanta* [Online],
         5, 6 paragraphs. Available Gopher: gopher.contrib.andrew.cmu.edu/
         magazines/quanta/issues/1993-dec [1995, July 15].

5. HTTP

Basic Forms

Author. (Year, month day). Title. *Magazine* [Type of medium], *volume number* (if
    given), inclusive paging (if given), or other indicator of length. Available: URL
    [Access date].

Title. (Year, month day). *Magazine* [Type of medium], *volume number* (if given),
    inclusive paging (if given), or other indicator of length. Available: URL
    [Access date].

                    • When author is not available, use the second basic form.
                    • Give the date: *year, month* for monthly publications, and *year,
                      month day* for weekly publications.
                    • Type of medium statement follows directly after the magazine
                      title, without punctuation.
                    • For information on management of paging, see the detailed
                      guidelines in Section I.B.1., under Basic Forms of this chapter
                      (page 33).
                    • When providing URL, indicate the WWW site, search path, and
                      file name.
                    • It is not necessary to repeat the protocol (HTTP) on the WWW
                      after the "available" statement since it is stated in the URL.

<A124>   Greg Roach: The bard of CD-ROM [Interview]. (1995, April/May). *Media West Magazine* [Online], 20 paragraphs. Available: http://www.wimsey.com/Media_Wave/current/Features/Greg_Roach.html [1995, July 16].

- Supplementary bibliographic information is supplied, in brackets, after the article title.
- Note the reference has no volume and issue numbers.

<A125>   Kadrey, R. (1995, July 16). Horse latitudes. *InterText* [Online], *5*, 36 paragraphs. Available: http://etext.archive.umich.edu/Zines/Inter Text/v5n4/latitudes.html [1995, July 17].

<A126>   Pique, J. (1993, Winter). San Diego dreaming. *TwentyNothing* [Online], 17 paragraphs. Available: http://afs/athena.mit.edu/user/t/h/thomasc/Public/twenty/wint93/pique.html [1995, June 17].

- Note the reference has no volume and issue numbers.

<A127>   Viviano, F. (1995, May/June). The new Mafia order. *Mother Jones Magazine* [Online], 72 paragraphs. Available: http://www.mojones.com/MOTHER_JONES/MJ95/viviano.html [1995, July 17].

6. Telnet

Basic Forms

Author. (Year, month day). Title. *Magazine* [Type of medium], *volume number* (if given), inclusive paging (if given), or other indicator of length. Available Telnet: Telnet site**/login**:**/password**:/search path/file [Access date].

Title. (Year, month day). *Magazine* [Type of medium], *volume number* (if given), inclusive paging (if given), or other indicator of length. Available Telnet: Telnet site**/login**:**/password**:/search path/file [Access date].

- When author is not available, use the second basic form.
- Give the date: *year, month* for monthly publications, and *year, month day* for weekly publications.
- Type of medium statement follows directly after the magazine title, without punctuation.
- For information on management of paging, see the detailed guidelines in Section I.B.1., under Basic Forms of this chapter (page 33).
- If log-in information and password are required in order to establish the Telnet session, include information in the "available" statement.

<A128> Quin, L. R. E. (No date). Summary of metafonts available. *TeXMag*
         [Online], *4*, 5–16. Available Telnet: library.unc.edu/**login**: LIBRARY/
         Electronic Journals/Texmag/texmag.4.06 [1995, July 5].
           • Write "No date" if the creation date for the electronic form is
             not available.

<A129> Overmyer, E. (1995, June). Serving the reference needs of children.
         Wilson Library Bulletin [Online], *69*, 16 paragraphs. Available
         Telnet: dewey.lib.ncsu.edu/Electronic Texts/Magazines/Wilson
         Library Bulletin/June 1995 [1995, July 21].

C. Newsletter Articles

1. CD-ROM and Commercial Online Databases

Basic Forms

Author. (Year, month day). Title. *Newsletter* [Type of medium], *volume*, paging if
    given, or other indicator of length. Available: Supplier/Database name/Identifier
    or number if available/item or accession number [Access date].

Title. (Year, month day). *Newsletter* [Type of medium], *volume*, paging if given, or
    other indicator of length. Available: Supplier/Database name/Identifier or num-
    ber if available/item or accession number [Access date].

           • Give date as it is given in reference.
           • Include volume if given, otherwise issue number (if given).
             Volume number will be underlined or italicized; the issue num-
             ber will not.
           • Give page range whenever possible. If that is not available,
             apply these rules:

1. When the initial page is known, (a) in parentheses, indicate the article length
after the initial page, e.g., 10(12 pp.), 10(80 paragraphs), 10(24 screens),
10(300 lines), 10(3,000 words); or (b) use notation "ff" for "and following
pages."

2. When the initial page is not available, indicate the article length (the number
of paragraphs, screens, lines, or words). No parentheses are needed.

<A130> Conway, C. (1995, January/February). Commentary: MDCP grants can
         promote strategic thinking in state trade development. *Clearinghouse
         on State International Policies: Newsletter of the State International
         Policy Network* [CD-ROM], *5*(1), 5 paragraphs. Available: National

Economic, Social, and Environmental Data Bank/Economic Con-
version Information Exchange (Program)/DA OECI CFED1 [1995,
July 13].

<A131> EU/Japan: Sir Leon leads European business delegation to Japan. (1995,
June 9). *Multinational Service* [Online], 9 paragraphs. Available:
Dialog/PTS Newsletter DB/636/02835122 [1995, July 13].

<A132> Fairweather, F. (1995, April). The beauty of our industry and the burden
of animal testing [Transcript of speech]. *European Cosmetic Markets*
[Online], 151ff. Available: Mead Nexis/EUROPE/ALLEUR [1995,
July 13].

<A133> Hansen, T. C. (1995, June 30). Trademark created for Indian-made
products. *News from Indian Country* [CD-ROM], *8*, 3. Available:
Softline Information/Ethnic Newswatch [1995, July 10].
   • Since this item has no identifying accession number, only supplier and database name are listed.

<A134> Sports: NBA announces it will lock out players until parties reach con-
tract agreement. (1995, July 5). *Daily Labor Report* [Online], *128*,
d15ff. Available: Mead Nexis/EASY/NEWS [1995, July 13].

<A135> Tricks of the trade: How to register a company in Russia (1994, April/
May). *BISNIS Bulletin (Newly Independent States)* [CD-ROM], 11
paragraphs. Available: National Trade Data Bank/BISNIS Bulletin
(Newly Independent States)/IT BISBUL APRMAY94ART8 [1995,
July 11].
   • This item lacks volume, issue number, and paging. Article
   length is given as a paragraph count following the type of
   medium statement.

2. E-mail

a. Archived Works

Basic Forms

Author. (Year, month day). Title. *Newsletter* [Type of medium], *volume number,*
inclusive paging (if given), or other indicator of length. Available E-mail:
LISTSERV/Get [Access date].

Title. (Year, month day). *Newsletter* [Type of medium], *volume number,* inclusive
paging (if given), or other indicator of length. Available E-mail: LISTSERV/
Get [Access date].

- When author is not available, use the second basic form.
- Give the date: *year, month* for monthly publications, and *year, month day* for weekly publications.
- Type of medium statement follows directly after the newsletter title, without punctuation.
- For information on management of paging, see the detailed guidelines in Section I.C.1., under Basic Forms of this chapter (page 41).
- In the "available" statement, provide the LISTSERV network address and the file name with its extension in the "Get" message.

<A136> EFF analysis of Communications Decency Act as passed by Senate. (1995, June 16). *EFFector Online* [Online], *8*, 38 paragraphs. Available E-mail: LISTSERV@eff.org/Get eff v08n10 [1995, July 18].
- The act title is capitalized as it is a proper noun.

<A137> Justice ponders Microsoft network. (1995, July 18). *EDUPAGE* [Online], 12 lines. Available E-mail: LISTSERV@educom.edu/Get edupage-07.18.95 [1995, July 21].
- Note the reference does not have volume information.

<A138> Women of Anabaptist traditions in historical perspective. (1994, March 21). *Historian's Newsletter* [Online], *2*, 7 paragraphs. Available E-mail: LISTSERV@ukanvm.cc.ukans.edu/Get histnews_2_9.txt [1995, July 21].

<A139> Zonneveld, C. (1995, June 7). [Review of the book *Dynamic energy budget in biological systems: Theory and applications in ecotoxicology*]. *Society for Mathematical Biology Digest* [Online], *95*, 6 paragraphs. Available E-mail: LISTSERV@fconvx.ncifcrf.gov/Get smb net v95n08 [1995, July 21].
- This is an example of a book review. For reviews of other media, change the statement in brackets accordingly, for example, [Review of the film *The postman*].

b. Real-Time Works

Basic Forms

Author. (Year, month day). Title. *Newsletter* [Type of medium], *volume number*, inclusive paging (if given), or other indicator of length. Available E-mail: DISCUSSION GROUP@address [Access date].

Title. (Year, month day). *Newsletter* [Type of medium], *volume number,* inclusive paging (if given), or other indicator of length. Available E-mail: DISCUSSION GROUP@address [Access date].

- When author is not available, use the second basic form.
- Give the date: *year, month* for monthly publications, and *year, month day* for weekly publications.
- Type of medium statement follows directly after the newsletter title, without punctuation.
- For information on management of paging, see the detailed guidelines in Section I.C.1., under Basic Forms of this chapter (page 41).
- In the "available" statement, indicate the discussion group/LIST-SERV and its Internet/BITNET address.

<A140>   EFF analysis of Communications Decency Act as passed by Senate. (1995, June 16). *EFFector Online* [Online], *8,* 38 paragraphs. Available E-mail: EFF@eff.org/Get eff v08n10 [1995, June 16].
- The act title is capitalized as it is a proper noun.

<A141>   Justice ponders Microsoft network. (1995, July 18). *EDUPAGE* [Online], 12 lines. Available E-mail: EDUPAGE@educom.edu [1995, July 18].
- Note the reference does not have volume and issue information.

<A142>   Women of Anabaptist traditions in historical perspective. (1994, March 21). *Historian's Newsletter* [Online], *2,* 7 paragraphs. Available E-mail: HISTNEWS@ukanvm.cc.ukans.edu [1994, March 21].

<A143>   Zonneveld, C. (1995, June 7). [Review of the book *Dynamic energy budget in biological systems: Theory and applications in ecotoxicology*]. *Society for Mathematical Biology Digest* [Online], *95,* 6 paragraphs. Available E-mail: SMBNET@fconvx.ncifcrf.gov [1995, June 7].
- This is an example of a book review. For reviews of other media, change the statement in brackets accordingly, for example, [Review of the film *The postman*].

3. FTP

Basic Forms

Author. (Year, month day). Title. *Newsletter* [Type of medium], *volume,* paging if given, or other indicator of length. Available FTP: address/path/file [Access date].

Title. (Year, month day). *Newsletter* [Type of medium], *volume*, paging if given, or other indicator of length. Available FTP: address/path/file [Access date].

- When author is not available, use the second basic form.
- Give date as it is given in reference.
- Include volume if given, otherwise issue number (if given). Volume number will be underlined or italicized; the issue number will not.
- For information on management of paging, see the detailed guidelines in Section I.C.1., under Basic Forms of this chapter (page 41).
- It is not necessary to repeat the protocol (FTP) on the WWW after the "available" statement since it is stated in the URL.

<A144a> Agre, P. (1995, January). The Internet meets the Constitution. *The Network Observer* [Online], 2, 13 paragraphs. Available FTP: ftp. eff.org/pub/Publications/E-journals/TNO/tno02.01 [1995, July 7].

<A144b> Agre, P. (1995, January). The Internet meets the Constitution. *The Network Observer* [Online], 2, 13 paragraphs. Available: ftp:// ftp.eff.org/pub/Publications/E-journals/TNO/tno02.01 [1995, July 7].
- If an FTP site is reached via the WWW, use the URL in the "available" statement.

<A145> Elbl, M. (1992, April). [Abstract of Tracking economic 'long waves' in medieval Mediterranean commerce, A paper presented at the Academy's Chicago 1991 Meeting]. *The American Academy of Research Historians of Medieval Spain Newsletter* [Online], *18*, 1–2. Available FTP: hnsource.cc.ukans.edu/pub/history/Journals/aarhms/vol18no2_april92 [1995, June 15].
- This is an abstract of a paper. Abstract of. . . precedes the paper title, along with information on the meeting; the whole statement is placed in brackets.

<A146> McManus, N. (1995, February 20). Letting publishers be publishers [Editorial], *Digital Media Perspective* [Online], 9 paragraphs. Available FTP: ftp.eff.org/pub/Publications/E-journals/DMP/950220.dmp [1995, July 7].
- Note indicating that this is an editorial follows the title in brackets.

<A147> Muktupavels, V. (1995, May 25). CDs: Recent Latvian releases. *Ethnomusicology Research Digest* [Online], *6*, 2-6. Available FTP: inform. umd.edu/inforM/EdRes/ReadingRoom/Newsletters/EthnoMusicology /Digest/95-207.erd [1995, June 16].

4. Gopher

Basic Forms

Author. (Year, month day). Title. *Newsletter* [Type of medium], *volume*, inclusive paging (if given), or other indicator of length. Available Gopher: gopher site/search path/file [Access date].

Title. (Year, month day). *Newsletter* [Type of medium], *volume*, inclusive paging (if given), or other indicator of length. Available Gopher: Gopher site/search path/file [Access date].

- When author is not available, use the second basic form.
- Give the date: *year, month day* for newsletter publications.
- Type of medium statement follows directly after the newsletter title, without punctuation.
- Include volume if given, otherwise, issue number (if given). Volume number will be underlined or italicized; the issue number will not.
- For information on management of paging, see the detailed guidelines in Section I.C.1., under Basic Forms of this chapter (page 41).
- When providing the "available" information, indicate the Gopher site, search path, and file name.
- It is not necessary to repeat the protocol (Gopher) on the WWW after the "available" statement since it is stated in the URL.

<A148> Cornell introduces project to teach kids about ecology. (1995, June 30). *ES-USDA Extension Service Newsletter* [Online], 4 paragraphs. Available: gopher://gopher-ext.mes.umn.edu:1000/00/Internal/ES-USDA/4635 [1995, July 18].
- No volume or issue number is supplied in the original document.

<A149> Government Performance and Results Act (GPRA) of 1993. (1994, May). *Integrated Pest Management Newsletter* [Online], *1*, 4 paragraphs. Available: gopher://psupena.psu.edu:70/0%24d%20290012 [1995, July 18].

<A150> More attacks on BBC regime. (1994, April 12). *AM/FM Online Edition* [Online], 3 paragraphs. Available Gopher: gopher.cic.net/Electronic Serials/AM/FM-UK Radio News [1995, July 17].
- No volume number is supplied in the original document.

<A151> Peterson, K. (1995, Spring). Motivating volunteers: The 1994 Midwinter LITA Leadership Development Session. *LITA Newsletter* [Online], *15*, 9 paragraphs. Available: gopher://vega.lib.ncsu.edu:70/0ftp%3Aftp.

lib.ncsu.edu@/pub/stacks/lita/lita-v15n02-peterson-motivating [1995, July 18].

5. HTTP

Basic Forms

Author. (Year, month day). Title. *Newsletter* [Type of medium], *volume number* (if given), inclusive paging (if given), or other indicator of length. Available: URL [Access date].

Title. (Year, month day). *Newsletter* [Type of medium], *volume number* (if given), inclusive paging (if given), or other indicator of length. Available: URL [Access date].

- When author is not available, use the second basic form.
- Give the date: *year, month* for monthly publications, and *year, month day* for weekly publications.
- Type of medium statement follows directly after the magazine title, without punctuation.
- For information on management of paging, see the detailed guidelines in Section I.C.1., under Basic Forms of this chapter (page 41).
- In the "available" statement, give the WWW site, search path, and file name.
- It is not necessary to repeat the protocol (HTTP) on the WWW after the "available" statement since it is stated in the URL.

<A152>   Mars planetary rover. (1994, Fall). *The M2RC Newsletter* [Online], *5*, 6 paragraphs. Available: http://www.mmrc.ncsu.edu/Newsletters/v5n1/v5n1.html#Rover [1995, July 18].

<A153>   Murphy, H. J. (1995, July 5). Duty of care broadened. *Law NOTES Canadian Legal News Letter* [Online], *7*, 7 paragraphs. Available: http://www.discribe.ca/murco [1995, July 18].

<A154>   Obermeyer, J., Edwards, R., & Bledsoe, L. (1995, June 9). Bean leaf beetles and emerging soybeans. *Pest Management & Crop Production Newsletter* [Online], *12*, 5 paragraphs. Available: http://infor.aes.purdue.edu/entomology/Pest&Crop/P&C12.txt [1995, July 18].
- Issue number is presented, instead of volume, in this reference.

<A155>   Pare, M. (1995, July 17). Fall River loan program promotes small business. *Providence Business News: Southern New England's Business Weekly* [Online], *10*, 24 paragraphs. Available: http://www.pbn.com/w071795/crecon.html [1995, July 18].

6. Telnet

Basic Forms

Author. (Year, month day). Title. *Newsletter* [Type of medium], *volume number* (if given), inclusive paging (if given), or other indicator of length. Available Telnet: Telnet site/**login**:/**password**:/search path/file [Access date].

Title. (Year, month day). *Newsletter* [Type of medium], *volume number* (if given), inclusive paging (if given), or other indicator of length. Available Telnet: Telnet site/**login**:/**password**:/search path/file [Access date].

- When author is not available, use the second basic form.
- Give the date: *year, month* for monthly publications, and *year, month day* for weekly publications.
- Type of medium statement follows directly after the magazine title, without punctuation.
- For information on management of paging, see the detailed guidelines in Section I.C.1., under Basic Forms of this chapter, (page 41).
- If log-in information and password are required in order to establish the Telnet session, include information in the "available" statement.

<A156>   EFF analysis of Communications Decency Act as passed by Senate. (1995, June 16). *EFFector Online* [Online], *8*, 38 paragraphs. Available Telnet: nicol.jvnc.net/**login**: nicol/news/Newspaper, Magazines, and Newsletters/Computer Publications/EFF/June, 1995 [1995, July 18].

- The act title is capitalized as it is a proper noun.

<A157>   International Symposium on Floristic Diversity and Characteristics of East Asia. (1995, December). *The Bean Bag* [Online], *40*, 7–9. Available Telnet: library.unc.edu/**login**: LIBRARY/Electronic Journals/UNC-CH Internet Library/The Bean Bag: Leguminosae Research Newsletter/Bean Bag, December 1994 [1995, July 19].

<A158>   One step closer to producing anti-atoms. (1995, July 6). *Physics News Update* [Online], 232, 34 lines. Available Telnet: dewey.lib.ncsu.edu/ Electronic Texts/Newsletters/Physics News/Physics News Update 232 [1995, July 21].

- The source lacks volume information. Thus, the issue number is provided in the reference.

D. Newspaper Articles

Basic Forms

Author. (Year, Month day). Title. *Newspaper* (edition, if given), [Type of medium], page or pages (or starting page and length). Available: Supplier/Database name/Identifier or number if available/item or accession number [Access date].

Title. (Year, Month day). *Newspaper* (edition, if given), [Type of medium], page or pages (or starting page and length). Available: Supplier/Database name/Identifier or number if available/item or accession number [Access date].

- When author is not available, give the second basic form.
- Give page range whenever possible. If that is not available, apply these rules:

1. When the initial page is known, (a) in parentheses indicate the article length after the initial page, e.g., 10(12 pp.), 10(80 paragraphs), 10(24 screens), 10(300 lines), 10(3,000 words); or (b) use the notation "ff" for "and following pages."

2. When the initial page is not available, indicate the article length (the number of paragraphs, screens, lines, or words). No parentheses are needed.

- It is not necessary to repeat the protocol (HTTP, Gopher, or FTP) used on the WWW after the "available" statement since it is stated in the URL.

<A159a> Asi-Jew, S. (1995, February 3). [Review of the book *The concubine's children*]. *Northwest Asian Quarterly* [CD-ROM], p. 20(24 paragraphs). Available: Softline Information/Ethnic Newswatch [1995, July 15].
- This is an example of a book review. For reviews of other media, change the statement in brackets accordingly, for example, [Review of the film *The postman*].

<A159b> Asi-Jew, S. (1995, February 3). [Review of the book *The concubine's children*]. *Northwest Asian Quarterly* [Electronic], p. 20(24 paragraphs). Available: Softline Information/Ethnic Newswatch [1995, July 15].
- This is an example of a book review. For reviews of other media, change the statement in brackets accordingly. For example, [Review of the film *The postman*].
- It is not always possible to tell whether one is accessing a networked CD-ROM or an online source. If this cannot be determined, use "Electronic" in the type of medium statement.

<A160> Bagwell, K. (1995, June 11). "Green" goods proliferate in varied
        shades. *The Arizona Daily Star* [Online], 46 paragraphs. Available:
        http://www.azstarnet.com/public/pubstar/134-3994.html [1995, July
        24].

<A161> Campbell, K. K. (1994, October 13). Courting Courtney on the net. *Eye
        Weekly* [Online], p. 1(20 paragraphs). Available: ftp://ftp.eff.org/pub/
        Publications/E-journals/Eye/941013.eye [1995, June 17].
        • This is an example of an document at an FTP site, reached on
          the WWW. In such a case, use the URL in the "available" state-
          ment.

<A162> Henneberger, M. (1995, June 8). Republicans battle party on arts funds.
        The New York Times (Late ed.), [Online], p. B6. Available: Mead
        Nexis/NEWS/NYT [1995, June 15].

<A163> Howard, J. (1994, June 17). Let the global game begin: Eyes, passions
        of soccer fans everywhere turn to U.S. *The Washington Post* (Final
        ed.), [Online], p. A1. Available: Dialog/The Washington Post/146/
        2198133 [1995, July 16].

<A164> Howell, V., & Carlton, B. (1993, August 29). Growing up tough: New
        generation fights for its life: Inner-city youths live by rule of ven-
        geance. *Birmingham News* [CD-ROM], p. 1A(10 pp.). Available:
        1994 SIRS/SIRS 1993 Youth/Volume 4/Article56A [1995, July 16].
        • This example shows the notation used when the number of
          pages in the electronic source is known.

<A165> Johnson, T. (1994, December 5). Indigenous people are now more com-
        bative, organized. *Miami Herald* [Online], p. 29SA(22 paragraphs).
        Available: gopher://summit.fiu.edu/Miami Herald—Summit-Related
        Articles/ 12/05/95—Indigenous People Now More Combative, Or-
        ganized [1995, July 16].
        • This reference gives beginning page and the number of para-
          graphs. This information is useful to refer to material in text ref-
          erences.
        • If a document is retrieved at a WWW site, give the URL in the
          "available" statement.

<A166> Jones, B. (1995, June 30). "Smoke" has substance [Movie review]. *The
        Phoenix Gazette* (Final section), [Online], p. C4(12 paragraphs).
        Available: Dialog/The Arizona Repub-Phoenix Gaz/492/08181238
        [1995, July 16].

• This is an example of a movie review where the review article has its own title. Otherwise, the article title is presented as: [Review of the film *Smoke*].

<A167a> LaFranchi, H. (1994, December 8). Miami Summit: The bonding of a continent. *Christian Science Monitor* [Online], p. WORLD1(20 paragraphs). Available: gopher://summit.fiu.edu:70/11/Monitor/ 12/08/94—Miami Summit: The Bonding of a Continent [1995, July 16].

<A167b> LaFranchi, H. (1994, December 8). Miami Summit: The bonding of a continent. *Christian Science Monitor* [Online], p. WORLD1(20 paragraphs). Available: http://summit.fiu.edu:70/00/Monitor/monitor.4 [1995, July 24].

• Examples A167a and A167b show the same document retrieved by different methods on different dates.

<A168> Moving up the charts. (1995, May 26). *South China Morning Post* [Online], Friday Entertainment, p. 24(26 paragraphs). Available: Mead Nexis/ASIAPC/SCHINA [1995, July 17].

• This is an example of an article from a special section of the newspaper.

<A169> 1994, a mixed bag in Indian country [Editorial]. (1994, December 30). *The Ojibwe News* [CD-ROM], p. 4(52 lines). Available: Softline Information/Ethnic Newswatch [1995, July 15].

• This is an example of an editorial.

• Line count is given to indicate article length.

• Note that numbers file alphabetically in a reference list as if they were spelled out.

<A170> Stout, H. (1995, May 24). Oregon tries its own welfare reform: Offering companies an incentive to put people to work. *Wall Street Journal* [Online], p. A16(1,330 words). Available: Dow Jones News Retrieval Service/TextM/Wall Street Journal [1995, July 16].

<A171> U.N. must fight back [Editorial]. *The Toronto Star* (Final ed.), [Online], p. A16(13 paragraphs). Available: Dow Jones News Retrieval Service/TextM/International Publications—Newspapers & General Publications [1995, July 16].

<A172> U.N. strike could change the rules for peacekeeping. (1993, June 13). *St. Petersburg Times* [CD-ROM], p. 1A(2 pp.). Available: 1994 SIRS/SIRS 1993 World Affairs/Article 65C [1995, July 16].

II. CITE AN ENTIRE WORK

This section provides a few examples of citations for electronic serials. The selection has been limited to publications that exist only in an electronic format. For an extensive listing of electronic serials, see *Directory of Electronic Journals, Newsletters, and Academic Discussion Lists* (Washington, D.C.: Association of Research Libraries, 1995).

Basic Form

Serial Title [Notes on serial, e.g., ISSN, frequency], [Type of medium]. (Date, first issue to date). Place of publication: Issuing agency. Available: address/path/file or message

> • Notes about the publication follow the title, in brackets.
> • Access date is not an essential element in this citation form.

<A173a> *Bryn Mawr Classical Review* [ISSN: 1063-2948; irregular], [Online]. (1990, November to date). Bryn Mawr, PA: Bryn Mawr College. Available Gopher: gopher.cic.net

<A173b> *Bryn Mawr Classical Review* [ISSN: 1063-2948; irregular], [Online]. (1990, November to date). Bryn Mawr, PA: Bryn Mawr College. Available E-mail: LISTSERV@cc.brynmawr.edu/SUBSCRIBE BMCR-L <firstname lastname>

<A174a> *Psycoloquy: A Refereed Journal of Peer Commentary in Psychology, Neuroscience and Cognitive Science* [Online]. (1990, February 1 to date). Princeton, NJ: Stephen Harnad (editor), Princeton University, and the American Psychological Association. Available E-mail: LIST SERV@pucc.princeton,edu/SUBSCRIBE PSYC <firstname last name>

<A174b> *Psycoloquy: A Refereed Journal of Peer Commentary in Psychology, Neuroscience and Cognitive Science* [Online]. (1990, February 1 to date). Princeton, NJ: Stephen Harnad (editor), Princeton University, and the American Psychological Association. Available Gopher: gopher.cic.net

<A175> *Surfaces* [Online]. (1991, October 31 to date). Montréal, PQ, Canada: Université de Montréal, Département de littérature comparée. Available FTP: ftp.umontreal.ca/Surfaces/Articles/ASCII, or MS-DOS or Macintosh

Discussion Lists, USENET Newsgroups, and Personal Mail

The *Publication Manual of the American Psychological Association* (4th edition, 1994) does not recommend including personal communications, i.e., personal electronic mail (E-mail) messages, messages on discussion lists and USENET newsgroups, in Reference Lists because of the difficulty of recovering them. Instead, the guide recommends citing the material only in the text (1994, p. 174). *Electronic Styles* differs with this approach and provides many examples for citing these types of resources in this chapter.

I. DISCUSSION LISTS

A. Cite a Message

Basic Forms

Author. (Year, Month day). Subject of message. *Discussion List* [Online]. Available E-mail: DISCUSSION LIST@e-mail address [Access date].

Author. (Year, Month day). Subject of message. *Discussion List* [Online]. Available E-mail: LISTSERV@e-mail address/Get [Access date].

> • If the reference is a real-time message, follow the first basic form. If the message is obtained by searching the list's archive, follow the second basic form.
> • If the message is unsigned, use the author's log-in name in uppercase letters.
> • Indicate the date when message was sent to the discussion list.
> • Paging or length statement is not required in this form.

53

- In uppercase letters, the names of discussion lists and LISTSERVs are present, followed by the lists' Internet or BITNET addresses (i.e., TWAIN-L or LISTSERV).

<A176a> Berkowitz, P. (1995, April 3). Sussy's gravestone. *Mark Twain Forum* [Online]. Available E-mail: TWAIN-L@yorkvml.bitnet [1995, April 3].

<A176b> Berkowitz, P. (1995, April 3). Sussy's gravestone. *Mark Twain Forum* [Online]. Available E-mail: LISTSERV@yorkvml.bitnet/Get twain-l log9504 [1995, July 31].
    - Reference is obtained by searching the list's archive.

<A177a> RRECOME. (1995, April 1). Top ten rules of film criticism. *Discussions on All Forms of Cinema* [Online]. Available E-mail: CINEMA-L@ american.edu [1995, April 1].

<A177b> RRECOME. (1995, April 1). Top ten rules of film criticism. *Discussions on All Forms of Cinema* [Online]. Available E-mail: LISTSERV@ american.edu/Get cinema-l log9504A [1995, August 1].
    - Reference is obtained by searching the list's archive.

B. Cite a Discussion: One Topic, Several Discussants

Basic Forms

Author. (Year, Month day). Subject of discussion [Discussion]. *Discussion List* [Online]. Available E-mail: DISCUSSION LIST@e-mail address [Access date].

Author. (Year, Month day). Subject of discussion [Discussion]. *Discussion List* [Online]. Available E-mail: LISTSERV@e-mail address/Get [Access date].

- If the reference is a real-time message, follow the first basic form. If the message is obtained by searching the list's archive, follow the second basic form.
- If the message is unsigned, use the author's log-in name in uppercase letters.
- Indicate the date when message was sent to the discussion list.
- In brackets, write Discussion after the subject of discussion, to indicate that the message is from a discussion with several discussants.
- Paging or length statement is not required in this form.
- Present, in uppercase letters, the names of discussion lists and LISTSERVs, followed by the lists' Internet or Bitnet addresses (i.e., SAFETY or LISTSERV).

<A178a> Boulton, R. (1995, July 21). Explosion proof refrigerator? [Discussion]. *Safety* [Online]. Available E-mail: SAFETY@uvmvm.uvm.edu [1995, July 21].

<A178b> Boulton, R. (1995, July 21). Explosion proof refrigerator? [Discussion]. *Safety* [Online]. Available E-mail: LISTSERV@uvmvm.uvm.edu/Get safety log9507D [1995, August 1].
  • This reference is obtained by searching the discussion list's archive.

<A179a> Voltz, J. (1995, July 20). Building codes [Discussion]. *Civil Engineering Research & Education* [Online]. Available E-mail: CIVIL-L@ unb.ca [1995, July 20].

<A179b> Voltz, J. (1995, July 20). Building codes [Discussion]. *Civil Engineering Research & Education* [Online]. Available E-mail: LISTSERV@unb. ca/Get civil-l log9507 [1995, July 31].
  • Reference is obtained by searching the list's archive.

C. Cite a Forwarded Message

1. Without Embellishments

Basic Forms

Forwarder. (Year, Month day). [Forwarded message original sender, *Discussion topic*]. *Discussion List* [Online]. Available E-mail: DISCUSSION LIST@e-mail address [Access date].

Forwarder. (Year, Month day). [Forwarded message original sender, *Discussion topics*]. *Discussion List* [Online]. Available E-mail: LISTSERV@e-mail address/Get [Access date].

  • If the reference is a real-time message, follow the first basic form. If the message is obtained by searching the list's archive, follow the second basic form.
  • If the message is unsigned, use the author's log-in name in uppercase letters.
  • Indicate the date when message was sent to the discussion list.
  • Enclose the original sender and discussion topic in brackets.
  • Paging or length statement is not required in this form.
  • Present, in uppercase letters, the names of discussion lists and LISTSERVs, followed by the lists' Internet or Bitnet addresses (i.e., CIVIL-L or LISTSERV).

<A180a> MANCA. (1995, July 20). [Forwarded message M. O. Khalifa, *Stop NUCLEAR experiments*]. *Civil Engineering Research & Education* [Online]. Available E-mail: CIVIL-L@unb.ca [1995, July 20].

　　• Author's log-in name, in uppercase, is given as the first element since the real name is not available.

<A180b> MANCA. (1995, July 20). [Forwarded message M. O. Khalifa, *Stop NUCLEAR experiments*]. *Civil Engineering Research & Education* [Online]. Available E-mail: LISTSERV@unb.ca/Get civil-l log9507 [1995, August 1].

　　• Reference is obtained by searching the list's archive.

<A181a> Presno, O. de. (1995, June 28). [Forwarded message A. Makuc, *New KIDFORUM topic*]. *KIDLINK Project List* [Online]. Available E-mail: KIDLINK@ndsuvm1.bitnet [1995, June 28].

<A181b> Presno, O. de. (1995, June 28). [Forwarded message A. Makuc, *New KIDFORUM topic*]. *KIDLINK Project List* [Online]. Available E-mail: LISTSERV@ndsuvm1.bitnet/Get kidlink log9506e [1995, August 2].

　　• Reference is obtained by searching the list's archive.

　　• The Spanish *de* is not used before the last name alone. For example, de Presno, becomes Presno, O. de.

2. With Embellishments

Basic Forms

Forwarder. (Year, Month day). Subject of new message [Original message Sender, *Discussion topic*]. *Discussion List* [Online]. Available E-mail: DISCUSSION LIST@e-mail address [Access date].

Forwarder. (Year, Month day). Subject of new message [Original message Sender, *Discussion topic*]. *Discussion List* [Online]. Available E-mail: LISTSERV@e-mail address/Get [Access date].

　　• If the reference is a real-time message, follow the first basic form. If the message is obtained by searching the list's archive, follow the second basic form.

　　• If the message is unsigned, use the author's log-in name in uppercase letters.

　　• Indicate the date when message was sent to the discussion list.

　　• Enclose the forwarded subject of message along with the original sender in brackets.

　　• Paging or length statement is not required in this form.

• Present, in uppercase letters, the names of discussion lists and LISTSERVs, followed by the lists' Internet or BITNET addresses (i.e., PACS-L or LISTSERV).

<A182a> Punia, D. T. (1995, August 2). Post-its destroy book [Original message J. Page, Post-It notes]. *Public-Access Computer Systems Forum* [Online]. Available E-mail: PACS-L@uhupvm1.uh.edu [1995, August 2].

<A182b> Punia, D. T. (1995, August 2). Post-its destroy book [Original message J. Page, Post-It notes]. *Public-Access Computer Systems Forum* [Online]. Available E-mail: LISTSERV@uhupvm1.uh.edu/Get pacs-l log9508 [1995, August 3].
 • Reference is obtained by searching the list's archive.

<A183a> Stone, S. (1995, April 2). E.T. the extraterrestrial [Original message HOWARDB, E.T. (1995, April 1)]. *Discussions on All Forms of Cinema* [Online]. Available E-mail: CINEMA-L@american.edu [1995, April 2].
 • If the original message is not forwarded to the discussion list on the same day it is created, include the original date after the original subject of message.

<A183b> Stone, S. (1995, April 2). E.T. the extraterrestrial [Original message HOWARDB, E.T. (1995, April 1)]. *Discussions on All Forms of Cinema* [Online]. Available E-mail: LISTSERV@american.edu/Get cinema-l log 9504A [1995, April 2].
 • If the original message is not forwarded to the discussion list on the same day it is created, include the original date after the original subject of message.
 • Reference is obtained by searching the list's archive.

II. USENET

A. Individual Works

Basic Forms

Author. (Year, Month day). *Title* (edition), [Type of medium]. Available USENET: newsgroup [Access date].

Title (edition), [Type of medium]. (Year, Month day). Available USENET: newsgroup [Access date].

 • If author or editor is not given, use the second basic form.

• Provide year, month, and day when the individual work (e.g., a message) is sent to the newsgroup.

<A184>   Jankowski, T. (1995, June 5). *Eastern Europe is being warned to return properties to Holocaust victims* [Online]. Available USENET: soc.culture.ukrainia [1995, June 8].

B. Journal Articles

Basic Forms

Author. (Year). Title. *Journal* [Type of medium], *volume*(issue), paging if given, or other indicator of length. Available USENET: newsgroup [Access date].

Title. (Year). *Journal* [Type of medium], *volume*(issue), paging if given, or other indicator of length. Available USENET: newsgroup [Access date].

> • When author is not given, use the second basic form.
> • It is sufficient to present just the year when the cited journal article was published.
> • Give page range whenever possible. If that is not available, apply these rules:

1. When the initial page is known, (a) in parentheses, indicate the article length after the initial page, e.g., 10(12 pp.), 10(80 paragraphs), 10(24 screens), 10(300 lines), 10(3,000 words; or (b) use notation "ff" for "and following pages."

2. When the initial page is not available, indicate the article length (the number of paragraphs, screens, lines, or words). No parentheses are needed.

<A185>   Horinouch, K., & Shiozawa, T. (1993). Analysis of dynamic behavior of an open-boundary Cherenkov laser [Text is in Japanese]. *IEICE Transactions on Electronics* [Online], *J76-C*(9), 331–336. Available USENET: comp.research.japan [1995, August 2].
> • Editorial note is placed after the title of article.
> • Provide volume information *J76-C* as it is presented in the publication.

C. Magazine Articles

Basic Forms

Author. (Year, month day). Title. *Magazine* [Type of medium], *volume* (if given), paging if given, or other indicator of length. Available USENET: newsgroup [Access date].

Title. (Year, month day). *Magazine* [Type of medium], *volume* (if given), paging if
given, or other indicator of length. Available USENET: newsgroup [Access date].

- When author is not given, use the second basic form.
- For information on paging or length, see Section II.B., Basic
  Forms on page 58 in this chapter.

<A186> Abayomi, T., & Ransome-Kuti, B. (1995, July 31). Legal concern/pris-
oners of conscience. *Amnesty International Urgent Action Bulletin*
[Online], 7 pars. Available USENET: misc.activism.progressive
[1995, August 2].
- Reference lacks volume information.

D. Newsletter Articles

Basic Forms

Author. (Year, month day). Title. *Newsletter* [Type of medium], *volume*(issue),
paging if given, or other indicator of length. Available USENET: newsgroup
[Access date].

Title. (Year, month day). *Newsletter* [Type of medium], *volume*(issue), paging if
given, or other indicator of length. Available USENET: newsgroup [Access date].

- When author is not given, use the second basic form.
- For information on paging or length, see Section II.B., Basic
  Forms on page 58 in this chapter.

<A187> Nader, R. (1995, July 31). Ralph Nader on Windows 95 problems
[Letter to President Bill Clinton]. *TAP-INFO: An Internet Newsletter
Available from Taxpayer Assets Project* [Online], 3–9. Available
USENET: comp.society.privacy [1995, August 2].
- Editorial note, indicating that this is a letter, is included in
  brackets after the article title.
- Reference lacks volume information.

III. PERSONAL E-MAIL

A. Correspondence

Basic Form

Sender (sender's E-mail address). (Year, month day). *Subject of message.* E-mail
to recipient (recipient's E-mail address).

- If the message is unsigned, use the author's log-in name in upper-case letters.
- Include both sender's and recipient's E-mail addresses in parentheses right after their names respectively.
- Use uppercase letters for log-in names.
- Indicate the date when message was sent.
- Access date is not required.

<A188>   Day, M (MDAY@sage.uvm.edu). (1995, July 30). *Review of the film— Bad Lieutenant.* E-mail to X. Li (XLI@moose.uvm.edu).

B. Forwarded Mail with Embellishment

Basic Form

Forwarder (Forwarder's E-mail address). (Year, Month day). *Subject of new message* [Original message sender, *Discussion topic*]. Forwarded message to recipient (recipient's E-mail address).

- If the message is unsigned, use the author's log-in name in uppercase letters.
- Indicate the date when message was forwarded.
- Include both forwarder's and recipient's E-mail addresses in parentheses right after their names respectively.
- Use uppercase letters with log-in names.
- Include the editorial note after the subject of a new message for information about the original message.
- Access date is not required.

<A189>   Archdeacon, D (DARCHDEA@uvmvm.uvm.edu). (1992, October 30). Update on Latvia [Original message M. Saule, *Life in the Baltics*]. Forwarded message to N. Crane (NCRANE@uvmvm.uvm.edu).

CHAPTER FIVE

U.S. Government Documents, Legal Sources, and International Documents

I. U.S. GOVERNMENT DOCUMENTS

This section is arranged by type of document or information.

The 4th edition of the *Publication Manual of the American Psychological Association* refers users to *The Bluebook: A Uniform System of Citation* (Cambridge: Harvard Law Rev. Assn., 15th ed., 1991) for citation of legal materials. *Electronic Styles* provides a choice, with legal sources presented in APA style in this section, and with examples of legal citation that follow *The Bluebook* style in the Legal Sources section.

If the basic form given in the section requires information on paging, the rules for paging mentioned in the preceding sections apply. That is, give page ranges whenever possible. Failing that, apply these rules:

1. When the initial page is known, (a) in parentheses indicate the document length after the initial page, e.g., 10(12 pp.), 10(80 paragraphs), 10(24 screens), 10(300 lines), 10(3,000 words); or (b) use notation "ff" for "and following pages."

2. When the initial page is not available, indicate the document length (the number of paragraphs, screens, lines or words). No parentheses are needed.

A. Bills, Resolutions

Basic Form

Legislative body. Number of Congress, Session. (Date). *Number of bill or resolution, Title*, Version if given [Type of medium]. Available (include protocol if relevant): Address/Path/File [Access date].

• Words in names of bills and resolutions should be capitalized.

<A190> U.S. House. 104th Congress, 1st Session. (1995, January 12). *H.R. 1, Congressional Accountability Act of 1995* [Popular title: *Contract with America*], [Online]. Available: gopher://marvel.loc.gov/U.S. Congress/Online Legislative Databases at the Library of Congress/ Connect to LOCIS/2/8/retrieve h.r. 1 [1995, August 8].

<A191> U.S. House. 104th Congress, 1st Session. (1995, January 28). *H.R. 26, Return of Excess Amounts from Official Allowances of Members of the House of Representatives to the Treasury for Deficit Reduction,* Version 1 [Online]. Available: Mead Lexis/GENFED/BILLS [1995, August 7].

<A192> U.S. Senate. 104th Congress, 1st Session. (1995, July 14). *S. Res. 149, Resolution Expressing the Sense of the Senate Regarding the Recent Announcement by the Republic of France That It Intends to Conduct a Series of Underground Nuclear Test Explosions Despite the Current International Moratorium on Nuclear Testing,* Version 1 [Online]. Available: Mead Lexis/LEGIS/BILLS [1995, August 10].

<A193> U.S. Senate. 104th Congress, 1st Session. (1995, June 28). *S. Res. 142, Resolution to Congratulate the New Jersey Devils for Becoming the 1995 NHL Champions and thus Winning the Stanley Cup,* Version 1 [Online]. Available: Mead Lexis/LEGIS/BILLS [1995, August 10].

B. Census

Basic Forms

Title of document [Type of medium]. (Date). Available (include protocol if relevant): Address or source/Path/File [Access date].

Or

Title of section, table or chapter. (Date). In *Title of document(s)* [Type of medium]. Available (include protocol if relevant): Address or source/Path/File [Access date].

<A194> Alaska. (No date). In *1990 census of population and housing* [Online]. Available: gopher://gopher.inform.umd.edu:10/00/EdRes/Topic/ UnitedStatesAndWorld/United_States/National_Agencies/Executive Branch/Census-90/alaska [1995, August 8].

> • This is a reference to a file within a database.
> • This source does not note a publication date; citation reflects this with "No date" statement.

- It is not necessary to repeat the protocol (Gopher) used on the WWW after the "available" statement since it is stated in the URL.

<A195> Asian or Pacific Islander females. (1992). In *1990 census of population and housing: Summary tape file 3A* [CD-ROM]. Available: 1990 census of population and housing: Summary tape 3A/Vermont/Burlington, VT MSA/Race by sex by age/Asian or Pacific Islander females [1995, August 14].

<A196> Computers and office accounting machines, MA35R. (1993). In *Current Industrial Reports* [Online]. Available: http://www.census.gov/ftp/ pub/industry/ma35r93.txt [1995, August 8].
- *Current Industrial Reports* is an annual (periodical) publication so it is proper to capitalize significant words in the title.

<A197> Table 3: Cities with 200,000 or more population ranked [Data on Asian or Pacific Islander populations]. (1994). In *County and city data book* [Online]. Available: http://www.census.gov/stat_abstract/ccdb/ www/ccdb305.txt [1995, August 8].
- Example uses note in brackets to describe coverage more fully.

C. Congressional Record

Basic Form

Last name of speaker, title, [Home state—abbreviated]. (Date). Title. *Congressional Record* [Type of medium], *volume*, paging or length of item. Available (include protocol): Address or source/Path/File [Access date].

<A198> Jeffords, Sen. [VT]. (1995, August 1). Jeffords (and others) Amendment No. 2054. *Congressional Record* [Online], *141*, S11120(3 screens). Available: Mead Lexis/LEGIS/RECORD [1995, August 9].
- The *Congressional Record* does not give initials of speakers as a rule so initials are replaced with title: Representative (Rep.) or Senator (Sen.). A note giving the legislator's home state further identifies the speaker.

D. Constitution (U.S.)

Basic Form

Article and section numbers: Title of section. (Date). In *Version of Constitution* [Type of medium]. Available (include protocol if relevant): Address or source/ Path/File [Access date].

<A199>   Amendment XIII: Abolition of slavery. (1993, March 14). In *The Constitution of the United States of America* [Online]. Available: http://www.law.cornell:80/constitution/constitution.amendmentxiii.html [1995, August 8].

> • The date given, in this case, is the load date of this electronic version.
> • It is not necessary to repeat the protocol (HTTP) on the WWW after the "available" statement since it is stated in the URL.

<A200>   USCS Constitution Preamble. (1994). In *United States Code Service: Constitution of the United States of America* [Online]. Available: Mead Lexis/GENFED/USCNST [1995, August 9].

E. Court Decisions

Basic Form

Name of case. (Date of decision). *Reporting service* (Jurisdiction if relevant), [Type of medium], *volume*, paging or length of item. Available (include protocol if relevant): Address or source/Path/File [Access date].

Note: The reporting services of U.S. District and Appeals court cases are not government documents. However, the citation patterns for cases in these federal jurisdictions have been included in this section for the convenience of users citing this information.

1. U.S. District Courts

<A201>   Johnson v. Miller. (1994, September 12). *Federal Supplement* (Southern District, Georgia), [Online], *864*, 1354(137 screens). Available: Mead Lexis/GENFED/COURTS [1995, August 7].

> • Cite the case name exactly as it is given in the source.
> • It is important to give the district in which the case was heard but not the division. In this instance, Southern District, Georgia is sufficient.

2. U.S. Court of Appeals

<A202>   Hetzel v. Bethlehem Steel Corp. (1995, April 24). *Federal Reporter*, 3rd (5th Circuit), [Online], 50, 360ff. Available: Mead Lexis/GENFED/USAPP [1995, August 10].

> • Give circuit in which case is heard.

• This example uses the notation "ff." to indicate "and following pages." Should it be necessary to quote information from this source, more exact information on number of pages, screens, or paragraphs will expedite citing to a specific part of the decision.

3. Supreme Court of the United States

<A203> Regents of the University of California v. Bakke. (1978, June 28). *United States Reports* [Online], *438*, 265(277 screens). Available: Mead Lexis/GENFED/US [1995, August 11].

<A204> Robert E. Rubin, Secretary of the Treasury, Petitioner v. Coors Brewing Company. (Preliminary print, Project Hermes). (1995, April 19). *United States Reports* [Online], 29 paragraphs. Available: ftp://ftp. cwru.edu/hermes/ascii/93-1631.ZO.filt [1995, August 8].
   • Volume and paging for this item are not available for this preliminary print of *United States Reports*.
   • It is not necessary to repeat the protocol (FTP) on the WWW after the "available" statement since it is stated in the URL.

<A205a> Miller v. Johnson. (1995, June 29). *U.S. Lexis* [Online], 4462(79 screens). Available: Mead Lexis/GENFED/US [1995, August 7].
   • See A205b and A205c for parallel citations to the *United States Supreme Court Reports, Lawyers' Edition* and *U.S. Law Week*.

<A205b> Miller v. Johnson. (1995, June 29). *United States Supreme Court Reports, Lawyers' Edition, 2d* [Online], *132*, 762(79 screens). Available: Mead Lexis/GENFED/US [1995, August 7].

<A205c> Miller v. Johnson. (1995, June 29). *U.S. Law Week* [Online], *63*, 4726(79 screens). Available: Mead Lexis/GENFED/US [1995, August 7].

F. House or Senate Reports

Basic Form

Legislative body. Committee. (Date). *Title* (House/Senate Report number), [Type of medium]. Available (include protocol if relevant): Address or source/Path/ File [Access date].

<A206> U.S. House. Committee on Rules. (1995, August 1). *Providing for the consideration of H.R. 1555, The Communications Act of 1995* (House Report 104–223), [Online]. Available: Mead Lexis/GENFED/ CMTRPT [1995, August 8].

<A207> U.S. Senate. Committee on Energy and Natural Resources. (1995, May 19). *To transfer a parcel of land to the Pueblo Indians of New Mexico* (Senate Report 104-85), [Online]. Available: Mead Lexis/GENFED/CMTRPT [1995, August 8].

G. Laws, Statutes

1. United States Code

Basic Form

Title of section. (Date). *Version of code* [Type of medium], Title (Tit.) number, Part (Pt.) number. Available (include protocol if relevant): Address or source/Path/File [Access date].

<A208> Abrogation of Treaties [with Indians]. (No date). *United States Code* [Online], Tit. 25, Pt. 72. Available HTTP: http://www.law.cornell.edu/uscode/25/72.html [1995, August 8].

<A209> Bringing in and Harboring Certain Aliens. (1994). *United States Code Service* [Online], Tit. 8, Pt. 1324. Available: Mead Lexis/GENFED/USCODE [1995, August 7].

2. United States Statutes at Large

Basic Form

Title of Act, Public Law (PL) Number. (Date). *United States Statutes at Large* [Type of medium], *volume*, paging or length of item. Available (include protocol if relevant): Address or source/Path/File [Access date].

<A210> Cancer Registries Amendment Act, PL 102–515. (1992). *United States Statutes at Large* [Online], *106*, 3372(13 screens). Available: Mead Lexis/GENFED/PUBLAW [1995, August 7].

<A211> Chinese Student Protection Act of 1992, PL 102-404. (1992). *United States Statutes at Large* [Online], *106*, 1969(2 pp.). Available: WESTLAW Database: US-PL [1992, October 15].

H. Patents

Basic Form

Name of the invention, by inventor's name. (Date). *Patent Number* [Type of medium]. Available (include protocol if relevant): Address or source/Path/File [Access date].

• When citing patents, the most important element is the name of the invention, which is given first, followed by the inventor's name.

<A212>   Apple tree "Vermont Gold", by W. H. Luginbuhl. (1991, August 13). *United States Patent PP 7618* [Online]. Available: Mead Lexis/PATENT/PLANT [1995, August 8].

• The date given is the issue date of the patent.

<A213>   Targeted drug delivery via phosphonate derivatives, by N.S. Bodor. (1993, January 5). *United States Patent 5177064* [Online]. Available: http://concord.cnidr.org/cgi-bin/agw?AIDSPAT+05177064+F [1995, August 8].

I. Periodicals

Basic Form

Author. (Year, month day). Title. *Magazine* [Type of medium], *volume* (if given), paging or length. Available (include protocol if relevant): Address or source/Path/File [Access date].

<A214>   Niles, T. M. T. (1992, August 17). US position and proposed actions concerning the Yugoslav crisis. *Department of State Dispatch* [Online], 12 screens. Available: Mead Lexis/GENFED/DSTATE [1995, August 11].

J. Presidential Documents

Basic Form

Documents in **Weekly Compilation**

Title [Nature of document, e.g., proclamation, speech]. (Date of publication). *Weekly Compilation of Presidential Documents* [Online], *volume*, paging or length. Available (include protocol if relevant): Address or source/Path/File [Access date].

• The name of the president, as author, is unnecessary because the date indicates the administration.

<A215>   Remarks on the 50th Anniversary of the United Nations Charter in San Francisco, California [Speech]. (1995, June 26). *Weekly Compilation of Presidential Documents* [Online], *31*, 1121(16 screens). Available: Mead Lexis/GENFED/PRESDC [1995, August 8].

Documents Not Issued in Weekly Compilation

Title [Nature of document, e.g.., proclamation, speech]. (Date of publication). Available (include protocol if relevant): Address or source/Path/File [Access date].

<A216>   *Statement by the President: I strongly support the Work First Bill* [Press release]. (1995, August 3). Available: gopher://info.tamu.edu:70/00/. data/politics/1995/welfare.0803 [1995, August 8].

K. Rules, Regulations

1. Code of Federal Regulations

Basic Form

Title or name of section. (Date). *Code of Federal Regulations* [Type of medium], Title (Tit.) number, Part (Pt.) number. Available (include protocol if relevant): Address or source/Path/File [Access date].

<A217>   Dietary Supplements [For U.S. Nationals incarcerated abroad]. (1993). *Code of Federal Regulations* [Online], Tit. 22, Pt. 71.12. Available: Mead Lexis/GENFED/CFR93 [1995, August 7].

2. Federal Register

Basic Form

Title or name of the section (agency report number if given). (Year, month day). *Federal Register* [Type of medium], *volume*, paging or length. Available (include protocol if relevant): Address or source/Path/File [Access date].

<A218>   Food labeling: General Requirements for Nutrition Labeling of Dietary Supplements; General Requirements for Nutrient Content Claims for Dietary Supplements. (1995, February 9). *Federal Register* [Online], *60*, 7711(11 screens). Available: Mead Lexis/GENFED/FEDREG [1995, August 7].

II. LEGAL SOURCES

Legal citation style varies significantly from APA style. The accepted practice in legal materials is to cite references in footnotes. The *Publication Manual of the American Psychological Association* indicates that "references to legal materials . . . which include court decisions, statutes, and other legislative materials, and various secondary sources, will be more useful to the reader if they include the information in the conventional format of legal citations" (1994, p. 223). The APA recommends that *The Bluebook: A Uniform System of Citation* (15th ed., 1991) be used as a guide when citing legal sources. This section gives a few examples using the legal style of citation. Consult *The Bluebook* for a complete elaboration of this approach.

A. Bills, Resolutions

Basic Form

Title, Bill, or resolution number, Congress, Session. (Date) (Electronic supplier, path).

<A219> Congressional Accountability Act of 1995 (Popular title: Contract with America), H.R. 1, 104th Cong., 1st Sess. (1995) (LOCIS, gopher:// marvel.loc.gov/U.S. Congress/Online Legislative Databases at the Library of Congress/Connect to LOCIS/2/8/retrieve h.r. 1).

<A220> Return of Excess Amounts from Official Allowances of Members of the House of Representatives to the Treasury for deficit reduction, H.R. 26, 104th Cong., 1st Sess. (1995) (LEXIS, Genfed, Bills).

<A221> Resolution Expressing the Sense of the Senate Regarding the Recent Announcement by the Republic of France That It Intends to Conduct a Series of Underground Nuclear Test Explosions Despite the Current International Moratorium on Nuclear Testing, S. Res. 149, 104th Cong., 1st Sess. (1995) (LEXIS, Legis, Bills).

B. Codes of Law, Statutes

Basic Form

Official or Popular Name (or both), Title number Source Section (\S\) number (Date) (Electronic supplier, path).

1. State Codes

Basic Form

The proper citation form for codes of law varies from state to state and with reporting service. A few examples are given below to show this variation. Consult *The Bluebook* (15th ed., 1991) for a complete guide to title abbreviations for each state service and the style of capitalization (large and small capitals) for specific titles.

<A222>   Application, Administration and Enforcement of Wildlife Laws: General Provisions, OR. REV. STAT. \S\ 496.004 (1991) (LEXIS, Codes, Orcode).

<A223>   Vermont Water Resources Board: Duties and Powers, VT. STAT. ANN. tit. 10, \S\ 905 (1991) (LEXIS, Codes, Vtcode).

2. United States Code

<A224>   Abrogation of Treaties, 25 U.S.C. \S\72 (No date) (Cornell Law, http://www.law.cornell.edu/uscode/25/72.html).

<A225>   Bringing in and Harboring Certain Aliens, 8 U.S.C.S. \S\1324 *et seq.* (1994) (LEXIS, Genfed, Uscode).
   • *Et seq.* means "and following" and indicates that the item starts at 1324 but continues for subsequent sections.

3. United States Statutes at Large

Basic Form

Title of Act, Pub. L. No. Volume Stat. Page (Date) (Electronic supplier, path).

<A226a> Cancer Registries Amendment Act, Pub. L. No. 102–515, 106 Stat. 3372 (1992) (LEXIS, Genfed, Publaw).

<A226b> Cancer Registries Amendment Act, Pub. L. No. 102–515, \S\ 399H, 106 Stat. 3372 (1992) (LEXIS, Genfed, Publaw).
   • This example shows how to cite a particular section (\S\ 399H) in the act.

<A227>   Chinese Student Protection Act of 1992, Pub. L. No. 102–404, 106 Stat. 1969 (1992) (WESTLAW, US-Pl).

C. Court Decisions

1. State Courts

The proper citation form for citing court decisions varies from state to state. A few examples are given below to show this variation. Consult *The Bluebook* (15th ed., 1991) for guidance in citing these materials.

Basic Form

Name of case, Source(s) using legal citation style, (Date) (Electronic supplier, path).

<A228>   General Telephone Company of California v. Public Utilities Com-
         mission; City of Santa Monica, Real Party in Interest, 34 Cal. 3d
         817, 670 P.2d 349, 195 Cal. Rptr. 695 (1983) (LEXIS, Cal, Cal).
                  • The practice is to cite all of the decision-reporting services,
                    whenever possible.

<A229>   Tina Labello, as Parent and Natural Guardian, Appellant v. Albany Medi-
         cal Center Hospital, et al., Respondent, 1995 N.Y. Int. 128 (1995)
         (Cornell Law, http://www.law.cornell.edu/ny/ctap/085_0701.htm).

2. Federal Courts

Basic Form

Name of case. Volume Source Starting Page (Jurisdiction Date) (Electronic suppli-
    er, path).

                  • Jurisdiction, district or circuit, is included in the date statement
                    for District and Appeals court decisions respectively.

a. *U.S. District Courts*

<A230>   Johnson v. Miller, 864 F. Supp. 1354 (S.D. Ga 1995) (LEXIS, Genfed,
         Courts).
                  • It is important to give the district in which the case was heard,
                    in this instance Southern District, Georgia, which is abbreviat-
                    ed as "S.D. Ga."

b. *U.S. Court of Appeals*

<A231>   Hetzel v. Bethlehem Steel Corp, 50 F.3d 360 (5th Cir. 1995) (LEXIS,
         Genfed, USApp).
                  • Give circuit in which case is heard.

<A232>   United States of America v. Daniel B. Hughes, a/k/a "Sonny", 716 F.2d
         234 (4th Cir. 1983) (WESTLAW, Allfeds).

c. *Supreme Court of the United States*

<A233>   Regents of the University of California v. Bakke, 438 U.S. 265, 98 S.
         Ct. 2733, 1978 U.S. LEXIS 5, 57 L.Ed. 2d 750, (1978) (LEXIS,
         Genfed, US).
                  • This example shows citations for all of the major Supreme Court
                    reporting services.

<A234>   Robert E. Rubin, Secretary of the Treasury, Petitioner v. Coors Brewing
         Company, Preliminary print, Project Hermes, U.S. (1995) (Case

Western Reserve University, ftp://ftp.cwru/edu/hermes/ascii/93-1631.
ZO.filt).
  • Volume and paging for this item are not available yet for this
    preliminary print of *United States Reports* (U.S.).

D. Periodicals

Basic Form

Author(s), *Title*, Volume Journal Page (Date) (Electronic supplier, path).
  • APA style and legal citation style vary considerably. For in-
    stance, legal citation gives the author's first *and then* last name,
    italicizes the article title, abbreviates journal titles, puts journal
    titles in large and small capitals, and places the date near the end
    of the reference.

<A235> Donald E. Lively & Stephen Plass, *Equal Protection: The Jurisprudence
        of Denial and Evasion*, 40 AM. U.L. REV. 1307 (1991) (LEXIS, Law-
        rev, Allrev).
  • This is an example with more than one author.
  • Refer to *The Bluebook* (15th ed., 1991) for periodical abbrevia-
    tions and form for capitalization of a particular title.

<A236> Christopher D. Stone, *Beyond Rio: "Insuring" Against Global Warming*,
        86 A.J.I.L. 445 (1992) (LEXIS, Lawrev, Allrev).

E. Rules, Regulations

1. Code of Federal Regulations

Basic Form

Name of Section, Title number C.F.R. Part number (Date) (Electronic supplier,
    path).

<A237> Dietary Supplements. 22 C.F.R. 71.12 (1993) (LEXIS, Genfed, CFR93).

2. Federal Register

Basic Form

Title or Name of the Section, Volume Fed. Reg. Page (Date) (to be codified at title
    C.F.R. part statement) (Electronic supplier, path).

<A238>   Food Labeling: General Requirements for Nutrition Labeling of Dietary
         Supplements; General Requirements for Nutrient Content Claims for
         Dietary Supplements, 60 Fed. Reg. 7711 (1995) (to be codified at 21
         C.F.R. \S\ 101) (LEXIS, Genfed, Fedreg).

III. INTERNATIONAL AND FOREIGN GOVERNMENT DOCUMENTS

This section has a sampling of international agency and non-U.S. governmental doc-
uments. For a more comprehensive representation of citations for this area, see *A
Complete Guide to Citing Government Information Resources: A Manual for
Writers & Librarians* by D. L. Garner and D. H. Smith (Rev. ed., 1993).

A. International Organization Documents

1. North Atlantic Treaty Organization

Basic Form

Periodical Article

Author. (Date). Article title. Journal title [Type of medium], *volume*(issue), paging
   or length. Available (include protocol if relevant): Address/Path/File [Access
   date].

<A239>   Ray, R. (1995). Australia's strategic approach. *NATO Review* [Online],
         43(3), 25-30. Available: gopher://marvin.stc.nato.int:70/00/natodata/
         NATOREVIEW/1995-1996/9503-5 [1995, August 14].

2. United Nations

a. *Conferences*

Basic Form

United Nations. Conference on. . ., Location, Date of Conference. (Date of publication). *Title* [Type of medium]. Available (include protocol if relevant):
   Address/Path/File [Access date].

<A240>   United Nations. Fourth World Conference on Women, Beijing, China,
         4–15, September 1995. Committee on the Elimination of Discrimi-
         nation Against Women. (1995, June 21). *Progress achieved in the
         implementation of The Convention on the Elimination of All Forms of*

Discrimination Against Women [Report by the Committee], [Online].
Available: gopher://undp.org:70/00/unconfs/women/off/a-7.en [1995,
August 14].

> • This item was prepared by a committee for the conference.
> • The name of the convention, referred to in the title, should be
>   capitalized.

b. *Official Proceedings, Reports*

Basic Form

United Nations. Organ, Meeting number of Session. (Date). *Title* [Type of medi-
um]. Available (include protocol if relevant): Address/Path/File [Access date].

<A241>   United Nations. General Assembly, 50th Session. (1995). *Strengthening
of the coordination of humanitarian and disaster relief assistance of
the United Nations, including special economic assistance: Special
economic assistance to individual countries or regions: Assistance to
Yemen* [Report of the Secretary-General], [Online]. Available: gopher:
//undp.org:70/00/undocs/gad/A/50/95_08/301 [1995, August 14].

c. *Item in a Collection*

Basic Form

United Nations. Organ, Meeting number of Session. (Date). Title. In *Source* [Type
of medium], paging or some other indicator of location in source. Available
(include protocol if relevant): Address/Path/File [Access date].

d. *Resolutions*

Basic Form

United Nations. Organ. Subsidiary Body (if given), Meeting number or Session.
(Date). *Resolution Number: Title* [Type of medium]. Available (include protocol if relevant): Address/Path/File [Access date].

<A242>   United Nations. General Assembly, 49th Session. (1995). *Resolution
215: Assistance in mine clearance* [Online]. Available: gopher://
undp.org:70/11/undocs/gad/RES/49/9576321E [1995, August 11].

<A243>   United Nations. Security Council, 2940th Meeting. (1990). *Resolution
667*: [Recalling the Vienna Conventions on diplomatic and consular
relations of which Iraq was a party], [Online]. Available: http://wire-
tap.spies.com/ftp.items/GOV/UN/un-667.res [1995, August 11].

> • Some resolutions do not have titles; in such cases, supply a title
>   that approximates content and place in brackets.

e. *Resolution in a Collection*

Basic Form

United Nations. Organ. Subsidiary Body (if given), Meeting number or Session. (Date). Resolution Number: Title. In *Source* [Type of medium]. Available (include protocol if relevant): Address/Path/File [Access date].

f. *Treaties*

Basic Form

Title of Treaty, Date—entered into force, Registry No. (Publication Date). *Title of Compendium* [Type of medium], volume, paging. Available (include protocol if relevant): Address/Path/File [Access date].

<A244>   Protocol Additional to the Geneva Conventions of 12 August 1949, and Relating to the Protection of Victims on Non-International Armed Conflicts (Protocol II), 7 December 1978, No. 17513. [This version gives information, as or April 1990, on parties ratifying the Protocols and year of ratification]. (No date). *United Nations Treaty Series* [Online], *1125*, 609ff. Available: http://wiretap.spies.com/ftp.items/ GOV/Treaties/Geneva/protocol2 [1995, August 15].

   • Names of treaties are proper nouns; significant words are capitalized.

3. World Health Organization

Basic Form

Work by Title

Title [Type of medium]. (Date). Available (include protocol if relevant): Address/ Path/File [Access date].

<A245>   *Country profile for Burundi: UNDP/UNFPA/WHO/WORLD BANK special programme of research, development and research training in human reproduction* [Online]. (1993). Available Gopher: who.org/ WHO's Major Programmes/Human Reproduction Programme (HRP)/ Country Profiles—1993/WHO/HRP Country Profile for Burundi— 1993 [1995, August 15].

     • This publication was retrieved via the WHO Gopher, although it is produced by the combined efforts of several international agencies.

B. National Documents (Non-U.S.)

a. *Constitutions*

Basic Form

Title (edition or version), [Type of medium]. (Date). Available (include protocol if relevant): Address/Path/File [Access date].

<A246>   *Constitution of the Republic of Macedonia* [Online]. (1992). Available: http://wiretap.spies.com:80/ftp.items/GOV/World/macedonia.con [1995, August 14].

b. *Department or Agency Publications*

Basic Form

Nation. Department. (Date). *Title* [Type of medium], (Series name and number, if part of a series). Available (include protocol if relevant): Address/Path/File [Access date].

<A247>   Canada. Environment Canada. (1992). *Water—Vulnerable to climate change* [Online], (Freshwater Series A-1). Available: http:// www.cciw. ca/glimr/data/water-fact-sheets/facta9-e.html [1995, August 15].

   • This is an example of an item in a series. Series note, in parentheses, follows immediately after title and type of medium statement.

c. *Parliamentary Documents*

Basic Form

Nation. Parliament. House of Parliament. Committee name. (Date). Title. In *Source* [Type of medium]. Available (include protocol if relevant): Address/Path/File [Access date].

<A248>   Canada. Parliament. House of Commons. Standing Committee on Aboriginal Affairs and Northern Development. (1995, June 15). Consideration of the expenditure plans and priorities in future fiscal years as described in the Departmental Outlook. In *Minutes of Evidence and Proceedings, Meeting No. 50* [Online]. Available: http://www.parl.gc. ca/committees/iand/iand-50-cover-e.html and http://www.parl.gc.ca/ committees/iand/iand50_blk101.html [1995, August 15].

   • This item is a split file. To retrieve the whole document, both Uniform Resource Locators must be used.

d. *Special Multilateral Governmental Reports*

Basic Form

Title [Type of medium]. (Date). Available (include protocol if relevant): Address/ Path/File [Access date].

<A249> *Consensus report on the Constitution: Charlottetown, August 28, 1992* [Popular title: *Charlottetown Constitutional Accord*], [Online]. (1992). Available: http//wiretap.spies.com/ftp.items/GOV/Canada/ Charlottetown.acc [1995, August 15].

CHAPTER SIX

Other Sources

I. ENTIRE SERVICES

A. CD-ROM and Commercial Online Full-Text Databases

Basic Forms

Author/editor. (Date). *Database* (Version), [Type of medium]. Producer (optional). Available: Supplier/Database identifier or number [Access date].

Database (Version), [Type of medium]. (Date). Producer (optional). Available: Supplier/Database identifier or number [Access date].

> • See also Chapter Two, Section I. Cite an Entire Work, A. CD-ROM and Commercial Online Databases (page 9 forward).
> • When author or editor is not available, use the second basic form.
> • Indicate the date when a database is produced. If a database is under regular revision, use the date of the last revision if that can be determined. For a serial publication, give the starting date.
> • Database version or edition information is included in parentheses directly after the database title.
> • When evaluating a database, it is useful to have information on the producer who contributes to the content of the database. If this information is readily available, supply it before the "available" statement.

<A250> *New York Times* [Online]. (1980, June–). New York Times Company (Producer). Available: Mead Nexis/NEWS/NYT [1995, August 10].
> • Producer is given in this reference.

<A251>   *Academic American encyclopedia* [Online]. (1995). Available: Dow
Jones News Retrieval Service/ENCYC [1995, May 27].

<A252>   Sternberg, M. L. A. (1994). *The American sign language dictionary on
CD-ROM* (Windows version), [CD-ROM]. Available: HarperCollins
[1995, May 25].

B. Bibliographic Databases

Basic Forms

Author/editor. (Date). *Database* [Bibliographic database], (Version), [Type of
medium]. Producer (optional). Available: Supplier/Database identifier or number [Access date].

Database [Bibliographic database], (Version), [Type of medium]. (Date). Producer
(optional). Available: Supplier/Database identifier or number [Access date].

- Include the date when the database is created. If a database is
under regular revision, use the date of the last revision if that can
be determined. For a serial publication, give the starting date.
- Give an optional note, indicating that this is a bibliographic
database, after the database title.
- When evaluating a database, it is often useful to have information on the producer who contributes to the content of the database. If this information is readily available, supply it before the
"available" statement.

<A253>   *Kompass Asia/Pacific* [Bibliographic database], [Online]. (1995).
Kompass International Management Corp. (Producer). Available:
DIALOG/592 [1995, May 28].
- Give the producer if different from the distributor.

<A254>   *Social Science Index* [Bibliographic database], [CD-ROM]. (1983–). H.
W. Wilson (Producer). Available: UMI/Social Science Index [1995,
July 10].
- Since this reference is serial in nature, capitalize first letters of
words in title and give the starting date of the electronic form.

<A255>   *AGRICOLA* [Bibliographic database], [CD-ROM]. (1987–). National
Agricultural Library (Producer). Available: SilverPlatter [1992,
October 28].
- Since this title is a serial, give the starting date.
- Cite the producer only if it is not the direct supplier of the data-
base.

C. FTP Sites

Basic Forms

Author/editor. (Last update). *FTP Site* [Online]. Available FTP: FTP site [Access date].

FTP Site [Online]. (Last update). Available FTP: FTP site [Access date].

> • If author or editor is not available, use the second basic form.
> • Use the date of the last revision if that can be determined; otherwise, use "n.d."
> • Treat FTP sites as edited or compiled works, nonserial in nature. The names of sites and services should be treated as proper nouns.

<A256a> *University of Virginia Electronic Text Center* [Online]. (1995, June 18–last update). Available FTP: etext.virginia.edu [1995, August 21].

<A256b> *University of Virginia Electronic Text Center* [Online]. (1995, June 18–last update). Available: ftp://etext.virginia.edu [1995, August 21].
> • If the information is retrieved on the World Wide Web (WWW), write URL in the "available" statement.

D. Gopher Sites

Basic Forms

Author/editor. (Last update). *Gopher Site* [Online]. Available Gopher: Gopher site [Access date].

Gopher Site [Online]. (Last update). Available Gopher: Gopher site [Access date].

> • If author or editor is not available, use the second basic form.
> • Use the date of the last revision if that can be determined; otherwise, use "n.d."
> • Treat Gopher sites as edited or compiled works, nonserial in nature. The names of sites and services should be treated as proper nouns.

<A257a> *E-Text Archives Services* [Online]. (1995, July 25 – last update). Available Gopher: gopher.etext.org [1995, August 15].

<A257b> *E-Text Archives Services* [Online]. (1995, July 25 – last update). Available: gopher://gopher.etext.org:70/ [1995, August 15].
> • If the information is retrieved on the WWW, provide the URL in the "available" statement.

E. Telnet Sites

Basic Forms

Author/editor. (Last update). *Telnet Site* [Online]. Available Telnet: domain/**login** (if required) [Access date].

Telnet Site [Online]. (Last update). Available Telnet: domain/**login** (if required) [Access date].

- If author or editor is not available, use the second basic form.
- Use the date of the last update if that can be determined; otherwise use "n.d."
- Treat Telnet sites as edited or compiled works, nonserial in nature. The names of sites and services should be treated as proper nouns.

<A258>   *Sage: The Information Gateway for the UVM Libraries and Media Services* [Online]. (1995, May 15 – last update). Available Telnet: sageunix.uvm.edu/**login**: sage [1995, August 20].

F. WWW Homepages

Basic Forms

Author/editor. (Last update or copyright date). *Homepage Title* [Homepage of . . .], [Online]. Available: URL [Access date].

Homepage Title [Homepage of . . .], [Online]. (Last update or copyright date). Available: URL [Access date].

- When author or editor is not available, use the second basic form.
- Treat homepages as edited or compiled works, nonserial in nature. The names of sites and services should be treated as proper nouns.
- If citing an editor or editors as the first element, include a note "Ed." or "Eds." in parentheses.
- Indicate the last update for the homepage if available. Otherwise, give the copyright date.
- Provide a note indicating the information supplier in the form of "Homepage of information supplier."
- It is not necessary to repeat the protocol (HTTP) on the WWW after the "available" statement since it is stated in the URL.

<A259>   Altis, K., & Tindle, N. (Eds.). (1995, August 14–last update). *City Net* [Homepage of City Net Express], [Online]. Available: http://www. city.net/ [1995, August 14].

<A260>   Mother Jones Interactive (Ed.). (1995–copyright). *MoJo Wire* [Homepage of Mother Jones Interactive], [Online]. Available: http://www. mojones.com/ [1995, August 14].

<A261>   Wall Street Journal (Ed.). (1995, August 14–last update). *Money & Investing Update* [Homepage of Dow Jones & Company], [Online]. Available: http://update.wsj.com/ [1995, August 14].

II. AUDIOVISUAL MATERIALS

A. Works of Art

Basic Forms

Author (Responsibility). (Date). Title of work [Nature of work], [Medium]. Available (include protocol if relevant): Address/Path/File [Access date].

Title [Nature of work], [Medium]. (Date). Available (include protocol if relevant): Address/Path/File [Access date].

- If author is not available, use the second basic form.
- Indicate, in parentheses, the responsibility of the author, for example, painter, photographer, computer graphic artist, or cartoonist.
- If available, give the date when electronic image is created.
- Specify the nature of work, in brackets, after the title of work, for example, drawing, painting, photograph, computer image, cartoon, or slide.
- Provide the electronic medium for the work such as online and CD-ROM.

<A262>   Daniels, M. (Photographer). (1991). *Corinthian: Handle at right* [Photograph], [CD-ROM]. Available: Perseus 1.0/Art and Archaeology/Pottery/Yale 1988.80.37 [1995, August 19].

<A263>   Sprangers, H. (Painter). (1993). *Untitled: Faces in the crowd no. 1* [Image of oil painting], [Online]. Available: http://www.fwi.uva.nl/ ~boncz/artvark/faces/face1.jpg [1995, August 17].

B. Film Clips

Basic Form

Producer. (Date). Title of the clip. In Director, *Film title* [Film], [Type of medium]. Distributor. Available (include protocol if relevant): Address/Path/File [Access date].

<A264>   Gibson, M., Davey, B., Ladd, A., Jr. & Gibson, M. (Producers). (1995). Defied the world. In M. Gibson (Director), *Braveheart* [Film], [Online]. Paramount (Distributor). Available: http://www.voyager. paramount.com/video/BHPRV02.mov [1995, August 25].
- Give the producer(s) as the first element of the citation.
- Provide the note *film*, in brackets, after the film title. Other examples are videotapes, audiotapes, slides, charts, and works of art, based on the fourth edition of the APA *Publication Manual*.
- Specify the distributor. If it is a small and less-known one, include the location of distributor.

C. Sound Recordings

Basic Form

Writer/composer. (Date of electronic recording). Title of specific piece from recording. [Recorded by artist if different from writer]. On *Title of recording* [Medium of original recording], [Type of electronic medium]. Producer (optional). Available (include protocol if relevant): Address/Path/File [Access date].

- Provide the date of electronic recording as the second element, immediately after the writer/composer.
- For the medium of original recording, specify if the recording is on, for example, compact disc, cassette, or record.
- Indicate the medium type for the electronic version of the recording, such as online, or CD-ROM.
- Include the supplier of the electronic recording.
- In the "available" statement, specify the protocol, domain, and path, if the piece is retrieved on the Internet. If the piece is available from a commercial electronic supplier, indicate the database, search path, and file name.

<A265>   Puccini, G. (No date). Che gelida manina [From *La Boheme*], [Recorded by P. Domingo]. On *The Placido Domingo album* [CD], [Online]. BMG Classics (Producer). Available: http://classicalmus. com/av/domingo.mp2 [1995, Aug. 25].

- Write "No date" if it is not certain when the electronic version was created.
- Information about the recording should be enclosed in brackets.

D. Maps

Basic Forms

Cartographer. (Date). *Title of map* [Map, Scale: if known]. In *Source* [Type of medium]. Available protocol: give sufficient information for retrieval.

Title of map [Map, Scale: if known]. In *Source* [Type of medium]. (Date). Available protocol: give sufficient information for retrieval.

<A266>   Turkey: Elevations [Map, Scale: 1:100 km]. In *Turkey* [Diskette] (1992, October). Available: PC Globe/Country/Turkey/Elevations [1995, May 28].

III. MEETING PROCEEDINGS AND SYMPOSIA

A. Paper in a Proceedings

Basic Form

Author. (Date). Paper title. In *Proceedings title* [Type of medium]. Paging or length. Available (include protocol if relevant): Address/Path/File [Access date].

- Give a page range whenever possible. If this inclusive paging information is lacking, apply these rules:

1. When the initial page is known, (a) in parentheses, indicate the article length after the initial page, e.g., 10(12 pp.), 10(80 paragraphs), 10(24 screens), 10(300 lines), or 10(3,000 words); or (b) use the notation "ff" for "and following pages."

2. When the initial page is not available, indicate the article length (the number of paragraphs, screens, lines, or words). No parentheses are needed.

- In the "available" statement, specify the protocol, domain, and path, if the piece is retrieved on the Internet. If the piece is available from a commercial electronic supplier, indicate the database, search path, and file name.

<A267>   Silberberg, D. P., & Semmel, R. D. (1994). The StarView flexible query mechanism. In *Astronomical Data Analysis Software and Systems III*

ASP Conference Series, Vol. 61, 1994 [Online]. 12 paragraphs. Available: http://cadcwww.dao.nrc.ca/ADASS/adass_proc/adass3/papers/silberbergd/silberbergd.html [1995, August 23].
   • Capitalize the name of a symposium as it is a proper name.

B. Entire Proceedings of a Conference

Basic Forms

Author/editor. (Date). *Proceedings title* [Type of medium]. Available (include protocol if relevant): Address/Path/File [Access date].

Proceedings title [Type of medium]. (Date). Available (include protocol if relevant): Address/Path/File [Access date].

> • In the "available" statement, specify the protocol, domain, and path, if the piece is retrieved on the Internet. If the piece is available from a commercial electronic supplier, indicate the database, search path, and file name.

<A268> *Proceedings of the Third International World Wide Web Conference: Technology, Tools and Applications, April 10–14, Darmstadt, Germany* [Online]. (1995). Available: http://www.igd.fhg.de/www/www95/proceedings/proceedings.html [1995, August 22].

IV. RADIO/TELEVISION TRANSCRIPTS AND WIRE SERVICE REPORTS

Basic Form

Transcripts

Author/reporter/anchor. (Date). Title/topic [Type of transcript]. *Source* [Type of medium]. Paging or length. Available (include protocol if relevant): Address/Path/File [Access date].

> • Give a page range whenever possible. If this inclusive paging information is lacking, apply these rules:

1. When the initial page is known, (a) in parentheses, indicate the article length after the initial page, e.g., 10(12 pp.), 10(80 paragraphs), 10(24 screens), 10(300 lines), or 10(3,000 words); or (b) use the notation "ff" for "and following pages."

2. When the initial page is not available, indicate the article length (the number of paragraphs, screens, lines, or words). No parentheses are needed.

- In the "available" statement, specify the protocol, domain, and path, if the piece is retrieved on the Internet. If the piece is available from a commercial electronic supplier, indicate the database, search path, and file name.

\<A269\>   Dobbs, L. (1995, August 18). Wall Street analyst discusses global telecommunications [Television transcript, interview with M. Gabelli]. *CNN Moneyline* [Online]. 2,386 words. Available: Mead Nexis/News/Script [1995, August 18].

Wire Service Reports

Author. (Date). Title/topic [Wire Service]. *Source* [Type of medium]. Paging or length. Available (include protocol if relevant): Address/Path/File [Access date].

- See Basic Form, Transcript, above, for information on paging or length of the report.

\<A270\>   Worsnip, P. (1995, August 25). U.S. assures Bosnia NATO will defend Gorazke [Wire Service]. *Reuters North American Wire, BC Cycle* [Online]. 945 words. Available: Mead Nexis/News/Wires [1995, August 26].

V. THESES AND DISSERTATIONS

A. Section of a Thesis/Dissertation

Basic Form

Author. (Year). Section title. In *Thesis/dissertation title* (Master's thesis/Doctoral dissertation, University), [Type of medium]. Paging or length. Available (include protocol if relevant): Address/Path/File [Access date].

- Give a page range whenever possible. If this inclusive paging information is lacking, apply these rules:

1. When initial page is known, (a) in parentheses, indicate the article length after the initial page, e.g., 10(12 pp.), 10(80 paragraphs), 10(24 screens), 10(300 lines), or 10(3,000 words); or (b) use the notation "ff" for the phrase, "and following pages."

2. When the initial page is not available, indicate the article length (the number of paragraphs, screens, lines, or words). No parentheses are needed.

- In the "available" statement, specify the protocol, domain, and path, if the piece is retrieved on the Internet. If the piece is available from a commercial electronic supplier, indicate the database, search path, and file name.

<A271>   Bierwagen, P. (1995). Chapter III: Molecular mechanics investigations of syndiospecific zirconocene-based ziegler-natta catalysis. In *Computational studies of ziegler-natta catalysis and concurrent resonance computations* (Doctoral dissertation, California Institute of Technology, Pasadena, California), [Online]. 24 paragraphs. Available: http://www.wag.caltech.edu/theses/epb/Ch3.ps [1995, August 29].

B. Entire Thesis/Dissertation

Basic Form

Author. (Year). *Thesis/dissertation title* (Master's thesis/Doctoral dissertation, University), [Type of medium]. Available (include protocol if relevant): Address/Path/File [Access date].

- In the "available" statement, specify the protocol, domain, and path, if the piece is retrieved on the Internet. If the piece is available from a commercial electronic supplier, indicate the database, search path, and file name.

<A272>   Lim, K. T. (1995). *Mega-molecular dynamics on highly parallel computer: methods and application* (Doctoral dissertation, California Institute of Technology, Pasadena, California), [Online]. Available: http://www.wag.caltech.edu/theses/ktl/ToC.html [1995, August 18].

VI. ABSTRACTS

A. Monograph or Individual Work

Basic Form

Author. (Year). [Abstract of *Individual work*], [Type of medium]. Available (include protocol if relevant): Address/Path/File [Access date].

- In the "available" statement, specify the protocol, domain, and path if the piece is retrieved on the Internet. If the piece is available from a commercial electronic supplier, indicate the database, search path, and file name.

<A273>   Kutner, L. A, & Mares, R. (1994). [Abstract of *Environmental discri-
mination*, Council Planning Librarians Bibliography No. 306],
[Online]. Available: OCLC FirstSearch/PAIS Decade/94-1201535
[1995, September 1].

> • Include any relevant information to describe the original source
> in a note, in brackets.

B. Journal Article

Basic Form

Author. (Year). [Abstract of Article title, *Journal*, *Volume*(issue)], [Type of medi-
um]. Available (include protocol if relevant): Address/Path/File [Access date].

> • In the "available" statement, specify the protocol, domain, and
> path, if the piece is retrieved on the Internet. If the piece is avail-
> able from a commercial electronic supplier, indicate the database,
> search path, and file name.

<A274>   Sengers, P. (1995). [Abstract of Madness and automation: On institu-
tionalization, *Postmodern Culture*, 5(Contents3)], [Online]. Available
FTP: ftp.ncsu.edu/pub/ncsu/pmc/pmc-list/contents.595 [1995, June
15].

> • Information about the source of the article, including journal
> title, volume, and issue numbers, are provided after the abstract.

C. Magazine Article

Basic Form

Author. (Year, Month day). [Abstract of Article title, *Magazine*, Volume], [Type of
medium]. Available (include protocol if relevant): Address/Path/File [Access
date].

> • In the "available" statement, specify the protocol, domain, and
> path, if the piece is retrieved on the Internet. If the piece is avail-
> able from a commercial electronic supplier, indicate the database,
> search path, and file name.

<A275>   Ying, Tong. (1995, June 5). [Abstract of Singapore airlines moves into
intelligent systems, *Computerworld*], [Online]. Available: DIALOG/
Magazine Database/17344962 [1995, August 20].

> • The reference lacks the magazine volume number.

D. Newspaper Article

Basic Form

Author. (Year, Month day). [Abstract of Article title, *Newspaper*], [Type of medium]. Available (include protocol if relevant): Address/Path/File [Access date].

> • In the "available" statement, specify the protocol, domain, and path, if the piece is retrieved on the Internet. If the piece is available from a commercial electronic supplier, indicate the database, search path, and file name.

<A276> Purdum, T. S. (1995, August 17). [Abstract of Hard choice for White House on Hillary Clinton and China, *New York Times*], [Online]. Available: Information Access/Expanded Academic ASAP/ A17187821 [1995, September 1].

CHAPTER SEVEN

Reference Citations in Text

The system of documentation recommended by the APA is called the author-date system. References in the text direct readers to the source of a quotation or work under discussion in the alphabetically arranged Reference List at the end of an article, chapter, book, or dissertation. This chapter gives some of the more common examples of "in-text citation."

I. WORK BY A SINGLE AUTHOR

Example 1: Merlan's work (1994) on Aboriginal narrative . . .

Example 2: Australia's Minister of Defense, Robert Ray, maintains that "In the next century a new pattern of strategic relationships will evolve in which the Asia-Pacific region will become more strategically self-contained" (1995, p. 25).

Example 3: "A philosopher is always someone for whom philosophy is not given, someone who in essence must question him or herself about the essence and destination of philosophy" (Derrida, 1994, paragraph 15).

Example 4: I. Holst's view of the move by the Norwegian Parliament to "ban" the national language is soon made clear: "The 1938 language reform bill served the heritage of the National Language the way Pol Pot served Cambodia; if the map and reality don't agree, then change reality" (No date, paragraph 4).

> • Examples 2, 3, and 4 each cite to a specific place in a work. In Examples 3 and 4, the references specify the location of the quotation in the document by giving the paragraph number.

91

• Example 4 shows the referencing method for an item with no publication date. The abbreviation "n.d." can be substituted for "no date" in both the text and Reference List.

II. WORK BY TWO OR MORE AUTHORS

Example 1: Sikula and Costa used a large sample of college students to study the issue of gender and ethical values (1994).

Example 2: The study finds that ". . . among today's youth of normal college age, there are no significant differences between ethical values of male and female students" (Sikula & Costa, 1994, p. 859).

Example 3a:Mardeusz, Reit and Robertson (1995) report . . .

Example 3b:The findings in a recent study (Mardeusz, Reit, & Robertson, 1995) indicate. . .

Example 4: If a work being cited has six or more authors, cite only the first author, followed by "et al." For example, a work by Barickman, Brew, Day, Kutner, Mardeusz, Reit, Robertson, and Ross published in 1995 would be cited as: (Barickman et al., 1995).

III. WORK BY A CORPORATE AUTHOR

Example 1: The United Nation's Fourth World Conference on Women will consider a report by the Committee on the Elimination of Discrimination Against Women (CEDAW) which suggests. . . (1995).

Subsequent References

For corporate authors with lengthy names, subsequent references may be abbreviated:

(U.N., 4th World Conf. Women, CEDAW, 1995).

Example 2: *Resolution 215* of the United Nations, General Assembly, 49th Session recognizes "the tremendous humanitarian problem caused by the presence of mines and other unexploded devices . . . to humanitarian aid operations . . ." (1995, paragraph 3).

Subsequent References

(U.N., Gen. Assembly, 49th Sess., 1995, paragraph 12).

• If there are other materials in the Reference List from this session of the General Assembly, then part of the title of the work should be included to distinguish the item being cited from these other sources:

(U.N., Gen. Assembly, 49th Sess., *Resolution 215*, paragraph 12).

IV. WORKS LISTED BY TITLE (NO AUTHOR GIVEN)

Example 1: In "Women of Anabaptist traditions. . ." (1994) there is an interesting portrayal. . .

Example 2: In recent years, we have seen discussion of the landmark decision "Regents of the University of California v. Bakke" (1978) turn. . .

V. MULTIPLE WORKS CITED IN PARENTHESES

Example 1: An earlier study by Tsaikis and Oritz-Buonafini is at some variance with the findings of Sikula and Costa (1990; 1994).

Example 2: There are two studies that have relevance to this issue, but they present rather different findings (Tsaikis & Oritz-Buonafini, 1990; Sikula & Costa, 1994).

VI. PERSONAL COMMUNICATIONS

Personal communications include personal electronic mail (E-mail) messages, messages on discussion lists and electronic bulletin boards. The *Publication Manual of the American Psychological Association* (4th edition, 1994) does not recommend including these resources in reference lists because of the difficulty of recovering them. Instead, the guide recommends citing the material only in the text (1994, p. 174). *Electronic Styles* differs with this approach and provides many examples for citing these kinds of resources. However, providing "personal communication" in the text note is a useful indicator of the kind of information under discussion.

Example 1: M. Day (personal communication, July 30, 1995) finds the film *Bad Lieutenant* meets several criteria.

Example 2: RRECOME presents ten rules of film criticism in a recent message on CINEMA-L (personal communication, April 1, 1995).

• RRECOME represents the author's log-in name. The convention is to present that name in uppercase letters if the writer's name cannot be determined.

REFERENCE LIST

American Psychological Association. (1994). *Publication manual of the American Psychological Association* (4th ed.). Washington, DC: Author.

Benson, A. C. (1995). *The complete Internet companion for librarians.* New York: Neal-Schuman.

The bluebook: A uniform system of citation (15th ed.). (1991). Cambridge, MA: The Harvard Law Review Association.

Boe, T., Graubart, C. B., & Cappo. M. (1995). *World desk: A student handbook to Gopher and the World-Wide Web.* Santa Cruz, CA: Learning in Motion.

Directory of Electronic Journals, Newsletters and Academic Discussion Lists (4th ed.), [Compiled by L. A. King & D. Kovacs]. (1995). Washington, DC: Association of Research Libraries.

ETEXTCTR [Discussion list for electronic text centers], [Online]. (No date). Available E-mail: LISTSERV@RUTVM1.RUTGERS.EDU

Gale Directory of Databases (Vols. 1–2). (1995, January). Detroit: Gale Research.

Gale Guide to Internet Databases. (1995). Detroit: Gale Research.

Garner, D. L., Smith, D. H., Cheney, D., & Sheehy, H. (1993). *The complete guide to citing government information resources: A manual for writers & librarians* (Rev. ed.). Bethesda, MD: Congressional Information Service for the Government Documents Round Table, American Library Association.

Gibaldi, J. (1995). *MLA handbook for writers of research papers* (4th ed.). New York: Modern Language Association.

Hahn, H. (1994). *The Internet yellow pages.* Berkeley, CA: Osborne-McGraw Hill.

International Organization for Standardization. Technical Committee 46. Subcommittee 9. (1995). *ISO/DIS 690-2: Information and documentation—Bibliographic references—Electronic documents or parts thereof* [Draft standards]. Geneva: Author.

The Internet directory. (1994). New York: Fawcett Columbine.

Internet world's on the Internet. (1994). Westport, CT: Mecklermedia.

Li, X., & Crane, N. B. (1993). *Electronic style: A guide to citing electronic information.* Westport, CT: Mecklermedia.

PACS-L [Public-Access Computer Systems Forum], [Online]. (No date). Available E-Mail: LISTSERV@UHUPVM1.UH.EDU

Patrias, K. (1991). Electronic information formats. In *National Library of Medicine recommended formats for bibliographic citation* (pp. 101–162). Bethesda, MD: National Library of Medicine.

Rosa, A., & Eschholz, P. (1994). *The writer's brief handbook.* New York: Macmillan Publishing Company.

Stout, N. R. (1993). *Getting the most out of your U.S. history course: The history student's vade mecum.* Lexington, MA: D.C. Heath.

Turabian, K. L. (1987). *A manual for writers of term papers, theses, and dissertations* [Revised and enlarged by B. Birtwistle], (5th ed.). Chicago: University of Chicago Press.

University of Chicago Press. (1993). *The Chicago manual of style* (14th ed.). Chicago: Author.

Part Two

MLA Embellished Style

CHAPTER EIGHT

Organization and Use of MLA Embellished Style

In Chapters Nine through Thirteen, *Electronic Styles* introduces examples using the MLA style of citation. To do this, these chapters generally give two basic forms for the kind of information being cited, one showing an author entry and the second showing title as the first element. Each form recommends the elements that should be included and the order in which they should be presented. The basic forms are followed by real citations drawn from various sources.

Although these chapters adhere closely to the MLA style of citation, in them we have stressed some elements more. For example, "available" statements are essential for locating the material being referenced. We have also found it necessary to expand some elements. The options given in this work for paging or some indicator of length augment what is offered in *MLA Handbook* (4th ed.).

The operative principle in making reference to an item, whether in print or electronic format, is to give enough information so that it can be located and no more than that. Another important principle is to make reference to that information in the source in hand. As a rule, it is not necessary to provide supplementary information that has to be located elsewhere. These principles have guided us when we make recommendations on the elements for inclusion in a particular kind of reference.

The following paragraphs provide considerable detail on the MLA style and add explanations for elements that describe electronic sources more completely. They also outline and justify those points where this guide differs from current MLA practice.

AUTHOR(S)

Author is the first element of a citation. When an author is not available, title becomes the first element.

- **Personal Author(s)**

Give last name, followed by the first name and middle initial, if available, (example: Dunlop, William L.). When there are two or three authors, they are listed in the order given in the source. For example:

> Mieder, Wolfgang, and George B. Bryan.

> Ross, Lyman, Janet Reit, and Craig Robertson.

Note that only the first listed author's name is inverted, and that the names are separated by commas. If more than three authors are listed, it is permissible to list only the first author, followed by "et al.", (e.g., Mardeusz, Patricia, et al.). You can also list all the names as they appear in the source, following the pattern for three authors, shown above.

- **Corporate Authors**

Corporate authors can replace personal authors as the first element of a citation. A corporate author is defined as a "commission, an association, a committee, or any other group whose individual members are not identified on the title page" (Gibaldi 117). For example:

> American Institute for Conservation. *Code of Ethics & Guidelines for Practice.*

- **Government Bodies and International Organizations**

Government bodies and international organizations can also be treated as authors. If the writer of the document is not known, give the body or bodies responsible for the content. For example:

> United States. Department of State. . . .

> International Organization for Standardization. Technical Committee 46. Subcommittee 9. . . .

TITLES

- **Book Titles**

The first word and last word of all titles, and all important words in between, are capitalized; subtitles are treated similarly. Book titles are underlined or given in italics. We have chosen to italicize titles of materials presented in this part of the book, which describe resources in MLA style.

- **Article Titles**

  The first word and last word of all titles, and all important words in between, are capitalized; subtitles are treated similarly. The entire article title is enclosed in quotation marks.

- **Journal, Magazine, Newsletter, and Newspaper Titles**

  The convention is to capitalize all words but articles, prepositions, and conjunctions embedded in the title. Titles are underlined or given in italics.

- **Titles of Databases and Electronic Sites**

  Database names or electronic sites, such as Gopher sites or World Wide Web (WWW) homepages should be capitalized and italicized or underlined as books or serial titles are. Databases may or may not be serial titles; electronic sites are treated as edited or compiled works and are nonserial in nature. For example:

  Britannica Online (database)

  E-Text Archives Services (Gopher site)

  City Net (homepage)

EDITION OR VERSION STATEMENTS

Notations on editions or versions should follow directly after the title statement. For example:

Oxford English Dictionary Computer File: On Compact Disc. 2nd ed. . . .

Sternberg, Martin L. A. *The American Sign Language Dictionary on CD-ROM.* Windows Vers. . . . *(Note: The word Version may be abbreviated as Vers.).*

EDITORS, COMPILERS, AND TRANSLATORS

Information on editors, compilers, and translators follow the title of the work, or the edition or version statement if one of these is included. For example:

Ed. Birdie MacLennan. (Editorial responsibility).

Comp. Linda Brew. (Compiler).

Trans. Wichada Sukantarat. (Translator).

Octovian (Cambridge): A Machine-Readable Version. Ed. Frances McSparran.

PUBLICATION INFORMATION AND INFORMATION REQUIRED FOR RETRIEVAL OF INDIVIDUAL WORKS OR PARTS OF WORKS

The *MLA Handbook* (4th ed.) suggests that if the electronic work being cited has a print counterpart, the publication information for the print version should be given first, followed by information for the electronic version. Standard publication information should include place of publication, publisher, and year of publication. Electronic sources introduce other elements: a statement about medium; name of the database; publisher, producer, or supplier of the database; indication of the address, path, and file name, and item or accession number if relevant.[3] These elements, unique to electronic sources, will be discussed more fully below. There are several examples of these very complete citations:

> *Hoover's Handbook of World Business.* Austin, TX: Reference Press, 1995.
> *Hoover's Handbook of World Business.* Online. Mead Nexis. COMPNY/
> HVRWLD. . . .

> "Louis Comfort Tiffany Foundation." *The Foundation Directory.* New York: Foundation Center, 1995. *The Foundation Directory.* Online. Dialog. 26. 00004187. . . .

> - In the first example, Mead Nexis is the online information supplier, and COMPNY/WORLD are the names of the Library and File respectively.
> - The second example shows Dialog as the supplier, the database number (26), and the item number (00004187).
> - For many items, a print counterpart does not exist, or the information about it is not readily available from the electronic source. The advice given in the *MLA Handbook*, and in this work, is "to cite what is available" for the publication (Gibaldi 154). The following show the less complete but far more common citations that fall into this group:

Oxford English Dictionary Computer File: On Compact Disc. 2nd ed. CD-ROM. Oxford: Oxford UP, 1992.

Prizker, Thomas J. *An Early Fragment from Central Nepal.* N.d. Online. Ingress Communications. Available: http://www.ingress.com/~astanart/pritzker.html.

PUBLICATION DATE, VOLUME/ISSUE AND PAGING, AND INFORMATION REQUIRED FOR RETRIEVAL

- **Journals**

For electronic journals, supply volume and issue, separated by a period, then date (in parentheses), followed by a colon and some indicator of the location of the article in the electronic journal or a notation on length. Failing this, give "n. pag." for no pagination. This information is followed, in the case of commercial online databases and CD-ROMs, by medium statement, supplier, database name (italicized or underlined),[4] database number, and item identifier. For Internet sources the elements are medium and "available" statement, which includes address of supplier, path, and, file name.[5] For example:

> . . . *Antiquity* 68.261 (1994): 3 pp. Online. Information Access. *Expanded Academic ASAP.* A16352317. . . . (The item is 3 pages long).

> . . . *Siecus Report* 21.6 (1993): 6-10. CD-ROM. 1994 SIRS. *SIRS 1993 School.* Volume 4. Article 93A. (This item gives a page range).

Other page or length notations, in brief, are as follows:

> . . . *Environmental Green Journal* 2.1 (1995): 3 pars. . . . (3 pars. means 3 paragraphs)

> . . . *EJournal* 4.4 (1994): 462 lines. . . .

> . . . *EJournal* 4.4 (1994): 12 screens. . . .

> . . . *Journal of Abnormal Child Psychology* 23.1 (1995): n. pag. . . .

Note: Providing a citation to a particular part of a work is easier if paging, number of pages, paragraphs, lines, or screens is given in the reference. Use "n. pag." only as a last resort.

- **Magazines**

For electronic magazines, give the date of the issue, followed by a colon, and then pagination or some other indication of length. See the section Journals, above, for a more complete listing of these options. This information is followed, in the case of commercial online databases and CD-ROMs, by medium statement, supplier, database name (underlined), database number, and item identifier. For Internet sources the elements are medium and "available" statement, which includes: address of supplier, path, and file name. For example:

> . . . *American Health* Sept. 1991: 60–64. CD-ROM. 1994 SIRS. *SIRS 1992 Life Science.* Article 08A.

> . . . *DargonZine* 13 May 1995: 22 pars. Online. Available E-mail: LIST SERV@brownvm.bitnet/Get dargon v8n2. . . .

> . . . *Audubon* Jan. 1995: 75+. Online. Mead Nexis. NEWS/MAGS. . . .

MLA Handbook uses a plus (+) sign to indicate that the article starts on a specified page but is not printed on consecutive pages. *Electronic Styles* has adopted this notation to mean the article starts on this page and continues forward for an unspecified number of pages. This notation is particularly useful when counting pages, screens, paragraphs, or lines is difficult. It is no more useful, however, than "n. pag." when one wants to cite a particular part of an article.

- **Newsletters**

  Newsletters are treated the same as magazines. For example:

  > . . . *News from Indian Country* 30 June 1995: 3. CD-ROM. Softline Information. *Ethnic Newswatch.* . . .

  > . . . *Historian's Newsletter* 21 Mar. 1994: 7 pars. Online. Available E-mail: HISTNEWS@ukanvm.cc.ukans.edu. . . .

- **Newspapers**

  Newspaper references require inclusion of date, edition information, if given, and an indicator of pagination or length. For example:

  > . . . *New York Times* 8 June 1995, late ed.: B6. Online. Mead Nexis. NEWS/ NYT. . . .

  > . . . *Toronto Star* 12 July 1995, final ed.: A16. Online. Dow Jones News Retrieval Service. TextM/*International Publications—Newspapers & General Publications.* . . .

MEDIUM STATEMENT

This is an important, added element to the information appearing in references for electronic publications. Common medium statements are online, CD-ROM, online posting,[6] diskette, and magnetic tape. This work gives examples for all but magnetic tapes. We also introduce "electronic" as an option for situations where it is not possible to determine whether a networked CD-ROM or an online supplier is the source of an item being cited.

AVAILABLE STATEMENT

This is included with sources retrieved from remote hosts reached usually via the Internet and using protocols such as FTP, HTTP, Gopher, or Telnet, and for electronic discussion lists. It generally includes information on the protocol used, address of supplier, path (or directory), and file name (if relevant).

The *MLA Handbook* (4th ed.) indicates that the "available" statement is an optional or supplementary item in a reference to an electronic source (Gibaldi 167). This work differs with this point of view. An "available" statement or comparable information is required in order to retrieve the item, and so it is included it as a matter of course in the references presented in the following chapters.

ACCESS DATE

This is the final element of most citations and shows the date on which the electronic source was viewed or retrieved. Many online resources go through constant, even daily updating. Giving the access date pinpoints the period of time in which the item was used, and may shed important light on the version of the document seen. The form of this statement is as follows:

12 May 1995.

29 Nov. 1994.

CD-ROMs and disks usually carry information on edition or version. Access date is not needed and therefore not included with these resources.

NOTES

Notes, which are added to elaborate on the information being cited, are given at the end of the reference—after the access date. For example:

Nader, Ralph. "Ralph Nader on Windows 95 Problems." *TAP/INFO: An Internet Newsletter Available from Taxpayer Assets Project* 21 July 1995:3-9. Online posting. Newsgroup comp.society.privacy. Usenet. 2 Aug. 1995. Letter to President Bill Clinton.

PUNCTUATION

Main elements in references are generally separated by periods. Punctuation in "available" statements should be given just as it is found in the source. The only permissible supplied elements are the colon after Available, forward slashes (/) indicating levels in a path or directory, and a period at the end of the entire "available" statement. In the following examples, supplied punctuation is presented in bold-faced type for emphasis:

> Available**:** http://www.census.gov/ftp/pub/industry/ma35r93.txt**.**

> Available FTP**:** vacs.uwp.edu**/**pub**/**music**/**lyrics**/**b/byrds**/**greatest.hits**.**

UPPERCASE AND LOWERCASE LETTERS

The first word and last word of all titles and all important words in between are capitalized; subtitles are treated similarly (see the section Titles, above, for a more complete discussion).

In the examples given in the preceding section, all of the words in the address are given in lowercase letters. Care must be taken in "available" statements to give uppercase and lowercase letters in the address or message exactly as found in the source, or reference to the source. Some computer systems are extremely sensitive to uppercase and lowercase letters, and if exact notations are not supplied, the communication will fail.

Finally, present abbreviations for protocols, discussion list names, and users' log-in names in uppercase letters: FTP or HTTP, PACS-L or CINEMA-L, and RRECOME, respectively.

ITALICIZING

Titles of books, periodical titles, database names, and actual electronic sites, such as WWW homepages are italicized. A second choice, if italicizing is unavailable, is underlining.

ABBREVIATIONS

When months are presented in a reference, they may be abbreviated. However, May, June, and July are such short words that abbreviation is unnecessary; instead, they are commonly entered in full in a reference. The *MLA Handbook* (4th ed.) has an extensive list of words, in various categories, and their acceptable abbreviations (Gibaldi 207–227). The abbreviation "hp." for homepage is introduced in this guide.

Chapter Twelve deviates from MLA style in Section II. Legal Sources, following the advice of the *MLA Handbook* which says that if ". . . your paper requires many such references [legal documents], consult . . . *The Bluebook: A Uniform System of Citation*, an indispensable guide in this field" (Gibaldi 181). Therefore this section shows standard legal notation for bills, codes of law, court decisions, law reviews (periodicals), and regulations. As a result, the references in that section are very different from those in the rest of the handbook. However, this work gives items cited in the legal section another listing in the section conforming to MLA style for those who want to use this form of notation.

Chapter Fourteen presents, briefly, the parenthetical system of documentation recommended by MLA. Comparable to footnotes or endnotes in function, text references direct readers to the source of a quotation or other information in a "List of Works Cited" at the end of an article, chapter, book, or dissertation. A more detailed discussion of this method can be found in the *MLA Handbook* (Gibaldi 184–202). Since some people will still want, instead, to make use of endnotes or footnotes to give credit for information drawn from other sources, this chapter also shows several examples of this type of notation.

We have tried to be as faithful as we can to this excellent method of making reference to information, a style in use by thousands of people. The differences between the APA style, shown in the first seven chapters of this work, and MLA style are rather substantial, but both styles adapt well to the inclusion of information unique to electronic sources. Finally, the International Organization for Standardization has labored for some time to make recommendations on the documentation of electronic sources in their new draft standards *ISO/DIS 690–2: Information and Documentation— Bibliographic References—Electronic Documents or Parts Thereof.* We have studied this work with care to assure that the information presented in the following pages conforms, as much as possible, with these draft standards as well.

NOTES

3. The *MLA Handbook* (4th ed.) recommends including a network element for online sources, e.g., Internet or BITNET (163-167). We disagree with inclusion of an avenue in such common use. It is more important to include database name, supplier, and "available" statement, which are necessary elements for identification and retrieval of an item.

4. The *MLA Handbook* (4th ed.; Gibaldi 161-163) orders the information as database name, medium, supplier, etc. This seems to break the logical sequence or path one would need to retrieve an item. As a result, we recommend the slightly different sequence of elements—medium, supplier, database name, item numbers, etc.—for journals, magazines, newsletters, and newspapers.

5. This book recommends a somewhat different approach than *MLA Handbook.* Their recommended elements include medium and the computer network, e.g., Internet or BITNET (see preceding note on this issue) or service. The fuller approach that we recommend requires showing the exact path taken to retrieve the electronic document. This makes it much easier for readers of the written work in which the reference appears to refer back to the original electronic document.

6. Online postings are defined as personal electronic messages, messages posted on discussion lists (LISTSERVs), and USENET newsgroups.

CHAPTER NINE

Full-Text Databases: Individual Works, Books, Monographs, or Full-Length Works

I. CITE AN ENTIRE WORK

A. CD-ROM and Commercial Online Databases

Basic Forms

Author/editor. *Title of Print Version of Work*. Place of publication: publisher, date. Medium. Information supplier. *Title of Electronic Work*. File identifier or number. Access date.

Title of Print Version of Work. Place of publication: publisher, date. Medium. Information supplier. *Title of Electronic Work*. File identifier or number. Access date.

> • If no author is given, title becomes the first element of the reference, and the work is alphabetized in the Works Cited list by the first significant word in the title.
>
> • The citation should generally contain the name of the information supplier and the database identifier or number for ease of retrieval.

<M1>   *Academic American Encyclopedia*. 1995. Online. Dow Jones News Retrieval Service. *Academic American Encyclopedia*. ENCYC. 27 May 1995.

> • It is not necessary to give place of publication and publisher when citing well-known reference sources.

- When a print and online version of a work exist, it is proper to cite both, as indicated above. Note the name of the database is italicized.
- Access date is given as the last element. Since updating of online sources may be continuous, the access date gives the reader precise indication of when the document was used or referred to.

<M2>   *The Agrochemicals Handbook.* Cambridge, Eng.: Royal Chemical Society, 1993. Online. CompuServe Knowledge Index. *The Agricultural Handbook.* CHEM3. 16 Apr. 1995.
- Months should be abbreviated if they are more than four letters. Spell out, in full, the months May, June, and July.

<M3>   *The Foundation Directory.* New York: Foundation Center, 1995. Online. Dialog. *The Foundation Directory.* 26. 27 May 1995.

<M4>   *Hoover's Handbook of World Business.* Austin, TX: The Reference Press, 1995. Online. Mead Nexis. *Hoover's Handbook of World Business.* COMPNY/HVRWLD. 23 May 1995.
- This statement shows the characteristic path: Library: COMPNY and File: HVRWLD from this information supplier.

1. Citation Form When a Print Version Is Not Included in Reference

Basic Forms

Online Sources

Author/editor. *Title of Electronic Work.* Edition statement (if given). Date. Medium. Information supplier. File name or number. Access date.

Title of Electronic Work. Edition statement (if given). Medium. Information supplier. File name or number. Access date.

<M5>   *Art Gallery Forum.* N.d. Online. CompuServe. ARTGALLERY. 1 June 1995.
- No date is abbreviated as N.d.

CD-ROM Sources

Author/editor. *Title of Print Work* (if one exists). Edition statement (if given). *Title of Database.* Medium. Place of publication: publisher, date.

Title of Print Work (if one exists). Edition statement (if given). *Title of Database.* Medium. Place of publication: publisher, date.

• Note that the access date is omitted in these examples. If you are following MLA style, the proviso is to cite a nonperiodical CD-ROM as you would a book, with the inclusion of the "medium" statement.

<M6> *Grolier Prehistoria Computer File: A Multimedia Who's Who of Pre-historic Life.* Macintosh vers. 1.0.0. CD-ROM. Danbury, CT: Grolier, 1994.

      • Version is abbreviated as vers.

<M7> *Oxford English Dictionary Computer File: On Compact Disc.* 2nd ed. CD-ROM. Oxford: Oxford UP, 1992.

<M8> Sternberg, Martin L. A. *The American Sign Language Dictionary on CD-ROM.* Windows vers. CD-ROM. New York: HarperCollins, 1994.

B. Electronic Mail (E-mail)

1. Archived Works

Basic Forms

Author/editor. *Title.* Edition. Medium. Available E-mail: LISTSERV/Get. Access date.

Title. Edition. Medium. Available E-mail: LISTSERV/Get. Access date.

      • If author or editor is not given, use the second basic form.
      • Title of work should be italicized in both cases.
      • Provide edition information if the work is not the first edition.
      • No publication information (i.e., place of publication and publisher) is needed.
      • For medium, write "online posting."
      • In the "available" statement, give the LISTSERV network address and the file name with its extension in the "Get" message.

<M9> Gaylord, Harry. *ISO.* 2 June 1989. Online posting. Available E-mail: LISTSERV@BROWNVM.BITNET/Get ISO STANDRDS. 1 June 1995.

<M10> Hurlbut, Jesse D. *From Functional Feast to Frivolous Funhouse: Two Ideals of Play in the Burgundian Court.* Apr. 1992. Online posting. Available E-mail: LISTSERV@IUBVM.UCS.INDIANA.EDU/Get HURLBUT PAPER. 15 May 1995. Paper given at the 5th Annual

Indiana University Symposium on Medieval Studies: Work and Play in the Middle Age.

  • Supplementary bibliographic information appears in a note at the end of the entry.

<M11>   Pope, Stephen T. *Sound Anthology*. 30 May 1995. Online posting. Available E-mail: LISTSERV@AMERICAN.EDU/Get EMUSIC-L LOG9505E. 1 June 1995.

<M12>   Smith, Russell. *The Legend of Mark Twain*. 22 June 1994. Online posting. Available E-mail: LISTSERV%YORKVM1.BITNET/Get LEG END MT. 15 May 1995.

2. Real-Time Works

See Chapter Eleven, Section I. Discussion Lists, A: Cite a Message (page 155 forward).

C. FTP

Basic Forms

Author/editor. *Title*. Edition statement (if given). Publication information for printed source (if available). Medium. Source of electronic text (if available). Available FTP: site/path/file. Access date.

Title. Edition statement (if given). Publication information for printed source (if available). Medium. Source of electronic text (if available). Available FTP: site/path/file. Access date.

  • In an FTP available statement, the address or site will be the first segment and file the last. The path, usually several segments, lies between. The information required for log-in is so standard with FTP sites that it need not be repeated in the "available" statement.
  • Often the information in the address must be interpreted to extract the information on the source of the item.

<M13>   Byrds. *The Byrds' Greatest Hits*. Lyrics. Kenosha, WI: U of Wisconsin—Parkside, n.d. Online. Lyric and Discography Archive. Available FTP: vacs.uwp.edu/ pub/music/lyrics/b/byrds/greatest.hits. 3 June 1995.

  • The author, in this case, is a singing group, rather than a personal author.

- The item bears no date, so that is noted in the place of a specific publication date with "n.d."

<M14> *Octovian (Cambridge): A Machine-Readable Version*. Ed. Frances McSparran. Early English Text Soc. 289. London, New York: Oxford University Press, 1986. Online. U of Virginia Library Electronic Text Center. Available FTP: etext.virginia.edu/pub/texts/AnoOctC. 12 May 1995.

- This is an example of a work for which editorial responsibility is given. "Ed. first name last name" follows title element.

<M15> *Oxford Text Archive Snapshot*. Oxford: Oxford UP, [1990?]. Online. HNServer. Available FTP: hnsource.cc.ukans.edu/pub/history/ Europe/Modern/Britain/oxtext.bib. 1 June 1995.

- When date of publication is approximated, indicate that by following the date with a question mark and inserting the statement in brackets.

<M16a> Robinson, Mary. *Sappho and Phaon in a Series of Legitimate Sonnets, with Thoughts on Poetical Subjects, and Anecdotes of the Grecian Poetess*. London: Gosnell, 1796. Online. U of Virginia Library Electronic Text Center. Available FTP: etext.virginia.edu/pub/britpo/ sappho/RobSapp. 12 May 1995.

- The electronic text of this version was loaded in 1993. This information is not necessary for inclusion; important dates are original publication and access dates.

<M16b> Robinson, Mary. *Sappho and Phaon in a Series of Legitimate Sonnets, with Thoughts on Poetical Subjects, and Anecdotes of the Grecian Poetess*. Charlottesville, VA: U of Virginia, 1993 [load date]. Online. U of Virginia Library Electronic Text Center. Available FTP: etext.vir ginia.edu/pub/britpo/sappho/RobSapp. 12 May 1995.

- It may not always be possible to identify the original source to cite in the electronic version. In this instance, publication information is taken from the electronic source. This supplied information is enclosed in brackets. Identify the date as "load date" as shown above.

<M17> Savetz, Kevin M. *The Unofficial Internet Book List: The Most Extensive Bibliography of Books about the Internet*. N.p.: [Northcoast Internet-Services?], 1994. Online. Murdoch U (Murdoch, West. Austral.). Available: ftp://infolib.murdoch.edu.au/pub/bib/savetz.bib. 12 May 1995.

- When no place of publication can be determined, use "N.p."

> • The source document does not clearly identify the publisher of this item; since there is some uncertainty, the information on the publisher is followed by a question mark, and enclosed in brackets.

<M18> *TWU Woman's Collection.* Denton, TX: Texas Woman's U, 1992. Online. [U Michigan Lib.?]. Available FTP: una.hh.lib.umich.edu/newstuff/ diversity/abouttwu. 15 May 1995.

> • If you supply information of which you are unsure, put a question mark after the segment and enclose the information in brackets.

D. Gopher

Basic Forms

Author/editor. *Title.* Edition. Place of publication: publisher, date. Medium. Available Gopher: Gopher site/search path/file. Access date.

Title. Edition. Place of publication: publisher, date. Medium. Available Gopher: Gopher site/search path/file. Access date.

> • If no author or editor is given, use the second basic form.
> • In the "available" statement, provide Gopher site or address, directory/directories, and file name.
> • It is not necessary to repeat the protocol (Gopher) on the WWW after the "available" statement since it is stated in the URL.

<M19> Barrie, James Matthew. *Peter Pan.* A Millennium Fulcrum ed. N.p.: Duncan Research, 1991. Online. Gutenberg Project. Available Gopher: gopher.tc.umc.edu/Libraries/Electronic Books/Peter Pan. 1 June 1995.

> • If no place of publication is given, write "N.p."

<M20> Descartes, Rene. *Discourse on the Method of Conducting the Reason, and Seeking Truth in the Sciences.* N.d. Online. Carnegie Mellon U. Available Gopher: english-server.hss.cmu.edu/Philosophy/Descartes-on Method. 12 June 1995.

> • This shows the form when a print version is not included in the reference.

<M21> *The Japanese Surrender Documents—WWII.* N.p.: n.p., 1945. Online. Gutenberg Project. Available Gopher: gopher.tc.umn.edu/Libraries/ Electronic Books/Historical Documents/Japanese Surrender. 25 May 1995.

> • If no place of publication is given, write "N.p." If no publisher is given, write "n.p." after the colon.

<M22>   Shelly, Mary Wollstonecraft. *Frankenstein*. Boston: Sever, Francis, & Co., 1869. Online. Gutenberg Project. Available: gopher://gopher. etext.org/Gutenberg/etext93/frandk10.txt. 2 June 1995.

E. HTTP

Basic Forms

Author/editor (if given). *Title*. Edition. Place of publication: publisher, date. Source of electronic information (if available). Medium. Available: URL. Access date.

Title. Edition. Place of publication: publisher, date. Source of electronic information (if available). Medium. Available: URL. Access date.

> • If no author or editor is given, use the second basic form.
> • The Uniform Resource Locator (URL) should include the WWW site, path, and file name.
> • It is not necessary to repeat the protocol (HTTP) on the WWW after the "available" statement since it is stated in the URL.

<M23>   American Institute for Conservation. *Code of Ethics & Guidelines for Practice*. Revised Draft. Washington, D.C.: American Institute for Conservation of Historic and Artistic Works, 1994. *Conservation Online (CoOL)*. Online. Stanford U. Available: http://palimpsest.stan ford.edu/byorg/aic/aicethics/ethdraf2.html. 13 June 1995.

> • Example shows name of database and source of the electronic document (Stanford U.).

<M24>   *Educating America for the 21st Century: Developing a Strategic Plan for Educational Leadership for Columbia University—1993–2000*. Initial Workshop Draft. New York: Columbia U., 1994. Online. Columbia U. Available: http://www.ilt.columbia.edu/CONF/EdPlan. html. 16 May 1995.

> • Start entry with title of work if author is not given.

<M25>   Lehman, Bruce A., and Ronald H. Brown. *Intellectual Property and the National Information Infrastructure*. Washington, D.C.: Information Infrastructure Task Force, 1994. Online. U.S. Patent and Trademark Office. Available: http://www.uspto.gov/nii/ipwg.html. 15 May 1995.

> • The second joint author appears first name first, followed by last name.

<M26>   Prizker, Thomas J. *An Early Fragment from Central Nepal.* N.d. Online.
Ingress Communications. Available: http://www.ingress.com/~asta
nart/pritzker /pritzker.html. 8 June 1995.
- This is a citation form when the print version is not included in
the reference.

F. Telnet

Basic Forms

Author/editor. *Title.* Edition. Place of publication: publisher, date. Medium. Source
of electronic information (if available). Available Telnet: Telnet site/**login**:/
password:/path/file. Access date.

Title. Edition. Place of publication: publisher, date. Medium. Source of electronic
information (if available). Available Telnet: Telnet site/**login**:/**password**:/path/
file. Access date.

- If no author or editor is given, use the second basic form.
- Medium statement follows directly after the publication infor-
mation.
- If log-in and password are required in order to establish the
Telnet session, provide those in the "available" statement.

<M27>   Bowles, Paul. *The Paul Bowles Moroccan Music Collection.* Washing-
ton, D.C.: Library of Congress, 1994. Online. Library of Congress.
Available Telnet: marvel.loc.gov/Research and Reference/Dance
Heritage Coalition Network/Dance Research Resources/Library of
Congress Dance Resources. 15 May 1995.

<M28>   *Depression Primer.* Washington, D.C.: George Washington U., 1994.
Online. George Washington U. Available Telnet: cap.gwu.edu/**login**:
gwis/**password**: guest/Health Center/Information by Topic/Depres
sion. 14 May 1995.

<M29>   *Educating America for the 21st century: Developing a Strategic Plan for
Educational Leadership for Columbia University—1993–2000.* Initial
Workshop Draft. New York: Columbia U., 1994. Online. Columbia U.
Available Telnet: columbianet.columbia.edu/**login**: guest/Handbooks,
Reports/Educating America For the 21st Century. 16 May 1995.

<M30>   Shakespeare, William. *A Midsummer Night's Dream.* Arthur Bullen's
Stratford Town ed. Stratford-on-Avon: Shakespeare Head, 1911.
Online. Dartmouth Coll. Lib. Available Telnet: library.dartmouth.
edu/shakespeare plays/a midsummer night's dream. 2 June 1995.

G. USENET

See Chapter Eleven, Section II. USENET, A. Individual Works (page 159 forward).

H. Wide-Area Information Server (WAIS)

Basic Forms

Author/editor. *Title*. Edition. Place of publication: publisher, date. Medium. Source of electronic information (if available). Available WAIS: WAIS site**/login:/user identifier**:**/terminal**:/path/file. Access date.

Title. Edition. Place of publication: publisher, date. Medium. Source of electronic information (if available). Available WAIS: WAIS site**/login:/user identifier**:/ **terminal**:/path/file. Access date.

> • If no author or editor is given, use the second basic form.
> • Boldfaced words in the "available" statement are system prompts.

<M31>   Carroll, Lewis. *The Walrus and the Carpenter*. N.p.: n.p., n.d. Online. MIT. Available WAIS: quake.think**/login**: wais**/user identifier**: user@address**/term**: vt100/404: * [microworld.media.mit] poetry/ **keywords**: walrus/001: (Poetry) The Walrus and the Carpenter Lew. 9 Sept. 1995.

<M32>   *Our Environmental Resource Base*. N.p.: n.p., n.d. Online. Canada Dept. of the Environment. Available WAIS: quake.think**/login**: wais**/user identifier**: user@address**/term**: vt100/227: * [atlenv.ns.doe.CA] Environment Canada**/keywords**: rivers/017: (Environment_Can) http: //atlenv.bed.ns.doe.ca/soe/chapt1_2. 9 Sept. 1995. This document is presented in Hypertext Markup Language.

> • Note further explaining the source being referenced is placed after the access date.
> • Path includes directory information and a URL.

II. CITE PART OF A WORK

A. CD-ROM and Commercial Online Databases

Basic Forms

Author/editor. "Part Title." *Title of Print Version of Work*. Edition statement (if given). Place of publication: publisher, date. Medium. Information supplier.

Title of Electronic Work. File identifier or number. Accession or item number (if given). Access date.

"Part Title." *Title of Print Version of Work.* Edition statement (if given). Place of publication: publisher, date. Medium. Information supplier. *Title of Electronic Work.* File identifier or number. Accession or item number (if given). Access date.

- If no author is given, title becomes the first element of the reference, and the work is alphabetized in the list of works cited by the first significant word in the title.
- The citation should generally contain the name of the information supplier, the database identifier or number, and the item or accession number for ease of retrieval.

<M33>   Belloc, Hilaire. "The Early Morning." *Oxford Dictionary of Quotations.* 3rd ed. Oxford: Oxford UP, 1979. Online. CompuServe Knowledge Index. *Quotations database.* REFR1. 00000814. 5 June 1995. Poem by Belloc.
- The "available" statement includes the database supplier, the database identifier, and the accession number of the specific item.
- Note of explanation is placed at the end of the citation.

<M34>   "Bosnia and Hercegovina." *Academic American Encyclopedia.* 1995. Online. Dow Jones News Retrieval Service. *Academic American Encyclopedia.* ENCYC. 5 June 1995.
- This is an article from an encyclopedia with no author given.
- It is not necessary to give place of publication and publisher when citing well-known reference sources.
- The database does not assign item numbers to specific articles, so citation lacks this information.

<M35>   College's Own In-Depth Description: University of Vermont. 1995. Online. Dow Jones News Retrieval Service. *Peterson's College Database.* COLLEGE. 5 June 1995. Title supplied.
- If the title is supplied, do not place it in quotations. In this example, a note gives the supplementary bibliographical information about the title.
- This is an example where no print counterpart is given.

<M36>   International Trade Administration. "IV. Political environment." *Ecuador: Country Commercial Guides.* 30 March 1995. CD-ROM. US Dept. of Commerce. Country Commercial Guides. *National Trade Data Bank—The Export Connection (R).* IT CCG ECUADOR04. Apr. 1995.

- This is an example of a corporate author.
- This cites only the electronic version of the information.

<M37>   "Kuru." *Mosby's Medical, Nursing, and Allied Health Dictionary*. 4th ed. N.p.: Mosby-Year Book, 1994. *Mosby's Medical, Nursing, and Allied Health Dictionary*. Electronic. Information Access. *InfoTrac—Health Reference Center*. Kuru—Dictionary definition. 7 June 1995.

   - The source does not give the location of the publisher, so the citation shows the use of "N.p."
   - Sometimes it is not possible to tell whether one is accessing an online source or a networked CD-ROM. If this is the case, substitute "Electronic" for the medium statement.
   - This database does not give accession numbers for the items found in a search, so citation shows the search path in lieu of an accession number; include access date.

<M38>   "Louis Comfort Tiffany Foundation." *The Foundation Directory*. New York: Foundation Center, 1995. Online. Dialog. *The Foundation Directory*. 26. 00004187. 7 June 1995.

<M39>   "Nestle Ltd." *Hoover's Handbook of World Business*. Austin, TX: Reference Press, 1995. Online. Mead Nexis. *Hoover's Handbook of World Business*. COMPNY/HVRWLD. 23 May 1995. (1995).

B. E-mail

1. Archived Works

Basic Forms

Author/editor. "Part Title." *Source*. Edition statement (if given). Medium. Source of electronic text (if available). Available E-mail: LISTSERV/Get. Access date.

"Part Title." *Source*. Edition statement (if given). Medium. Source of electronic text (if available). Available E-mail: LISTSERV/Get. Access date.

   - If no author or editor is given, use the second basic form.
   - Publication information (i.e., place of publication and publisher) is not necessary in the reference.
   - For the medium element, write "Online posting."
   - In the "available" statement, give the LISTSERV network address; file name, with its extension, is given in the "Get" message.

<M40>   Bailey, Charles W. "Electronic Serials and Related Topics." *Directory of Electronic Journals and Newsletters*. 2nd edition. Washington, D.C.: ARL Office of Scientific & Academic Publishing, 1992. Online posting. Available E-mail: LISTSERV@UOTTAWA.BITNET/Get EJOURNL1 DIRECTRY. 8 June 1995.
   • Include publication information of the print version if available.

<M41>   Gaylord, Harry. "Four Fundamental Options in Building up Multi-Character Sets." *ISO*. 2 June 1989. Online posting. Available E-mail: LISTSERV@BROWNVM.BITNET/Get ISO STANDRDS. 8 June 1995.

<M42>   Russell, Barry. "Parisian Fairground Theatre." *PERFORM LOG9505*. 1 June 1995. Online posting. Available E-mail: LISTSERV@IUBVM.UCS.INDIANA.EDU/Get PERFORM LOG9505. 8 June 1995.

<M43>   Twain, Mark. "The Balloon Ascension." *Tom Sawyer Abroad*. May 1993. Online posting. Available E-mail: LISTSERV@YORKVM1.BITNET/Get TSA TEXT. 15 May 1995.

2. Real-Time Works

See Chapter Eleven, Section I. Discussion Lists, A. Cite a Message (page 155 forward).

C. FTP

Basic Forms

Author/editor. "Part Title." *Source*. Edition statement (if given). Publication information for printed source (if available). Medium. Source of electronic text (if available). Available FTP: address or site/path/file. Access date.

"Part Title." *Source*. Edition statement (if given). Publication information for printed source (if available). Medium. Source of electronic text (if available). Available FTP: address or site/path/file. Access date.

   • In an FTP available statement, the *address* will be the first segment and *file* the last. The *path*, usually several segments, lies between. Log-in information for FTP sites is so standard one need not repeat it in the "available" statement.

<M44>   Byrds. "So You Want to Be a Rock 'N' Roll Star." *The Byrds' Greatest Hits*. Lyrics. Kenosha, WI: U of Wisconsin—Parkside, n.d. Online.

Lyric and Discography Archive. Available FTP: vacs.uwp.edu/ pub/ music/lyrics/b/byrds/greatest.hits. 3 June 1995.
- •The authors are, in this case, a singing group.
- • Statement following the title indicates special nature of this information.
- • The item bears no date, so that is noted in the place of a specific publication date with "n.d."

<M45>   Holst, Ingar. "Language Reform 1907–1958." *How the Norwegian Parliament Banned the National Language.* N.p.: n.p., n.d. Online. Finnish University and Research Network. Available FTP: nic.funet. fi/pub/culture/text/ingar-holst/murder-of-norw-language. 11 June 1995.

<M46a>   Robinson, Mary. Preface. *Sappho and Phaon in a Series of Legitimate Sonnets, with Thoughts on Poetical Subjects, and Anecdotes of the Grecian Poetess.* By Robinson. London: Gosnell, 1796. Online. U of Virginia Library Electronic Text Center. Available FTP: etext. virginia.edu/pub/britpo/sappho/RobSapp. 12 May 1995.
- • For an introduction, foreword, preface, or afterword of a work, give that information without enclosure in quotes, and cite the author of that work after the title. If the writer of the piece is the author of the whole work, give just the person's last name. If the piece is by a different author, give the full time (e.g., By John Smith).

<M46b>   Robinson, Mary. Preface. *Sappho and Phaon in a Series of Legitimate Sonnets, with Thoughts on Poetical Subjects, and Anecdotes of the Grecian Poetess.* By Robinson. Charlottesville, VA: U of Virginia, 1993 [load date]. Online. U of Virginia Library Electronic Text Center. Available FTP: etext.virginia.edu/pub/britpo/sappho/RobSapp. 12 May 1995.
- • It may not always be possible to identify the original source to cite in parallel with the electronic version. Cite what is available (e.g., "load date" of the electronic information) and so indicate with a note in brackets.
- • See note in <M46a> for a discussion of citation forms for prefaces, introductions, forewords, and afterwords.

<M47>   "Title 1: Common Provisions." *Treaty on European Union (Maastricht Treaty).* Luxembourg: EEC, 1992. Online. Available FTP: src.doc.ic. ac.uk/politics/EEC/Maastricht/title1. 5 June 1995.
- • Supplier of the electronic document is not given in this reference.

D. Gopher

Basic Forms

Author/editor. "Part Title." *Source*. Edition statement (if given). Publication information for printed source (if available). Medium. Source of electronic text (if
available). Available Gopher: Gopher site/path/file. Access date.

"Part Title." *Source*. Edition statement (if given). Publication information for printed
source (if available). Medium. Source of electronic text (if available). Available
Gopher: Gopher site/path/file. Access date.

> • If no author or editor is given, use the second basic form.
> • Include publication information for printed source if available in
> the form of "Place of publisher: publisher, publication date."
> • In the "available" statement, provide Gopher site, search path,
> and file name.

<M48>   Bacon, Francis. "Of Truth." *The Essays*. N.p.: n.p., 1601. Online.
Carnegie Mellon U. Available Gopher: english-server.hss.cmu.edu/
Philosophy/Bacon-The Essays. 13 June 1995.

> • Write "N.p." and "n.p." if no place of publication and publisher
> are given.

<M49>   Carroll, Lewis. "Chapter XI: Who Stole the Tarts?" *Alice's Adventures
in Wonderland*. The Millennium Fulcrum edition 2.7a. N.p.: Duncan
Research, 1991. Online. Gutenberg Project. Available Gopher:
gopher.tc.umc.edu/Libraries/Electronic Books/Alice's Adventures in
Wonderland/Chapter XI. 12 June 1995.

> • Write "N.p." when the place of publication is not given.

<M50>   Embassy of India. "Demographic Background." *India 1993 Annual*.
Washington, D.C.: The Embassy of India, 1994. Online. India Network. Available Gopher: india.bgsu.edu/India-ANU/Land, people
and population. 13 June 1995.

> • This is a reference for a corporate author.

<M51>   "Will Caffeine Enhance Athletic Performance?" *Caffeine: Caffeine Ef-
fects on Academics and Athletics*. N.d. *The Drugs Database*. Online.
U Wisconsin. Available Gopher: hemp.uwec.edu/drugs/Caffeine/Caf
feine's Effects on Academics and Athletics. 13 June 1995.

> • This is a citation form when a print version is not included in
> the reference.

E. HTTP

Basic Forms

Author/editor. "Part Title." *Source*. Edition statement (if given). Publication information for printed source (if available). Medium. Source of electronic text (if available). Available: URL. Access date.

"Part Title." *Source*. Edition statement (if given). Publication information for printed source (if available). Medium. Source of electronic text (if available). Available: URL. Access date.

> • It is not necessary to repeat the protocol (HTTP) on the WWW after the "available" statement since it is stated in the URL.

<M52>   Armour, Ian D. "World Affairs: Special Report: Bosnia and Herzegovina." *Britannica Online: Book of the Year (1994)*. 1995. Online. Encyclopaedia Britannica. Available: http://www.eb.com:180/cgi-bin/g?DocF=boy/94/H03245.html. 14 June 1995.

> • It is not necessary to give place of publication and publisher when citing well-known reference sources.

<M53>   American Institute for Conservation. "Code of Ethics." *Code of Ethics and Guidelines for Practice*. Revised draft. Washington, D.C.: American Institute for Conservation of Historic and Artistic Works, 1994. *Conservation Online (CoOL)*. Online. Stanford U. Available: http://palimpsest.stanford.edu/byorg/aic/aicethics/ethdraf2.html. 13 June 1995.

> • This is an example with a corporate author.

<M54>   Aristotle. "Part I." *Poetics*. Trans. S. H. Butcher. N.p.: n.p., n.d. Online. The Tech Classics Archive. Available: http://the-tech.mit.edu/Classics/Aristotle/poetics.txt.Part_1.html. 13 June 1995.

> • When citing a translation, state the author's name first and give the translator's name, preceded by "Trans.," after the title of the source. This source does not give translator's full name; cite what is available.
>
> • Write "N.p." and "n.p.," and "n.d." when the place of publication, publisher, and date are not given.

<M55>   Daniel, Ralph Thomas. "The History of Western Music." *Britannica Online: Macropaedia*. 1995. Online. Encyclopaedia Britannica. Available: http://www.eb.com:180/cgi-bin/g:DocF=macro/5004/45/0.html. 14 June 1995.

> • It is not necessary to give place of publication and publisher when citing well-known reference sources.

<M56>   J.P. Morgan & Co. "Data Series Naming Standards." *Structure of the RiskMetrics Data Files.* New York: J.P. Morgan, n.d. Online. Risk-Metrics. Available: http://www.jpmorgan.com/RiskMetrics/About. html. 13 June 1995.
> • This is an example of a corporate author.
> • Write "n.d." when the publication date is not given.

<M57>   Muir, John. "Yosemite." *Britannica Online: Britannica Classics.* 1995. Online. Encyclopaedia Britannica. Available: http://www.eb.com: 180/cgi-bin/g?DocF=classic/C00014.html. 14 June 1995.
> • It is not necessary to give place of publication and publisher when citing well-known reference sources.

F. Telnet

Basic Forms

Author/editor. "Part Title." *Source.* Edition statement (if given). Publication infor-mation for printed source (if available). Medium. Source of electronic text (if available). Available Telnet: Telnet site/**login**:/**password**:/search path/file. Access date.

"Part Title." *Source.* Edition statement (if given). Publication information for print-ed source (if available). Medium. Source of electronic text (if available). Available Telnet: Telnet site/**login**:/**password**:/search path/file. Access date.

> • If no author or editor is given, use the second basic form.
> • If log-in and password are required in order to establish the Telnet session, provide those in the "available" statement.

<M58>   Dickens, Charles. "Chirp the First." *The Cricket on the Hearth.* N.d. Online. Online Book Initiative. Available Telnet: marvel.loc.gov/**login**: marvel/Research and Reference/Electronic Publications/Texts and Books/Online Book Initiative (OBI)/The Online Books/Charles Dickens/cricket.on.hearth.txt. 16 June 1995.
> • This is an example when a print version is not included in the reference.

<M59>   "Norway." *The World Factbook 1994.* Washington, D.C.: Central Intel-ligence Agency, 1994. Online. Dartmouth Coll. Lib. Available Telnet: LIBRARY.DARTMOUTH.EDU/World factbook/Norway. 16 June 1995.

<M60>   Shakespeare, William. "Act I, Scene II." *Hamlet*. Arthur Bullen's
         Stratford Town ed. Stratford-on-Avon: Shakespeare Head, 1911.
         Online. Dartmouth Coll. Lib. Available Telnet: LIBRARY.DART
         MOUTH.EDU/Shakespeare plays/Hamlet. 15 June 1995.

<M61>   "Synagogue." *Oxford English Dictionary*. 2nd ed. Oxford, Eng.: Clar-
         endon, 1989. Online. U Washington. Available Telnet: UWIN.U.
         WASHINGTON.EDU/I/REF/OED/synagogue. 16 June 1995.

G. USENET

See Chapter Eleven, Section II. USENET (page 159 forward).

H. WAIS

Basic Forms

Author/editor. "Part Title." *Source*. Edition. Place of publication: publisher, date.
   Medium. Source of electronic information (if available). Available WAIS:
   WAIS site/**login**:/**user identifier**:/**terminal**:/path/file. Access date.

"Part Title." *Source*. Edition. Place of publication: publisher, date. Medium.
   Source of electronic information (if available). Available WAIS: WAIS
   site/**login**:/**user identifier**:/**terminal**:/path/file. Access date.

- If no author or editor is given, use the second basic form.
- Underlined words in the "available" statement indicate system queries to which user must respond.

<M62>   "Lesotho." *World Factbook 1993*. N.p.: n.p., 1993. Online. U Western
         Ontario. Available WAIS: quake.think/**login**: wais/**user identifier**:
         user@address/**term**: vt100/547:* [gopher.uwo.ca] world-factbook93/
         keywords: lesotho/001: (world-factbook9) Lesotho Geography/
         Location: South. 9 Sept. 1995.

<M63>   "Water." *Our Environmental Resource Base*. N.p.: n.p., n.d. Online.
         Canada Dept. of the Environment. Available WAIS: quake.think/**login**:
         wais/**user identifier**: user@address/**term**: vt100/227: *[atlenv.ns.doe.
         CA] Environment Canada/**keywords**: rivers/017: (Environment_Can)
         http://atlenv.bed.ns.doe.ca/soe/chapt1_2. 9 Sept. 1995.

- The address, path, and file take the user only to the document level—not the part of the work being cited.
- The WAIS address includes a URL as the last element.

CHAPTER TEN

Full-Text Databases: Periodicals

The MLA prescribed order of elements has been changed somewhat in this chapter. The "database name" element has been relocated to follow supplier. This makes the path for retrieval clearer in those sections describing citation of CD-ROM and commercial online databases and more nearly matches the order of information in "available" statements.

I. CITE PART OF A WORK

A. Journal Articles

1. CD-ROM and Commercial Online Databases

Basic Forms

Author. "Article Title." *Journal Title* Volume number.Issue number (Year): Number of pages or paragraphs (if given), or n. pag. (for no pagination). Medium. Supplier. *Database name*. Database identifier or number if available. Item or accession number. Access date.

"Article Title." *Journal Title* Volume number.Issue number (Year): Number of pages or paragraphs (if given), or n. pag. (for no pagination). Medium. Supplier. *Database name*. Database identifier or number if available. Item or accession number. Access date.

- When author is not given, use the second basic form.
- There are several possibilities for indicating paging or length of the article, including the following:

(a) number of pages (e.g., 10 pp.)
(b) number of paragraphs (e.g., 10 pars.)
(c) page range (e.g., 10–20.)
(d) starting page known (e.g., 10+.)
(e) paging cannot be determined (e.g., n. pag. for no pagination)

Choices d and e do not provide the flexibility for citing to a particular part of an article that a, b, and c do.

> • Underline database name or give in all caps.
> • The elements following "supplier" may vary somewhat; include what makes sense for the particular system being searched.

<M64>   Achenbach, Thomas M. "Diagnosis, Assessment, and Comorbidity in Psychosocial Treatment Research." *Journal of Abnormal Child Psychology* 23.1 (1995): n. pag. Online. Mead Nexis. NEWS/ASAPII. 12 June 1995. Special Issue: Psychosocial Treatment Research.

> • This item has a special issue, which is noted in a statement directly after access date.
> • The number of pages in the article is not given, so the note, "n. pag.," for no pagination is substituted.
> • Mead Nexis references do not have item or accession numbers for individual stories, so this information will be lacking from citations. Library and file names are separated by a slash sign (/). Elements might also be separated with a period (e.g., NEWS. ASAPII.).

<M65>   Beaton, J. M. Rev. of *Sahul in Review: Pleistocene Archaeology in Australia, New Guinea and Island Melanesia*, by M. A. Smith, M. Spriggs, and B. Fankhauser. *Antiquity* 68.261 (1994): 3 pp. Online. Information Access. *Expanded Academic ASAP*. A16352317. 12 June 1995.

> • This is an example of a book review. Reviewer's name is given first, followed by the title of the review, in quotes, if there is a title. The *Rev. of* statement is the next element and includes the title of the work and the author statement.
> • Author's and reviewers' full names are not given in the source; cite what is given.
> • This review lacks a title.

<M66>   Bosselman, Fred. "Four Land Ethics: Order, Reform, Responsibility, Opportunity." *Environmental Law* 24 (1994): n. pag. Online. Mead Lexis. LAWREV/ENVLAW. June 12 1995.

> • This citation lacks an issue number.

• The number of pages in the article is not given, so the note, "n. pag.," for no pagination is substituted.

<M67> Brookfield, Harold, and Christine Padoch. "Appreciating Agrodiversity: A Look at Dynamism and Diversity of Indigenous Farming Practices." *Environment* 36.5 (1994): 15 pp. Online. Dialog. *Magazine Index*. 47. 15490130. 13 June 1995.

    • This example gives the format for citing more than one author.

<M68> Clark, Jeffrey K. "Complications in Academia: Sexual Harassment and the Law." *Siecus Report* 21.6 (1993): 6–10. CD-ROM. 1994 SIRS. *SIRS 1993 School*. Volume 4. Article 93A. 13 June 1995.

    • This is an example of an article from a CD-ROM database.

<M69> Heartney, Eleanor. "Contemporary Oracles. (Report from Greece)." *Art in America* 83.5 (1995): 3 pp. Online. Information Access. *Expanded Academic ASAP*. A16878539. 12 June 1995.

<M70> Merlan, Francesca. "Narratives of Survival in the Post-Colonial North." *Oceania* 65.2 (1994): 24 pp. Online. Information Access. *Expanded Academic ASAP*. A16998760. 12 June 1995.

<M71a> Monti, David, George Cicchetti, Thomas Goodkind, and Michael T. Ganci. "SPT: A New Methodology for Instruction. (Structured Presentation Technology)." *T H E Journal* 22.1 (1994): 3 pp. CD-ROM. Information Access. *Computer Select*. 16232996. 13 June 1995.

    • This is an example of multiple authors where all of the authors are given. It is also permissible, when there are more than three authors, to introduce "et al." See the next example.

<M71b> Monti, David, et al. "SPT: A New Methodology for Instruction. (Structured Presentation Technology)." *T H E Journal* 22.1 (1994): 3 pp. Electronic. Information Access. *Computer Select*. 16232996. 13 June 1995.

    • This example shows use of et al. when there are more than three authors. It is also permissible to list all of the authors, as in the example immediately preceding this one.

    • Sometimes it is not possible to tell whether one is accessing an online source or a networked CD-ROM. If this is the case, use "Electronic" in the medium statement.

<M72> Shostak, Arthur B. "The Nature of Work in the Twenty-First Century: Certain Uncertainties." *Business Horizons* (1993):n. pag. Online. Dow Jones News Retrieval Service. TextM. *Business Library*. 12 June 1995.

• This item lacks a volume and issue number, and an item or accession number.

<M73>   Shweder, Richard A. "'Why Do Men Barbecue?' and Other Postmodern Ironies of Growing Up in the Decade of Ethnicity." *Daedalus* 122.1 (1993): 30 pp. Online. Dialog. *Magazine Database*. 47. 13401091. 13 June 1995.

• Place single quotation marks around a quotation when it appears within a title requiring quotations marks.

<M74>   Sikula, Andrew, Sr., and Adelmiro D. Costa. "Are Women More Ethical Than Men?" *Journal of Business Ethics* 13.11 (1994): 859–871. Online. Dialog. *ABI Inform*. 15. 95-78695. 12 June 1995.

• The example above shows Sr. in the name and shows the format for citing more than one author.

2. E-mail

a. Archived Works

Basic Forms

Author. "Article Title." *Journal Title* Volume number.Issue number (Year): Number of pages or paragraphs (if given), or n. pag. (for no pagination). Medium. Available E-mail: LISTSERV/Get. Access date.

"Article Title." *Journal Title* Volume number.Issue number (Year): Number of pages or paragraphs (if given), or n. pag. (for no pagination). Medium. Available E-mail: LISTSERV/Get. Access date.

• When an author is not given, use the second basic form.
• For information on management of paging or length element, see pages 125-126 in this chapter.
• In the "available" statement, give the LISTSERV network address and the file name with its extension in the "Get" message.

<M75>   Brent, Douglas A. "Information Technology and the Breakdown of 'Places' of Knowledge." *EJournal* 4.4 (1994): 462 lines. Online. Available E-mail: LISTSERV@uacsc2.albany.edu. 29 June 1995.

• Names of discussion lists and the word LISTSERV are presented in uppercase letters.

<M76>   Carriveau, Kenneth L., Jr. Rev. of *Environmental Hazards: Marine Pollution*, by Martha Gonnan. *Environmental Green Journal* 2.1

(1995): 3 pars. Online. Available E-mail: LISTSERV@uidaho.edu/
Get egj log03. 21 June 1995.
- Example above shows Jr. in an author's name.
- This is a reference for a book review.
- Paragraph count instead of paging is given (i.e., "3 pars." for 3 paragraphs).

<M77> Hawks, Carol Pitts. "OhioLINK: Implementing Integrated Library Services Across Institutional Boundaries." *The Public-Access Computer Systems Review* 6.2 (1995): 5–26. Online. U of Houston Libraries. Available E-mail: LISTSERV@uhupvm1.bitnet/Get pacs-review v6n295. 29 June 1995.

<M78> Huo, Yang. H., and Francis Kwansa. "Effect of Operating and Financial Leverage on Firm's Risk." *Journal of the International Academy of Hospitality Research.* 8 (1994): 2–17. Online. Available E-mail: LISTSERV@VTVM1.CC.VT.EDU/Get JIAHR8 TEXT. 19 June 1995.
- This is a reference with no volume number.

<M79> Olaniran, Bolanle A. "Individual Differences and Computer Mediated Communication: The Role of Perception/Les Differences Individuelles et la Communication Informatisee: Le Role de la Perception." *The Electronic Journal of Communication/La Revue Electronique de Communication.* 3.2 (1993): n. pag. Online. Available E-mail: LISTSERV@Vm.Its.Rpi.Edu/Get Olaniran V3N293. 28 June 1995.
- Provide all the languages in which the article title is presented.
- Write "n. pag." if no paging information is given.

b. Real-Time Works

Basic Forms

Author. "Article Title." *Journal Title* Volume number.Issue number (Year): Number of pages or paragraphs (if given), or n. pag. (for no pagination). Medium. Available E-mail: DISCUSSION GROUP@address. Access date.

"Article Title." *Journal Title* Volume number.Issue number (Year): Number of pages or paragraphs (if given), or n. pag. (for no pagination). Medium. Available E-mail: DISCUSSION GROUP@address. Access date.

- When an author is not given, use the second basic form.
- For information on management of paging or length element, see pages 125-126 in this chapter.

• In the "available" statement, indicate the discussion group/LIST-SERV and its Internet/BITNET address.

<M80>   Arens, William. Rev. of *Reproduction & Succession: Studies in Anthropology, Law and Society*, by Robin Fox. *Law and Politics Book Review* 3.5 (1993): n. pag. Online. Available E-mail: PSRT-L@MIZ ZOU1.MISSOURI.EDU. 5 May 1993.

• This is a reference to a book review.

<M81>   Herring, Susan C. "Gender and Democracy in Computer-Mediated Communication/Sexe et Democratie Dans la Communication Informatisee." *The Electronic Journal of Communication/La Revue Electronique de Communication* 3.2 (1993): n. pag. Online. Available E-mail: EJCREC@Vm.Its.Rpi.Edu. 15 April 1993.

• Provide all the languages in which the article title is presented.

<M82>   Israel, Glenn D., and Thomas W. Ilvento. "Everybody Wins: Involving Youth in Community Needs Assessment." *Journal of Extension* 33.2 (1995): n. pag. Online. Available E-mail: JOE@joe.uwex.edu. 15 April 1995.

• This is a reference with two authors.

<M83>   Wilson, Thomas. C. "Culture Clash on the Infobahn: Paradise Lost?" *Telecommunications Electronic Reviews (TER)* 2.2(1995): n. pag. Online. Available E-mail: LITA-L@uicvm.uic.edu. 21 June 1995.

3. FTP

Basic Forms

Author. "Article Title." *Journal Title* Volume number.issue number (Year or date of publication): number of pages or paragraphs (if given) or n. pag. (for no pagination). Medium. Available FTP: address/path/file. Access date.

"Article Title." *Journal Title* Volume number.issue number (Year or date of publication): number of pages or paragraphs (if given) or n. pag. (for no pagination). Medium. Available FTP: address/path/file. Access date.

• When author is not given, use the second basic form.
• For information on management of paging or length element, see pages 125-126 in this chapter.
• It is not unusual for important information to be lacking from material obtained at FTP sites. Try to present information that will help the reader retrieve the item from the source. The "available" statement is essential in this instance.

<M84>   Attfield, Robin. "Preferences, Health, Interests, and Value." *The Elec-
tronic Journal of Analytic Philosophy* (Spring 1995): 20 pp. Online.
Available FTP: tarski.phil.indiana.edu/ejap/1995.spring/attfield.1995.
spring.txt. 15 June 1995.

<M85>   Derrida, Jacques. "Of the Humanities and the Philosophical Discipline:
The Right to Philosophy from the Cosmopolitical Point of View: The
Example of an International Institution." Trans. Thomas Dutoit.
Surfaces 4.310 (1994): 34 pars. Online. Available FTP: harfang.cc.
umontreal.ca/Surfaces/Articles/Ascii/vol4/A_Derrida (ang).ascii. 15
June 1995.
    • This is an example of a reference when no pagination is given.
      A paragraph count is given instead.
    • Indication that this is a translation and translator's name are
      given after the article title.

<M86>   Massing, Walter. "Metaphysical Windmills in Robotland." Rev. of *What
Robots Can and Can't Be*, by Selmer Bringsjord. *Psycoloquy* 6.16
(1995): 27 pars. Online. Available FTP: princeton.edu/pub/harnad/
Psycoloquy/1995.volume.6/psycoloquy.95.6.16.robot-consciousness.
11.massing. 30 June 1995.
    • This is an example of a book review.
    • Pagination is not given, but in this case the paragraphs are num-
      bered and that information is easily used instead.

<M87>   Sengers, Phoebe. Abstract of "Madness and Automation: On Institu-
tionalization." *Postmodern Culture* 5.Contents 3 (1995): n. pag. Online. Available FTP: ftp.ncsu.edu/pub/ncsu/pmc/pmc-list/contents.595.
15 June 1995.
    • In this example, the contents of the journal, which was
      retrieved separately, includes abstracts. A note is made just pre-
      ceding the title of the paper to indicate that the abstract only is
      being cited.
    • There are no pages given in this document, so the notation "n.
      pag." (no pagination) is made.

4. Gopher

Basic Forms

Author. "Article Title." *Journal Title* Volume number.Issue number (Year): Number of pages or paragraphs (if given), or n. pag. (for no pagination). Medium.
Available Gopher: gopher site/search path/file. Access date.

"Article Title." *Journal Title* Volume number.Issue number (Year): Number of
pages or paragraphs (if given), or n. pag. (for no pagination). Medium. Available Gopher: gopher site/search path/file. Access date.

- When an author is not given, use the second basic form.
- For information on management of paging or length element,
  see pages 125-126 in this chapter.
- In the "available" statement, indicate the Gopher site, search
  path, and file name.
- It is not necessary to repeat the protocol (Gopher) on the WWW
  after the "available" statement since it is stated in the URL.

<M88>   Carriveau, Kenneth L., Jr. Rev. of *Environmental Hazards: Marine
        Pollution*, by Martha Gonnan. *Environmental Green Journal* 2.1
        (1995): 3 pars. Online. Available: gopher://gopher.uidaho.edu/11/
        UI_gopher/library/egj03/carriv01.html. 21 June 1995.
        - Example above shows Jr. in an author's name.
        - This is a reference for a book review.
        - For paging information, substitute number of paragraphs (i.e., "3
          pars." for three paragraphs) in this reference.
        - If the information is retrieved via a Gopher on the World Wide
          Web (WWW), indicate the Uniform Resource Locator (URL) in
          the "available" statement.

<M89a> Fitch, Roslyn Holly, and Victor H. Denenberg. "A Role for Ovarian
        Hormones in Sexual Differentiation of the Brain." *Psycoloquy* 6.5
        (1995): 56 pars. Online. Available Gopher: gopher.Princeton.EDU/
        pub/harnad/Psycoloquy/psyc.95.6.05.sex-brain.1.fitch. 29 June 1995.

<M89b> Fitch, Roslyn Holly, and Victor H. Denenberg. "A Role for Ovarian
        Hormones in Sexual Differentiation of the Brain." *Psycoloquy* 6.5
        (1995): 56 pars. Online. Available: gopher://gopher.Princeton.EDU:
        70/1ftp%3Aprinceton.edu@/pub/harnad/Psycoloquy/psyc.95.6.05.
        sex-brain.1.fitch. 29 June 1995.
        - If the information is retrieved via a Gopher on the WWW, indi-
          cate the URL in the "available" statement.

<M90a> Israel, Glenn D., and Thomas W. Ilvento. "Everybody Wins: Involving
        Youth in Community Needs Assessment." *Journal of Extension* 33.2
        (1995): 10 pars. Online. Available Gopher: sageunix.uvm.edu/Elec
        tronic Journals/Journal of Extension, April 1995 Volume 33. 15 April
        1995.

<M90b> Israel, Glenn D., and Thomas W. Ilvento. "Everybody Wins: Involving
        Youth in Community Needs Assessment." *Journal of Extension* 33.2

(1995): 10 pars. Online. Available: gopher://wussagi.ywex.edu:70/
00/joe/1995april/a1. 15 April 1995.

> • If the information is retrieved via a Gopher on the WWW, indi-
> cate the URL in the "available" statement.

\<M91\>   Wilson, Thomas C. "Culture Clash on the Infobahn: Paradise Lost?"
Telecommunications Electronic Reviews (TER) 2.2 (1995): 5 pars.
Online. Available Gopher: info.lib.uh.edu/Looking for Articles/
Electronic Journals/LITA/Telecommunications Electronic Reviews/
Volume 2. 21 June 1995.

5. HTTP

Basic Forms

Author. "Article Title." *Journal Title* Volume number.Issue number (Year): Number of pages or paragraphs (if given), or n. pag. (for no pagination). Medium.
Available: URL. Access date.

"Article Title." *Journal Title* Volume number.Issue number (Year): Number of pages
or paragraphs (if given), or n. pag. (for no pagination). Medium. Available: URL.
Access date.

> • When an author is not given, use the second basic form.
> • For information on management of paging or length element,
> see pages 125-126 in this chapter.
> • When providing the URL, indicate the WWW site, search path,
> and file name.
> • It is not necessary to repeat the protocol (HTTP) on the WWW
> after the "available" statement since it is stated in the URL.

\<M92\>   Carriveau, Kenneth L., Jr. Rev. of *Environmental Hazards: Marine
Pollution*, by Martha Gonnan. *Environmental Green Journal* 2.1
(1995): 3 pars. Online. Available: http://drseuss.lib.uidaho.edu:70/
docs/egj03/carriv01.html. 21 June 1995.
> • Example above shows Jr. in an author's name.
> • This is a reference for a book review.
> • For paging information, substitute number of paragraphs (i.e., "3
> pars." for three paragraphs in this reference).

\<M93\>   Inada, Kenneth. "A Buddhist Response to the Nature of Human Rights."
Journal of Buddhist Ethics 2 (1995): 9 pars. Online. Available: http://
www.cac.psu.edu/jbe/twocont.html. 21 June 1995.
> • Example lacks issue number.

<M94>   Weidman, John C. "Diversifying Finance of Higher Education Systems in the Third World: The Cases of Kenya and Mongolia." *Education Policy and Analysis* 3.5 (1995): 800 lines. Online. Available: http://info.asu.edu/asu-cwis/epaa/v3n5.html. 21 June 1995.

<M95>   Wilson, Thomas C. "Culture Clash on the Infobahn: Paradise Lost?" *Telecommunications Electronic Reviews (TER)* 2.2 (1995): 5 pars. Online. Available: http://chehalis.lib.washington.edu/ter/ter-2-2.html. 21 June 1995.

6. Telnet

Basic Forms

Author. "Article Title." *Journal Title* Volume number.Issue number (Year): Number of pages or paragraphs (if given), or n. pag. (for no pagination). Medium. Available Telnet: Telnet site/**login**:/**password**:/search path/file. Access date.

"Article Title." *Journal Title* Volume number.Issue number (Year): Number of pages or paragraphs (if given), or n. pag. (for no pagination). Medium. Available Telnet: Telnet site/**login**:/**password**:/search path/file. Access date.

> • When author is not given, use the second basic form.
> • For information on management of paging or length element, see pages 125-126 in this chapter.
> • If log-in information and password are required in order to establish the Telnet session, include information in the "available" statement.

<M96>   Chaya, Henry J. "Analysis of Alaskan Archeological Obsidian Artifacts." *Journal of World Anthropology* 1.2 (1994): 24 pars. Online. Available Telnet: library.unc.edu/**login**: LIBRARY/Electronic Journals/UNC-CH Internet Library/Journal of World Anthropology/JWA-Volume 1 Number 2/Analysis of Alaskan. . . . 30 June 1995. Paper presented at the Archaeometry Research Graduate Group Annual Symposium February 1994, University at Buffalo Anthropology Department.

> • Supplementary bibliographic information appears at the end of the reference.

<M97>   Gowing, Alain M. Rev. of *Caesar and the Crisis of the Roman Aristocracy*, by James S. Ruebel. *Bryn Mawr Classical Review* 95.2 (1995): 8 pars. Online. Available Telnet: ccat.sas.upenn.edu/Electronic Journals and Publications/Bryn Mawr Classical Review/95.2.10. Ruebel, Caesar and the Crisis of the Roman Aristocracy. 30 June 1995.

> • This is a reference to a book review.

<M98>   Mann, Paul. "Stupid Undergrounds." *Postmodern Culture* 5.3 (1995): 49
         pars. Online. Available Telnet: dewey.lib.ncsu.edu/Electronic Texts/
         Scholarly Journals/Postmodern Culture/v5/n3. 30 June 1995.

<M99>   Reynolds, Dennis J. "Evaluating Dial-up Internet Access Options."
         MeckJournal 3.4 (1993): 17 pars. Online. Available Telnet: nicol.
         jvnc.net/**login**: nicol/MeckJournal/Volume III, Issue 4. 22 June 1995.

B. Magazine Articles

1. CD-ROM and Commercial Online Databases

Basic Forms

Author. "Article Title." *Magazine Title* Date: Number of pages or paragraphs (if
    given), or n. pag. (for no pagination). Medium. Supplier. Database name. Data-
    base identifier or number if available. Item or accession number. Access date.

"Article Title." *Magazine Title* Date: Number of pages or paragraphs (if given), or
    n. pag. (for no pagination). Medium. Supplier. Database name. Database identi-
    fier or number if available. Item or accession number. Access date.

> • If author is not given, use the second basic form.
> • Volume and issue numbers are *not given* when citing magazine
>   articles.
> • If a magazine is published weekly, or every other week, give the
>   complete date (e.g., 1 July 1995).
> • If a magazine is published monthly, or at some other interval,
>   give month and year (e.g., June 1995).
> • For information on management of paging or length element,
>   see pages 125-126 in this chapter.

<M100>   Buhler, Patricia. "Understanding Cultural Diversity and Its Benefits.
         (Managing in the 90s)." *Supervision* 1 July 1993: 17+. Online. Dow
         Jones News Retrieval Service. TextM. *Business Library.* 12 June 1995.
> • This example is taken from a database that does not give item or
>   accession numbers. In such a case, one can only cite the infor-
>   mation given.

<M101>   Daly, Douglas. "The Perils of Collecting: Amazon Exploration." *Audubon*
         Jan. 1995: 78+. Online. Mead Nexis. NEWS/MAGS. 20 June 1995.

<M102>   Geipel, John. "Brazil's Unforked Tongue. (Portuguese Dialects)." *His-
         tory Today* Aug. 1993: 11+. Online. Dialog. *Magazine Database.* 47.
         14235390. 13 June 1995.

<M103> Goodstein, Carol. "Healers from the Deep." *American Health* Sept. 1991: 60-64. CD-ROM. 1994 SIRS. *SIRS 1992 Life Science.* Article 08A.
   • Access date is not needed when the medium is a CD-ROM.

<M104> "Half Price Hotels in '95: Deals Coast to Coast." *Consumer Reports Travel Letter* Mar. 1995: 52+. Online. Mead Nexis. NEWS/ASAPII. 12 June 1995. Includes related articles.
   • This is an example of an article lacking an author. Title becomes the first element in the entry.
   • Note describing the article follows immediately after the access date.

<M105> Heywood, Michael. "The Importance of Being Ern. (Ern Malley, Australian Hoax Poet)." *National Review* 17 Apr. 1995: 66+. Online. Information Access. *Expanded Academic ASAP.* A16823474. 30 June 1995.

<M106a> Mageau, Therese. "Listening to Multimedia: The (In)Sane Person's Guide to Multimedia in Education." *Electronic Learning* Nov.–Dec. 1994: 28+. CD-ROM. Information Access. *Computer Select.* 16289501. Includes glossary and related article on networking multimedia.
   • Note describing the article further follows immediately after the reference.
   • Access date is not necessary when the medium is a CD-ROM.

<M106b> Mageau, Therese. "Listening to Multimedia: The (In)Sane Person's Guide to Multimedia in Education." *Electronic Learning* Nov.–Dec. 1994: 28+. Electronic. Information Access. *Computer Select.* 16289501. 13 June 1995. Includes glossary and related article on networking multimedia.
   • Sometimes it is not possible to tell whether one is accessing an online source or a networked CD-ROM. If this is the case, use "Electronic" in the type of medium statement.
   • Note describing the article further follows immediately after the access date.

<M107> Portz-Shovlin, Eileen. "Our Annual Guide to Summer Running Camps: Directory." *Runner's World* Apr. 1995: 77+. Online. Mead Nexis. NEWS/ASAPII. 12 June 1995.

<M108> Reid, Howard. "Forest Rovers of the Amazon." *UNESCO Courier* Nov. 1994: 25+. Online. Mead Nexis. NEWS/ UNESCO. 20 June 1995.

<M109>   "Valve Replacement in the Elderly. (Mitral Valve)." *Patient Care* 15
        Oct. 1995: 26. CD-ROM. Information Access. *InfoTrac—Health
        Reference Center*/July '91–July '94. 11 May 1995.
            • This example has no identifying accession number.

2. E-mail

a. Archived Works

Basic Forms

Author. "Article Title." *Magazine Title* Date: Number of pages or paragraphs (if
    given), or n. pag. (for no pagination). Medium. Available E-mail: LISTSERV/
    Get. Access date.

"Article Title." *Magazine Title* Date: Number of pages or paragraphs (if given), or
    n. pag. (for no pagination). Medium. Available E-mail: LISTSERV/Get. Access
    date.

                    • If author is not given, use the second basic form.
                    • Volume and issue numbers are *not given* when citing magazine
                      articles.
                    • If a magazine is published weekly, or every other week, give the
                      complete date (e.g., 1 July 1995).
                    • If a magazine is published monthly, or at some other interval,
                      give month and year (e.g., June 1995).
                    • For information on management of paging or length element,
                      see pages 125-126 in this chapter.
                    • In the "available" statement, provide the LISTSERV network
                      address and the file name with its extension in the "Get" message.

<M110>   Owens, Jim. "A Lighter Burden." *DargonZine* 13 May 1995: 22 pars.
        Online. Available E-mail: LISTSERV@brownvm.bitnet/Get dargon
        v8n2. 17 June 1995.

<M111>   Snell, Jason. "Different Circumstances." *Quanta* Dec. 1993: 6 pars.
        Online. Available E-mail: LISTSERV@andrew.cmu.edu/Get quanta
        1293. 20 December 1994.

<M112>   Viviano, Frank. "The New Mafia Order." *Mother Jones Magazine*
        May–June 1995: 72 pars. Online. Available E-mail: MOTHER
        JONES-LIST@mojones.com/Get mojones MJ95. 17 June 1995.

b. Real-Time Works

Basic Forms

Author. "Article Title." *Magazine Title* Date: Number of pages or paragraphs (if given), or n. pag. (for no pagination). Medium. Available E-mail: DISCUS-SION GROUP@address. Access date.

"Article Title." *Magazine Title* Date: Number of pages or paragraphs (if given), or n. pag. (for no pagination). Medium. Available E-mail: DISCUSSION GROUP @address. Access date.

> • If author is not given, use the second basic form.
> • Volume and issue numbers are *not given* when citing magazine articles.
> • If a magazine is published weekly, or every other week, give the complete date (e.g., 1 July 1995).
> • If a magazine is published monthly, or at some other interval, give month and year (e.g., June 1995).
> • For information on management of paging or length element, see pages 125-126 in this chapter.
> • In the "available" statement, indicate the discussion group/LIST-SERV and its Internet/BITNET address.

<M113>   Owens, Jim. "A Lighter Burden." *DargonZine* 13 May 1995: 22 pars. Online. Available E-mail: DARGON-L@brownvm.bitnet. 13 May 1995.

<M114>   Snell, Jason. "Different Circumstances." *Quanta* Dec. 1993: 6 pars. Online. Available E-mail: QUANTA@andrew.cmu.edu. 20 December 1993.

<M115>   Viviano, Frank. "The New Mafia Order." *Mother Jones Magazine* May–June 1995: 72 pars. Online. Available E-mail: MOTHER JONES-LIST@mojones.com. 17 July 1995.

3. FTP

Basic Forms

Author. "Article Title." *Magazine Title* Date: Number of pages or paragraphs (if given), or n. pag. (for no pagination). Medium. Available FTP: address/path/file. Access date.

"Article Title." *Magazine Title* Date: Number of pages or paragraphs (if given), or n. pag. (for no pagination). Medium. Available FTP: address/path/file. Access date.

- If author is not given, use the second basic form.
- Volume and issue numbers are *not given* when citing magazine articles.
- If a magazine is published weekly, or every other week, give the complete date (e.g., 1 July 1995).
- If a magazine is published monthly, or at some other interval, give month and year (e.g., June 1995).
- For information on management of paging or length element, see pages 125-126 in this chapter.
- It is not necessary to repeat the protocol (FTP) on the WWW after the "available" statement since it is stated in the URL.

<M116> Atwood, Margaret. Interview with Robert Sward. *The Blue Penny Quarterly* Dec. 1994: 143–152. Online. Available FTP: ftp.etext.org/pub/ Zines/BluePennyQuarterly/BPQ_3.txt. 10 July 1995.
- This is an example of an interview. Note that the name of the person being interviewed is given as author. The name of the interviewer follows in a note. This interview is untitled so the descriptive statement is not enclosed in quotations.

<M117> Bealer, Dave. (1995, February). "Brighton Bealer Memoirs." *Random Access Humor* Feb. 1995: 3+. Online. Available FTP: ftp.clark.net/ pub/rah/rah9502.txt. 10 July 1995.
- This author writes using his nickname "Dave."

<M118> Holohan, Erin. "As Time Goes By." *My Town* Jan. 1995: 1–2. Online. Available FTP: quake.think.com/pub/scholastic/My Town (ASCII). 11 June 1995.

<M119a> Schrader, Esther. "A Giant Spraying Sound: Since NAFTA, Mexican Growers Are Spraying More Toxic Pesticides on Fruits, Vegetables—and Workers." *Mother Jones Magazine* Jan.–Feb. 1995: 34+. Online. Available FTP: mojones.com/pub/Mother_Jones_ Text/JF95/MotherJones_JF95:_A_Giant_Spraying_Sound. 1 July 1995.

<M119b> Schrader, Esther. "A Giant Spraying Sound: Since NAFTA, Mexican Growers Are Spraying More Toxic Pesticides on Fruits, Vegetables— and Workers." *Mother Jones Magazine* Jan.–Feb. 1995: 34+. Online. Available: ftp://mojones.com/pub/Mother_Jones_Text/JF95/Mother Jones_JF95:_A_Giant_Spraying_Sound. 1 July 1995.
- This is an example of an article obtained from an FTP site via the WWW. The "available" statement has a slightly different format.

4. Gopher

Basic Forms

Author. "Article Title." *Magazine Title* Date: Number of pages or paragraphs (if given), or n. pag. (for no pagination). Medium. Available Gopher: gopher site/search path/file. Access date.

"Article Title." *Magazine Title* Date: Number of pages or paragraphs (if given), or n. pag. (for no pagination). Medium. Available Gopher: gopher site/search path/file. Access date.

- If author is not given, use the second basic form.
- Volume and issue numbers are *not given* when citing magazine articles.
- If a magazine is published weekly, or every other week, give the complete date (e.g., 1 July 1995).
- If a magazine is published monthly, or at some other interval, give month and year (e.g., June 1995).
- For information on management of paging or length element, see pages 125-126 in this chapter.
- When providing the "available" statement, indicate the Gopher site, search path, and file name.
- It is not necessary to repeat the protocol (Gopher) on the WWW after the "available" statement since it is stated in the URL.

<M120> Holst, Kai. "The School of Life." *Twilight World* 14 May 1995: 53 pars. Online. Available Gopher: gopher.etext.org/Zines/Twilight_World/ twilight.world-2.3.gz. 16 July 1995.

<M121a> Owens, Jim. "A Lighter Burden." *DargonZine* 13 May 1995: 22 pars. Online. Available Gopher: gopher.cic.net/Electronic Serials/Dargon Zine/dargon v8n2. 17 July 1995.

<M121b> Owens, Jim. "A Lighter Burden." *DargonZine* 13 May 1995: 22 pars. Online. Available: gopher://gopher.cic.net/Electronic Serials/Dargon Zine/dargon v8n2. 17 July 1995.
- If the item is retrieved on the WWW, give the URL.

<M122> Schrader, Esther. "A Giant Spraying Sound." *The Mother Jones Magazine* Jan.–Feb. 1995: 42 pars. Online. Available: gopher://mojones. mojones.com.:70/00/JF95/MotherJones_JF95%3A_Giant_Spraying_ Sound. 30 May 1995.

<M123> Snell, Jason. "Different Circumstances." *Quanta* Dec. 1993: 6 pars. Online. Available Gopher: gopher.contrib.andrew.cmu.edu/magazines/ quanta/issues/1993-dec. 15 July 1995.

5. HTTP

Basic Forms

Author. "Article Title." *Magazine Title* Date: Number of pages or paragraphs (if given), or n. pag. (for no pagination). Medium. Available: URL. Access date.

"Article Title." *Magazine Title* Date: Number of pages or paragraphs (if given), or n. pag. (for no pagination). Medium. Available: URL. Access date.

- If author is not given, use the second basic form.
- Volume and issue numbers are *not given* when citing magazine articles.
- If a magazine is published weekly, or every other week, give the complete date (e.g., 1 July 1995).
- If a magazine is published monthly, or at some other interval, give month and year (e.g., June 1995).
- For information on management of paging or length element, see pages 125-126 in this chapter.
- In the "available" statement, give the WWW site, search path, and file name.
- When providing the URL, indicate the WWW site, search path, and file name.
- It is not necessary to repeat the protocol (HTTP) on the WWW after the "available" statement since it is stated in the URL.

<M124> Roach, Greg. Interview. "Greg Roach: The Bard of CD-ROM." *Media West Magazine* April–May 1995: 20 pars. Online. Available: http://www.wimsey.com/Media_Wave/current/Features/Greg_Roach.html. 16 July 1995.

<M125> Kadrey, Richard. "Horse Latitudes." *InterText* 16 July 1995: 36 pars. Online. Available: http://etext.archive.umich.edu/Zines/InterText/v5n4/latitudes.html. 17 July 1995.

<M126> Pique, Jen. "San Diego Dreaming." *TwentyNothing* Winter 1993: 17 pars. Online. Available: http://afs/athena.mit.edu/user/t/h/thomasc/Public/twenty/wint93/pique.html. 17 June 1995.

<M127> Viviano, Frank. "The New Mafia Order." *Mother Jones Magazine* May–June 1995: 72 pars. Online. Available: http://www.mojones.com/MOTHER_JONES/MJ95/viviano.html. 17 July 1995.

6. Telnet

Basic Forms

Author. "Article Title." *Magazine Title* Date: Number of pages or paragraphs (if given), or n. pag. (for no pagination). Medium. Available Telnet: Telnet site/**login**:/**password**:/search path/file. Access date.

"Article Title." *Magazine Title* Date: Number of pages or paragraphs (if given), or n. pag. (for no pagination). Medium. Available Telnet: Telnet site/**login**:/**password**:/search path/file. Access date.

> - If author is not given, use the second basic form.
> - Volume and issue numbers are *not given* when citing magazine articles.
> - If a magazine is published weekly, or every other week, give the complete date (e.g., 1 July 1995).
> - If a magazine is published monthly, or at some other interval, give month and year (e.g., June 1995).
> - For information on management of paging or length element, see pages 125-126 in this chapter.
> - If log-in information and password are required in order to establish the Telnet session, include information in the "available" statement.

<M128> Quin, Liam R. E. "Summary of Metafonts Available." *TeXMag* n.d.: 4–6. Online. Available Telnet: library.unc.edu/**login**: LIBRARY/ Electronic Journals/Texmag/texmag.4.06. 5 July 1995.
> - Write "n.d." if the publication date is not given.

<M129> Overmyer, Elizabeth. "Serving the Reference Needs of Children." *Wilson Library Bulletin* June 1995: 16 pars. Online. Available Telnet: dewey.lib.ncsu.edu/Electronic Texts/Magazines/Wilson Library Bulletin/June 1995. 21 July 1995.

C. Newsletter Articles

1. CD-ROM and Commercial Online Databases

Basic Forms

Author. "Article Title." *Newsletter Title* Date: Number of pages or paragraphs (if given), or n. pag. (for no pagination). Medium. Supplier. *Database name.* Database identifier or number if available. Item or accession number. Access date.

"Article Title." *Newsletter Title* Date: Number of pages or paragraphs (if given), or n. pag. (for no pagination). Medium. Supplier. *Database name.* Database identifier or number if available. Item or accession number. Access date.

- If author is not given, use the second basic form.
- Volume and issue numbers are *not given* when citing newsletter articles.
- If a newsletter is published weekly, or every other week, give the complete date (e.g., 1 July 1995).
- If a newsletter is published monthly, or at some other interval, give month and year (e.g., June 1995).
- For information on management of paging or length element, see pages 125-126 in this chapter.

<M130> Conway, Carol. "Commentary: MDCP Grants Can Promote Strategic Thinking in State Trade Development." *Clearinghouse on State International Policies: Newsletter of the State International Policy Network.* Jan.–Feb. 1995: 5 pars. CD-ROM. US Dept. of Commerce. *National Economic, Social, and Environmental Data Bank/Economic Conversion Information Exchange (Program).* DA OECI CFED1.

- When paging is not given in an electronic source, give some indicator of length (e.g., number of paragraphs).
- Access date is not necessary when the medium is a CD-ROM.

<M131> "EU/Japan: Sir Leon Leads European Business Delegation to Japan." *Multinational Service* 9 June 1995: 9 pars. Online. Dialog. *PTS Newsletter DB.* 636. 02835122. 13 July 1995.

<M132> Fairweather, Frank. "The Beauty of Our Industry and the Burden of Animal Testing." Speech. European Cosmetic, Toiletry and Perfumery Assoc. Information Day. Brussels. 29 Nov. 1994. *European Cosmetic Markets* Apr. 1995: 151+. Online. Mead Nexis. EUROPE/ALLEUR. 13 July 1995.

- This is an example of a citation for a speech. A descriptive note (speech) is given, along with the information on the meeting at which it was given.

<M133> Hansen, Terri C. "Trademark Created for Indian-Made Products." *News from Indian Country* 30 June 1995: 3. CD-ROM. Softline Information. *Ethnic Newswatch.*

- Since this item has no identifying accession number, only supplier and database name are listed.

<M134> "Sports: NBA Announces It Will Lock Out Players until Parties Reach Contract Agreement." *Daily Labor Report* 5 July 1995: d15+. Mead Nexis. EASY/NEWS. 13 July 1995.

<M135> "Tricks of the Trade: How to Register a Company in Russia." *BISNIS Bulletin (Newly Independent States)* Apr.–May 1994: 11 pars. CD-ROM. US Dept. of Commerce. *National Trade Data Bank/BISNIS Bulletin (Newly Independent States)*. IT BISBUL APRMAY94 ART8.

2. E-mail

a. Archived Works

Basic Forms

Author. "Article Title." *Newsletter Title* Date: Number of pages or paragraphs (if given), or n. pag. (for no pagination). Medium. Available E-mail: LISTSERV/ Get. Access date.

"Article Title." *Newsletter Title* Date: Number of pages or paragraphs (if given), or n. pag. (for no pagination). Medium. Available E-mail: LISTSERV/Get. Access date.

- If author is not given, use the second basic form.
- Volume and issue numbers are *not given* when citing newsletter articles.
- If a newsletter is published weekly, or every other week, give the complete date (e.g., 1 July 1995).
- If a newsletter is published monthly, or at some other interval, give month and year (e.g., June 1995).
- For information on management of paging or length element, see pages 125-126 in this chapter.
- In the "available" statement, provide the LISTSERV network address and the file name with its extension in the "Get" message.

<M136> "EFF Analysis of Communications Decency Act as Passed by Senate." *EFFector Online* 16 June 1995: 38 pars. Online. Available E-mail: LISTSERV@eff.org/Get eff v08n10. 18 July 1995.

<M137> "Justice Ponders Microsoft Network." *EDUPAGE* 18 July 1995: 12 lines. Online. Available E-mail: LISTSERV@educom.edu/Get edu page-07.18.95. 21 July 1995.

<M138> "Women of Anabaptist Traditions in Historical Perspective." *Historian's Newsletter* 21 Mar. 1994: 7 pars. Online. Available E-mail: LIST SERV@ukanvm.cc.ukans.edu/Get histnews_2_9.txt. 21 July 1995.

<M139> Zonneveld, Cor. Rev. of *Dynamic Energy Budget in Biological Systems: Theory and Applications in Ecotoxicology,* by S.A.L.M. Kooijman. *Society for Mathematical Biology Digest* 7 June 1995: 6 pars. Online. Available E-mail: LISTSERV@fconvx.ncifcrf.gov/Get smbnet v95n08. 21 July 1995.

> • This is a reference to a book review. Reviewer's name is given first, followed by the title of the review, in quotes, if there is a title. The *Rev. of* statement is the next element and includes the title of the work and the author statement. Since this item lacks a title, the element following the author is the Rev. of . . . statement.
> • Book author's full name is not given in electronic source; cite what is available.

b. Real-Time Works

Basic Forms

Author. "Article Title." *Newsletter Title* Date: Number of pages or paragraphs (if given), or n. pag. (for no pagination). Medium. Available E-mail: DISCUS-SION GROUP@address. Access date.

"Article Title." *Newsletter Title* Date: Number of pages or paragraphs (if given), or n. pag. (for no pagination). Medium. Available E-mail: DISCUSSION GROUP @address. Access date.

> • If author is not given, use the second basic form.
> • Volume and issue numbers are *not given* when citing newsletter articles.
> • If a newsletter is published weekly, or every other week, give the complete date (e.g., 1 July 1995).
> • If a newsletter is published monthly, or at some other interval, give month and year (e.g., June 1995).
> • For information on management of paging or length element, see pages 125-126 in this chapter.
> • In the "available" statement, indicate the discussion group/LIST-SERV and its Internet/Bitnet address.

<M140> "EFF Analysis of Communications Decency Act as Passed by Senate." *EFFector Online* 16 June 1995: 38 pars. Online. Available E-mail: EFF@eff.org. 18 July 1995.

<M141>   "Justice Ponders Microsoft Network." *EDUPAGE* 18 July 1995: 12 lines. Online. Available E-mail: EDUPAGE@educom.edu. 18 July 1995.

<M142>   "Women of Anabaptist Traditions in Historical Perspective." *Historian's Newsletter* 21 Mar. 1994: 7 pars. Online. Available E-mail: HIST NEWS@ukanvm.cc.ukans.edu. 21 March 1994.

<M143>   Zonneveld, Cor. Rev. of *Dynamic Energy Budget in Biological Systems: Theory and Applications in Ecotoxicology,* by S.A.L.M. Kooijman. *Society for Mathematical Biology Digest* 7 June 1995: 6 pars. Online. Available E-mail: smbnet@fconvx.ncifcrf.gov. 7 June 1995.

- This is a reference to a book review. Reviewer's name is given first, followed by the title of the review, in quotes, if there is a title. The *Rev. of* statement is the next element and includes the title of the work and the author statement. Since this item lacks a title, the element following the author is the Rev. of . . . statement.

- Book author's full name is not given in the electronic source; cite what is available.

3. FTP

Basic Forms

Author. "Article Title." *Newsletter Title* Date: Number of pages or paragraphs (if given), or n. pag. (for no pagination). Medium. Available FTP: address/path/file. Access date.

"Article Title." *Newsletter Title* Date: Number of pages or paragraphs (if given), or n. pag. (for no pagination). Medium. Available FTP: address/path/file. Access date.

- If author is not given, use the second basic form.
- Volume and issue numbers are *not given* when citing newsletter articles.
- If a newsletter is published weekly, or every other week, give the complete date (e.g., 1 July 1995).
- If a newsletter is published monthly, or at some other interval, give month and year (e.g., June 1995).
- For information on management of paging or length element, see pages 125-126 in this chapter.
- It is not necessary to repeat the protocol (FTP) on the WWW after the "available" statement since it is stated in the URL.

<M144a> Agre, Phil. "The Internet Meets the Constitution." *The Network Observer* Jan. 1995: 13 pars. Online. Available FTP: ftp.eff.org/pub/Publications/E-journals/TNO/tno02.01. 7 July 1995.

<M144b> Agre, Phil. "The Internet Meets the Constitution." *The Network Observer* Jan. 1995: 13 pars. Online. Available: ftp:// ftp.eff.org/pub/Publications/E-journals/TNO/tno02.01. 7 July 1995.

> • If an FTP site is reached via the WWW, use the URL in the "available" statement.

<M145> Elbl, Martin. Abstract of "Tracking Economic 'Long Waves' in Medieval Mediterranean Commerce." *The American Academy of Research Historians of Medieval Spain Newsletter* Apr. 1992: 1–2. Online. Available FTP: hnsource.cc.ukans.edu/pub/history/Journals/aarhms/vol18no2_april92. 15 June 1995. Paper presented at the Academy's Chicago 1991 Meeting.

> • This is an example of an abstract of a paper.

<M146> McManus, Neil. "Letting Publishers Be Publishers." Editorial. *Digital Media Perspective* 20 Feb. 1995: 9 pars. Online. Available FTP: ftp. eff.org/pub/Publications/E-journals/DMP/950220.dmp. 7 July 1995.

> • A note indicating that this item is an editorial follows directly after the title.

<M147> Muktupavels, Valdis. "CDs: Recent Latvian Releases." *Ethnomusicology Research Digest* 25 May 1995: 2–6. Available FTP: inform.umd.edu/inforM/EdRes/ReadingRoom/Newsletters/EthnoMusicology/Digest/9 5-207.erd. 16 June 1995.

4. Gopher

Basic Forms

Author. "Article Title." *Newsletter Title* Date: Number of pages or paragraphs (if given), or n. pag. (for no pagination). Medium. Available Gopher: gopher site/search path/file. Access date.

"Article Title." *Newsletter Title* Date: Number of pages or paragraphs (if given), or n. pag. (for no pagination). Medium. Available Gopher: gopher site/search path/file. Access date.

> • If author is not given, use the second basic form.
> • Volume and issue numbers are *not given* when citing newsletter articles.

- If a newsletter is published weekly, or every other week, give the complete date (e.g., 1 July 1995).
- If a newsletter is published monthly, or at some other interval, give month and year (e.g., June 1995).
- For information on management of paging or length element, see pages 125-126 in this chapter.
- When providing the "available" statement, indicate the Gopher site, search path, and file name.
- It is not necessary to repeat the protocol (Gopher) on the WWW after the "available" statement since it is stated in the URL.

<M148>   "Cornell Introduces Project to Teach Kids About Ecology." *ES-USDA Extension Service Newsletter* 30 June 1995: 4 pars. Online. Available: gopher://gopher-ext.mes.umn.edu:1000/00/Internal/ES-USDA/4635. 18 July 1995.

     • This is a reference with no author given.

<M149>   "Government Performance and Results Act (GPRA) of 1993." *Integrated Pest Management Newsletter* May 1994: 4 pars. Online. Available: gopher://psupena.psu.edu:70/0%24d%20290012. 18 July 1995.

<M150>   "More Attacks on BBC Regime." *AM/FM Online Edition* 12 Apr. 1994: 3 pars. Online. Available Gopher: gopher.cic.net/Electronic Serials/AM/FM-UK Radio News. 17 July 1995.

<M151>   Peterson, Kristina. "Motivating Volunteers: The 1994 Midwinter LITA Leadership Development Session." *LITA Newsletter* Spring 1994: 9 pars. Online. Available: gopher://vega.lib.ncsu.edu:70/0ftp%3Aftp.lib.ncsu.edu@/pub/stacks/lita/lita-v15n02-peterson-motivating. 18 July 1995.

5. HTTP

Basic Forms

Author. "Article Title." *Newsletter Title* Date: Number of pages or paragraphs (if given), or n. pag. (for no pagination). Medium. Available: URL. Access date.

"Article Title." *Newsletter Title* Date: Number of pages or paragraphs (if given), or n. pag. (for no pagination). Medium. Available: URL. Access date.

     • If author is not given, use the second basic form.
     • Volume and issue numbers are *not given* when citing newsletter articles.

- If a newsletter is published weekly, or every other week, give the complete date (e.g., 1 July 1995).
- If a newsletter is published monthly, or at some other interval, give month and year (e.g., June 1995).
- For information on management of paging or length element, see pages 125-126 in this chapter.
- In the "available" statement, give the URL which includes the site, search path, and file name.
- It is not necessary to repeat the protocol (HTTP) on the WWW after the "available" statement since it is stated in the URL.

<M152>   "Mars Planetary Rover." *The M2RC Newsletter* Fall 1994: 6 pars. Online. Available: http://www.mmrc.ncsu.edu/Newsletters/v5n1/v5n1.html#Rover. 18 July 1995.

<M153>   Murphy, Henry J. "Duty of Care Broadened." *Law NOTES Canadian Legal News Letter* 5 July 1995: 7 pars. Online. Available: http://www.discribe.ca/murco. 18 July 1995.

<M154>   Obermeyer, John., Rich Edwards, and Larry Bledsoe. "Bean Leaf Beetles and Emerging Soybeans." *Pest Management & Crop Production Newsletter* 9 June 1995, 5 pars. Available: http://infor.aes.purdue.edu/entomology/Pest&Crop/P&C12.txt. 18 July 1995.

<M155>   Pare, Michael. "Fall River Loan Program Promotes Small Business." *Providence Business News: Southern New England's Business Weekly* 17 July 1995: 24 pars. Online. Available: http://www.pbn.com/w071795/crecon.html. 18 July 1995.

6. Telnet

Basic Forms

Author. "Article Title." *Newsletter Title* Date: Number of pages or paragraphs (if given), or n. pag. (for no pagination). Medium. Available Telnet: Telnet site/**login**:/**password**:/search path/file. Access date.

"Article Title." *Newsletter Title* Date: Number of pages or paragraphs (if given), or n. pag. (for no pagination). Medium. Available Telnet: Telnet site/**login**:/**password**:/search path/file. Access date.

- If author is not given, use the second basic form.
- Volume and issue numbers are *not given* when citing newsletter articles.

- If a newsletter is published weekly, or every other week, give the complete date (e.g., 1 July 1995).
- If a newsletter is published monthly, or at some other interval, give month and year (e.g., June 1995).
- For information on management of paging or length element, see pages 125-126 in this chapter.
- If log-in information and password are required in order to establish the Telnet session, include information in the available statement.

<M156> "EFF Analysis of Communications Decency Act as Passed by Senate." *EFFector Online* 16 June 1995: 38 pars. Available Telnet: nicol.jvnc. net/**login**: nicol/news/Newspaper, Magazines, and Newsletters/ Computer Publications/EFF/June, 1995. 18 July 1995.

<M157> "International Symposium on Floristic Diversity and Characteristics of East Asia." *The Bean Bag* Dec. 1994: 7–9. Online. Available Telnet: library.unc.edu/**login**: LIBRARY/Electronic Journals/UNC-CH Internet Library/The Bean Bag: Leguminosae Research Newsletter/ Bean Bag, December 1994. 19 July 1995.

<M158> "One Step Closer to Producing Anti-atoms." *Physics News Update* 6 July 1995: 34 lines. Online. Available Telnet: dewey.lib.ncsu.edu/ Electronic Texts/Newsletters/Physics News/Physics News Update 232. 21 July 1995.

D. Newspaper Articles

Basic Forms

Author. "Article Title." *Newspaper Title* Date, Edition (if given): page(s) or some indicator of article length. Medium. Supplier. *Database name*. Database identifier or number if available. Item or accession number. Access date.

"Article Title." *Newspaper Title* Date, Edition (if given): page(s) or some indicator of article length. Medium. Supplier. *Database name*. Database identifier or number if available. Item or accession number. Access date.

For Sources Using One of the Internet Protocols

Author. "Article Title." *Newspaper Title* Date, Edition (if given): page(s) or some indicator of article length. Medium. Available (include protocol if relevant): Address or source/Path/File. Access date.

"Article Title." *Newspaper Title* Date, Edition (if given): page(s) or some indicator of article length. Medium. Available (include protocol if relevant): Address or source/Path/File. Access date.

- Volume and issue numbers are *not given* when citing newspaper articles.
- Paging information may be given as follows:

  (a) Page, often within a section (e.g., D5)

  (b) Starting page with a plus immediately following the numeral (e.g., D5+) which may or may not indicate continuous paging

  (c) Number of paragraphs (e.g., 56 pars.)

  (d) N. pag. (for no pagination)

- It is not necessary to repeat the protocol used on the WWW after the "available" statement since it is stated in the URL.

<M159a> Asi-Jew, Shalin. Rev. of *The Concubine's Children*, by Denise Chong. *Northwest Asian Quarterly* 3 Feb. 1995: 20. CD-ROM. Softline Information. *Ethnic Newswatch.*

- This is an example of a citation to a book review; review is untitled.
- Access date is unnecessary when the medium is a CD-ROM.

<M159b> Asi-Jew, Shalin. Rev. of *The Concubine's Children*, by Denise Chong. *Northwest Asian Quarterly* 3 Feb. 1995: 20. Electronic. Softline Information. *Ethnic Newswatch.* 15 July 1995.

- It is not always possible to tell whether one is accessing a networked CD-ROM or an online source. If this cannot be determined, use "Electronic" in the type of medium statement; include access date in this instance.

<M160> Bagwell, Keith. "'Green' Goods Proliferate in Varied Shades." *Arizona Daily Star* 11 June 1995: 46 pars. Online. Available: http://www. azstarnet.com/public/pubstar/134-3994.html. 24 July 1995.

- This example gives the length of the article in number of paragraphs. This makes it easier to cite the information in parenthetical documentation, footnotes, or endnotes.

<M161> Campbell, K. K. "Courting Courtney on the Net." *Eye Weekly* 13 Oct. 1994: 20 pars. Online. Available: ftp://ftp.eff.org/pub/Publications/ E-journals/Eye/941013.eye. 17 June 1995.

- Electronic source does not give author's full name. Provide the information that is available.

- This example gives the length of the article in number of paragraphs. This makes it easier to cite the information in parenthetical documentation, footnotes, or endnotes.
- Example of document at an FTP site, reached by the WWW. In such a case, use the URL in the "available" statement.

<M162> Henneberger, Melinda. "Republicans Battle Party on Arts Funds." *New York Times* 8 June 1995, late ed.: B6. Online. Mead Nexis. NEWS/ NYT. 15 June 1995.

<M163> Howard, Johnette. "Let the Global Game Begin: Eyes, Passions of Soccer Fans Everywhere Turn to U.S." *Washington Post* 17 June 1994, final ed.: A1. Online. Dialog. *The Washington Post.* 146. 2198133. 16 July 1995.

<M164> Howell, Vicki, and Bob Carlton. "Growing Up Tough: New Generation Fights for Its Life: Inner-city Youths Live by Rule of Vengeance." *Birmingham News* 29 Aug. 1993: 1A+. CD-ROM. 1994 SIRS. *SIRS 1993 Youth.* Volume 4. Article56A.

- The article, in this case, extends beyond one page.
- Access date is unnecessary if medium is a CD-ROM.

<M165> Johnson, Tim. "Indigenous People Are Now More Combative, Organized. *Miami Herald* 5 Dec. 1994:29SA. Online. Availabler: gopher://sum mit.fiu.edu/Miami Herald—Summit-Related Articles/ 12/05/95— Indigenous People Now More Combative, Organized. 16 July 1995.

- If a document is retrieved at a WWW site, give the URL in the "available" statement.

<M166> Jones, Bill. "'Smoke' Has Substance." Rev. of *Smoke*, dir. Wayne Wang. *Phoenix Gazette* 30 June 1995, final sec.: C4. Online. Dialog. *The Arizona Repub-Phoenix Gaz.* 492. 08181238. 16 July 1995.

- This is an example of a movie review.

<M167a> LaFranchi, Howard. "Miami Summit: The Bonding of a Continent." *Christian Science Monitor* 8 Dec. 1994: WORLD1. Online. Available: gopher://summit.fiu.edu:70/11/Monitor/ 12/08/94—Miami Summit: The Bonding of a Continent. 16 July 1995.

<M167b>LaFranchi, Howard. "Miami Summit: The Bonding of a Continent." *Christian Science Monitor* 8 Dec. 1994: WORLD1. Online. Available: http://summit.fiu.edu:70/00/Monitor/monitor.4. 24 July 1995.

- Examples M167a and M167b show the same document retrieved by different methods, on different dates.

<M168> "Moving Up the Charts." *South China Morning Post* 26 May 1995, Friday Entertainment: 24. Online. Mead Nexis. ASIAPC/SCHINA. 17 July 1995.
- This is an example of an article from a special section of the newspaper.

<M169> "1994, a Mixed Bag in Indian Country." Editorial. *Ojibwe News* 30 Dec. 1994: 4. CD-ROM. Softline Information. *Ethnic Newswatch.*
- This is an example of an editorial.
- Numbers file alphabetically in a reference list as if they were spelled out.

<M170> Stout, Hilary. (1995, May 24). "Oregon Tries Its Own Welfare Reform: Offering Companies an Incentive to Put People to Work." *Wall Street Journal* 24 May 1995: A16. Online. Dow Jones News Retrieval Service. TextM. *Wall Street Journal.* 16 July 1995.

<M171> "U.N. Must Fight Back." Editorial. *Toronto Star* 12 July 1995, final ed.: A16. Online. Dow Jones News Retrieval Service. TextM. *International Publications—Newspapers & General Publications.* 16 July 1995.

<M172> "U.N. Strike Could Change the Rules for Peacekeeping." *St. Petersburg Times* 13 June 1993: 1A. CD-ROM. 1994 SIRS. *SIRS 1993 World Affairs.* Article 65C.

II. CITE AN ENTIRE WORK

This section provides a few examples of citations for electronic serials. The selection has been limited to publications that exist only in an electronic format. For an extensive listing of electronic serials, see *Directory of Electronic Journals, Newsletters, and Academic Discussion Lists*, 4th ed. (Washington, D.C.: Association of Research Libraries, 1995).

Basic Form

Serial Title. Editor, if given. Medium. Place of publication: Issuing agency, date of first issue–. Available: address/path/file or message. Notes (optional) which may include standard number (ISSN), frequency of publication, etc.

- Note that access date is not an essential element in this citation form.

<M173a> *Bryn Mawr Classical Review.* Online. Bryn Mawr, PA: Bryn Mawr College, Nov. 1990–. Available Gopher: gopher.cic.net. ISSN: 1063-2948; issued irregularly.

• Note following the "available" statement gives standard number and frequency of publication.

<M173b> *Bryn Mawr Classical Review*. Online. Bryn Mawr, PA: Bryn Mawr College, Nov. 1990–. Available E-mail: LISTSERV@cc.brynmawr.edu/SUBSCRIBE BMCR-L <firstname lastname>. ISSN: 1063-2948; issued irregularly.

• Examples M173a and M173b show the same journal retrieved via different methods.

<M174a> *Psycoloquy: A Refereed Journal of Peer Commentary in Psychology, Neuroscience and Cognitive Science*. Ed. Stephen Harnad. Online. Princeton, NJ: Princeton University, and the American Psychological Association, 1 Feb. 1990-. Available E-mail: LISTSERV@pucc.princeton.edu/SUBSCRIBE PSYC <firstname lastname>.

<M174b> *Psycoloquy: A Refereed Journal of Peer Commentary in Psychology, Neuroscience and Cognitive Science*. Ed. Stephen Harnad. Online. Princeton, NJ: Princeton University, and the American Psychological Association, 1 Feb. 1990-. Available Gopher: gopher.cic.net.

• Examples M174a and M174b show the manner in which an editor is given.
• Examples show the same journal retrieved via different methods.

<M175> *Surfaces*. Online. Montréal, PQ, Canada: Université de Montréal, Département de littérature comparée, 31 Oct. 1991–. Available FTP: ftp.umontreal.ca/Surfaces/Articles/ASCII, or MS-DOS or Macintosh.

Discussion Lists, USENET Newsgroups, and Personal Mail

I. DISCUSSION LISTS

A. Cite a Message

Basic Forms

Author. "Subject of Message." Date. Online posting. Discussion List. Available E-mail: DISCUSSION LIST@e-mail address. Access date.

Author. "Subject of Message." Date. Online posting. Discussion List. Available E-mail: LISTSERV@e-mail address/Get. Access date.

> • If the reference is a real-time message, follow the first basic form. If the message is obtained by searching the list's archive, follow the second basic form.
>
> • If the message is unsigned, use the author's log-in name in uppercase letters.
>
> • Indicate the date when message was sent to the discussion list.
>
> • The statement of paging or length is not required, according to the *MLA Handbook* (4th ed.; Gibaldi 177–178).
>
> • Present in uppercase letters the names of discussion lists and LISTSERVs, followed by lists' Internet or BITNET addresses (i.e., TWAIN-L or LISTSERV).

<M176a> Berkowitz, Paul. "Sussy's Gravestone." 3 April 1995. Online posting. Mark Twain Forum. Available E-mail: TWAIN-L@yorkvm1.bitnet. 3 April 1995.

<M176b> Berkowitz, Paul. "Sussy's Gravestone." 3 April 1995. Online posting. Mark Twain Forum. Available E-mail: LISTSERV@yorkvm1.bit net/Get twain-l log9504. 31 July 1995.
  • Reference is obtained by searching the list's archive.

<M177a> RRECOME. "Top Ten Rules of Film Criticism." 1 April 1995. Online posting. Discussions on All Forms of Cinema. Available E-mail: CIN EMA-L@american.edu. 1 Apr. 1995.
  • Author's log-in name, in uppercase, is given as the first element.

<M177b> RRECOME. "Top Ten Rules of Film Criticism." 1 April 1995. Online posting. Discussions on All Forms of Cinema. Available E-mail: LISTSERV@american.edu/Get cinema-l log9504A. 1 Aug. 1995.
  • Reference is obtained by searching the list's archive.

B. Cite a Discussion: One Topic, Several Discussants

Basic Forms

Author. "Subject of Message." Date. Online posting. Discussion List. Available E-mail: DISCUSSION LIST@e-mail address. Access date. Discussion.

Author. "Subject of Message." Date. Online posting. Discussion List. Available E-mail: LISTSERV@e-mail address/Get. Access date. Discussion.

  • If the reference is a real-time message, follow the first basic form. If the message is obtained by searching the list's archive, follow the second basic form.
  • If the message is unsigned, use the author's log-in name in uppercase letters.
  • Indicate the date when message was sent to the discussion list.
  • The statement of paging or length is not required, according to the *MLA Handbook* (4th ed.; Gibaldi 177–178).
  • Present in uppercase letters the names of discussion lists and LISTSERVs, followed by lists' Internet or BITNET addresses (i.e., TWAIN-L or LISTSERV).
  • Additional description "Discussion" at the end of the reference indicates that this is from a discussion with several discussants.

<M178a> Boulton, Ron. "Explosion Proof Refrigerator?" 31 July 1995. Online posting. Safety. Available E-mail: SAFETY@uvmvm.uvm.edu. 31 July 1995. Discussion.

<M178b> Boulton, Ron. "Explosion Proof Refrigerator?" 31 July 1995. Online posting. Safety. Available E-mail: LISTSERV@uvmvm.uvm.edu/Get safety log9507D. 1 Aug. 1995. Discussion.
• Reference is obtained by searching the list's archive.

<M179a> Voltz, Jeff. "Building Codes." 20 July 1995. Online posting. Civil Engineering Research & Education. Available E-mail: CIVIL-L@unb.ca. 20 July 1995. Discussion.

<M179b> Voltz, Jeff. "Building Codes." 20 July 1995. Online posting. Civil Engineering Research & Education. Available E-mail: LIST SERV@unb.ca/Get civil-l log9507. 31 July 1995. Discussion.
• Reference is obtained by searching the list's archive.

C. Cite a Forwarded Message

1. Without Embellishments

Basic Forms
Forwarder. Forwarded message "Original Subject" by sender. Date. Online posting. Discussion List. Available E-mail: DISCUSSION LIST@e-mail address. Access date.

Forwarder. Forwarded message "Original Subject" by sender. Date. Online posting. Discussion List. Available E-mail: LISTSERV@e-mail address. Access date.

> • If the reference is a real-time message, follow the first basic form. If the message is obtained by searching the list's archive, follow the second basic form.
> • If the message is unsigned, use the author's log-in name in uppercase letters.
> • Indicate the date when message was sent to the discussion list.
> • Paging or length statement is not required, according to the *MLA Handbook* (4th ed.; Gibaldi 177–178).
> • Present in uppercase letters the names of discussion lists and LISTSERVs, followed by lists' Internet or BITNET addresses (i.e., TWAIN-L or LISTSERV).

<M180a> MANCA. Forwarded message "Stop NUCLEAR Experiments" by Mubarak Osman Khalifa. 20 July 1995. Online posting. Civil Engineering Research & Education. Available E-mail: CIVIL-L@unb.ca. 20 July 1995.
• Author's log-in name is given, in uppercase, as the first element.

<M180b> MANCA. Forwarded message "Stop NUCLEAR Experiments" by
   Mubarak Osman Khalifa. 20 July 1995. Online posting. Civil Engineering Research & Education. Available E-mail: LISTSERV@unb.
   ca/Get civil-l log9507. 1 Aug. 1995.
     • Reference is obtained by searching the list's archive.

<M181a> Presno, Odd de. Forwarded message "New KIDFORUM Topic" by
   Alenka Makuc. 29 June 1995. Online posting. KIDLINK Project List.
   Online. Available E-mail: KIDLINK@ndsuvml.bitnet. 28 June 1995.

<M181b> Presno, Odd de. Forwarded message "New KIDFORUM Topic" by
   Alenka Makuc. 29 June 1995. Online posting. KIDLINK Project List
   [Online]. Available E-mail: LISTSERV@ndsuvml.bitnet/Get kidline
   log9506e. 2 Aug. 1995.
     • In examples M181a and M181b, the name de Presno is given as
       prescribed by MLA. The "Spanish *de* is not used before the last
       name alone" (Gibaldi 88).

2. With Embellishments

Basic Forms

Forwarder. "Subject of New Message." Date. Online posting. Discussion List.
   Available E-mail: DISCUSSION LIST@e-mail address. Access date. Original
   message "Original Subject" by . . .

Forwarder. "Subject of New Message." Date. Online posting. Discussion List.
   Available E-mail: LISTSERV@e-mail address. Access date. Original message
   "Original Subject" by . . .

     • If the reference is a real-time message, follow the first basic
       form. If the message is obtained by searching the list's archive,
       follow the second basic form.
     • If the message is unsigned, use the author's log-in name in
       uppercase letters.
     • Indicate the date when message was sent to the discussion list.
     • Paging or length statement is not required.
     • Present in uppercase letters the names of discussion lists and
       LISTSERVs, followed by lists' Internet or BITNET addresses
       (i.e., TWAIN-L or LISTSERV).
     • Include the editorial note at the end of the reference for informa-
       tion about the original message.

<M182a> Punia, David. T. "Post-Its Destroy Book." 2 Aug. 1995. Online posting.
   Public-Access Computer Systems Forum. Available E-mail: PACS-

L@uhupvm1.uh.edu. 2 Aug. 1995. Original message "Post-It Notes" by Julie Page.

<M182b> Punia, David. T. "Post-Its Destroy Book." 2 Aug. 1995. Online posting. Public-Access Computer Systems Forum. Available E-mail: LIST SERV@uhupvm1.uh.edu/Get pacs-l log9508. 3 Aug. 1995. Original message "Post-It Notes" by Julie Page.
• Reference is obtained by searching the list's archive.

<M183a> Stone, Sasha. "E.T. the Extraterrestrial." 2 Apr. 1995. Online posting. Discussions on All Forms of Cinema. Available E-mail: CINEMA-L@american.edu. 2 Apr. 1995. Original message "E.T." by HO-WARDB on 1 Apr. 1995.
• If the original message is not forwarded to the discussion list on the same day it is created, include the original date after the author note.

<M183b> Stone, Sasha. "E.T. the Extraterrestrial." 2 Apr. 1995. Online posting. Discussions on All Forms of Cinema. Available E-mail: LISTSERV @american.edu/Get cinema-l log9504A. 2 Apr. 1995. Original message "E.T." by HOWARDB on 1 Apr. 1995.
• If the original message is not forwarded to the discussion list on the same day it is created, include the original date after the author note.
• Reference is obtained by searching the list's archive.

II. USENET

A. Individual Works

Basic Forms

Author/editor. "Title of work." Date. Medium. Newsgroup. Usenet. Access date.

"Title of work." Date. Medium. Newsgroup. Usenet. Access date.

• If author or editor is not given, use the second basic form.
• Title of work is given in quotation marks.
• No publication information (i.e., place of publisher and publisher) is needed.
• For the type of medium element, write "Online posting." This describes an individual's message posted to a newsgroup.

<M184> Jankowski, Tomek. "Eastern Europe Is Being Warned to Return Properties to Holocaust Victims." 5 June 1995. Online posting. Newsgroup soc.culture.ukrainia. Usenet. 8 June 1995.

B. Journal Articles

Basic Forms

Author. "Article Title." *Journal Title* Volume number.Issue number (Year): Inclusive pages (if given), or n. pag. (for no pagination). Medium. Newsgroup. Usenet. Access date.

"Article Title." *Journal Title* Volume number.Issue number (Year): Inclusive pages (if given), or n. pag. (for no pagination). Medium. Newsgroup. Usenet. Access date.

* When author is not given, use the second basic form.
* Use "Online" to indicate the medium.

<M185> Horinouch, Katsuhiho, and Toshiyuki Shiozawa. "Analysis of Dynamic Behavior of an Open-Boundary Cherenkov Laser." *IEICE Transactions on Electronics* J76-C.9 (1993): 331–336. Online. Newsgroup comp.research.japan. Usenet. 2 Aug. 1995. Text is in Japanese.
* Provide volume information "J76-C" as it is presented in the publication.
* Editorial note is placed at the end of the citation.

C. Magazine Articles

Basic Forms

Author. "Article Title." *Magazine Title* Date: number of pages or paragraphs (if given), or n. pag. (for no pagination). Medium. Newsgroup. Usenet. Access date.

"Article Title." *Magazine Title* Date: number of pages or paragraphs (if given), or n. pag. (for no pagination). Medium. Newsgroup. Usenet. Access date.

* When author is not given, use the second basic form.
* Use "Online" to indicate medium.

<M186> Abayomi, Tunji, and Beko Ransome-Kuti. "Legal Concern/Prisoners of Conscience." *Amnesty International Urgent Action Bulletin* 31 July 1995: 7 pars. Online. Newsgroup misc.activism.progressive. Usenet. 2 Aug. 1995.

D. Newsletter Articles

Basic Forms

Author. "Article Title." *Newsletter Title* Date: number of pages or paragraphs (if given), or n. pag. (for no pagination). Medium. Newsgroup. Usenet. Access date.

"Article Title." *Newsletter Title* Date: number of pages or paragraphs (if given), or n. pag. (for no pagination). Medium. Newsgroup. Usenet. Access date.

> • When author is not given, use the second basic form.
> • Use "Online" to indicate medium.

<M187>   Nader, Ralph. "Ralph Nader on Windows 95 Problems." *TAP-INFO: An Internet Newsletter Available from Taxpayer Assets Project* 31 July 1995: 3–9. Online. Newsgroup comp.society.privacy. Usenet. 2 Aug. 1995. Letter to President Bill Clinton.

> • A note, indicating that this is a letter, is included at the end of the reference.

III. PERSONAL E-MAIL

A. Correspondence

Basic Form

Sender (Sender's E-mail address). "Subject of Message." E-mail to recipient (recipient's E-mail address). Date of message.

> • If the message is unsigned, use the author's log-in name in uppercase letters.
> • Include both sender and recipient's E-mail addresses in parentheses right after their names respectively. This gives two options for locating a copy of this original message.
> • Capitalize the log-in names as they are proper names, followed by Internet or Bitnet addresses.
> • Indicate the date when message was sent.

<M188>   Day, Martha (MDAY@sage.uvm.edu). "Review of Film—*Bad Lieutenant*." E-mail to Xia Li (XLI@moose.uvm.edu). 30 July 1995.

B. Forwarded Mail with Embellishment

Basic Form

Forwarder (forwarder's E-mail address). "Subject of New Message." E-mail to recipient (recipient's E-mail address). Date of message. Original message, "Subject" by . . .

> • If the message is unsigned, use the author's log-in name in uppercase letters.

- Include both forwarder's and recipient's E-mail addresses in parentheses right after their names.
- Capitalize the log-in names as they are proper names, followed by Internet or Bitnet addresses.
- Indicate the date when message was sent.
- Include an editorial note at the end of the reference for information about the *original* message.

<M189>   Archdeacon, Dan (DARCHDEA@uvmvm.uvm.edu). "Update on Latvia." E-mail to Nancy Crane (NCRANE@uvmvm.uvm.edu). 30 Oct. 1992. Original message, "Life in the Baltics" by Mara Saule.

CHAPTER TWELVE

U.S. Government Documents, Legal Sources, and International Documents

I. U.S. GOVERNMENT DOCUMENTS

This section is arranged by type of document or information and draws sources from a variety of electronic resources.

The 4th edition of the *MLA Handbook* refers readers to *The Bluebook: A Uniform System of Citation* (Cambridge: Harvard Law Rev. Assn., 15th ed., 1991) for citation of legal materials. *Electronic Styles* provides a choice, with legal sources presented in MLA style in this section, and examples of legal citation following *The Bluebook* in the Legal Sources section, which starts on page 172.

A. Bills, Resolutions

Basic Forms

United States. Cong. House or Senate. *Title of Bill or Resolution*. Version (Vers.) if given. Number Cong., Number Sess., Number of bill or resolution. Date. Medium. Supplier. Path (separate levels with forward slashes). Access date.

Sources Retrieved Using One of the Internet Protocols

United States. Cong. House or Senate. *Title of Bill or Resolution*. Version (Vers.) if given. Number Cong., Number Sess., Number of bill or resolution. Date. Medium. Supplier. Available (include protocol if relevant): Address/Path/File. Access date.

<M190>   United States. Cong. House. *Congressional Accountability Act of 1995*. Vers. 1. 104th Cong., 1st Sess., H.R. 1. 12 Jan. 1995. Online. Library of Congress. Available: gopher://marvel.loc.gov/U.S. Congress/Online

Legislative Databases at the Library of Congress/Connect to LOCIS/ 2/8/retrieve h.r. 1. 8 Aug. 1995. Popular title: *Contract with America.*
- The "available" statement shows an example of a Gopher site accessed via the World Wide Web (WWW).
- It is not necessary to repeat the protocol (Gopher) on the WWW after the "available" statement since it is stated in the URL.

<M191> United States. Cong. House. *Return of Excess Amounts from Official Allowances of Members of the House of Representatives to the Treasury for Deficit Reduction.* Vers. 1. 104th Cong., 1st Sess., H.R. 26. 28 Jan. 1995. Online. Mead Lexis. GENFED/BILLS. 7 Aug. 1995.

<M192> United States. Cong. Senate. *Resolution Expressing the Sense of the Senate Regarding the Recent Announcement by the Republic of France That It Intends to Conduct a Series of Underground Nuclear Test Explosions Despite the Current International Moratorium on Nuclear Testing.* Vers. 1. 104th Cong., 1st Sess., S. Res. 149. 14 July 1995. Online. Mead Lexis. GENFED/BILLS. 10 Aug. 1995.

<M193> United States. Cong. Senate. *Resolution to Congratulate the New Jersey Devils for Becoming the 1995 NHL Champions and Thus Winning the Stanley Cup.* Vers. 1. 104th Cong., 1st Sess., S. Res. 142. 28 June 1995. Online. Mead Lexis. LEGIS/BILLS. 10 Aug. 1995.

B. Census

Basic Forms

Title of Document. Date. Medium. Supplier. Available (include protocol if relevant): Address or source/Path/File. Access date.

Title of Document. Date. Medium. Supplier. Path. Access date.

- This is the form for citing a whole document.

Or

"Title of Section, Table or Chapter." *Title of Document.* Date. Medium. Supplier. Available (include protocol if relevant): Address or source/Path/File. Access date.

"Title of Section, Table or Chapter." *Title of Document.* Date. Medium. Supplier. Path. Access date.

- This is the form for citing part of a work.
- It is not necessary to repeat the protocol (Gopher) on the WWW after the "available" statement since it is stated in the URL.

<M194> "Alaska." *1990 Census of Population and Housing*. N.d. Online. U of
         Maryland. Available: gopher://gopher.inform.umd.edu:10/00/EdRes/
         Topic/UnitedStatesAndWorld/United_States/National_Agencies/Exec
         utiveBranch/Census-90/alaska. 8 Aug. 1995.
         • No print counterpart is cited.

<M195> "Asian or Pacific Islander Females." *1990 Census of Population and
         Housing: Summary Tape File 3A*. CD-ROM. U.S. Bureau of the Cen-
         sus. 1990 Census of Population and Housing: Summary Tape 3A/
         Vermont/Burlington, VT MSA/Race by sex by age/Asian or Pacific
         Islander females. 1990.
         • The information provided for material on a CD-ROM varies
           somewhat from the basic forms given above. Note that the path
           is given, with segments separated by slashes, directly after the
           supplier of the information, for ease of retrieval.
         • No access date is required for information obtained from a CD-
           ROM.
         • Date of the work is the last element.

<M196> "Computers and Office Accounting Machines, MA35R." *Current Indus-
         trial Reports*. 1993. Online. U.S. Bureau of the Census. Available:
         http://www.census.gov/ftp/pub/industry/ma35r93.txt. 8 Aug. 1995.
         • No print counterpart is cited.

<M197> "Table 3: Cities with 200,000 or More Population Ranked." *County and
         City Data Book*. 1994. Online. U.S. Bureau of the Census. Available:
         http://www.census.gov/stat_abstract/ccdb/www/ccdb305.txt. 8 Aug.
         1995. Data on Asian or Pacific Islander populations.
         • No print counterpart is cited.
         • Note at end of entry describes coverage more fully.

C. Congressional Record

Basic Forms

Sen. or Rep. Last name of speaker (Home state—abbreviated). "Title." *Cong. Rec.*
  Date: paging. Medium. Supplier. Path. Access date.

Sources Retrieved Using One of the Internet Protocols

Sen. or Rep. Last name of speaker (Home state—abbreviated). "Title." *Cong. Rec.*
  Date: paging. Medium. Supplier. Available (include protocol if relevant): Address or source/Path/File. Access date.

<M198> Sen. Jeffords (VT). "Jeffords (and Others) Amendment No. 2054." *Cong. Rec.* 1 Aug. 1995: S11120. Online. Mead Lexis. LEGIS/RECORD. 9 Aug. 1995.

> • The *Congressional Record* does not give first names of speakers as a rule so first name is replaced with title: Representative (Rep.), or Senator (Sen.).

D. Constitution (U.S.)

Basic Forms

"Article and section numbers: Title of section." *Version of Constitution.* Date. Medium. Supplier. Available (include protocol if relevant): Address or source/Path/File. Access date.

Or

"Article and section numbers: Title of section." *Version of Constitution.* Date. Medium. Supplier. Path. Access date.

<M199> "Amendment XIII: Abolition of slavery." *Constitution of the United States of America.* 14 Mar. 1993 [load date]. Online. Cornell Law. Available: http://www.law.cornell:80/constitution/constitution. amendmentxiii.html. 8 Aug. 1995.

> • The date given, in this case, is the load date of this electronic version.

<M200> "USCS Constitution Preamble." *United States Code Service: Constitution of the United States of America.* 1994. Online. Mead Lexis. GENFED/USCNST. 9 Aug. 1995.

E. Court Decisions

Basic Forms

"Name of case." (Date of decision). *Reporting service* (Jurisdiction, if relevant) Volume (Date): paging or length of item. Medium. Supplier. Path. Access date.

Sources Retrieved Using One of the Internet Protocols

"Name of case." (Date of decision). *Reporting service* (Jurisdiction, if relevant) Volume (Date): first page or length of item. Medium. Supplier. Available (include protocol if relevant): Address or source/Path/File. Access date.

> • The convention when citing legal decisions is to give the first
> page on which the decision appears. If this is not available, give
> some measure of length, e.g., number of paragraphs (pars.),
> lines, screens, or words.

Note: The reporting services of U.S. District and Appeals court cases are not government documents. However, the citation patterns for cases in these federal jurisdictions have been included in this section for the convenience of users citing this information.

1. U.S. District Courts

<M201> "Johnson v. Miller." *Federal Supplement* (Southern District, Georgia) 864
(1994): 1354. Online. Mead Lexis. GENFED/COURTS. 7 Aug. 1995.
> • Cite the case name exactly as it is given in the source.
> • It is important to give the district in which the case was heard
> but not the division. In this instance, Southern District, Georgia
> is sufficient.

2. U.S. Court of Appeals

<M202> "Hetzel v. Bethlehem Steel Corp." *Federal Reporter, 3rd* (5th Circuit)
50 (1995): 360. Online. Mead Lexis. GENFED/USAPP. 10 Aug.
1995.
> • Give circuit in which case is heard.

3. Supreme Court of the United States

<M203> "Regents of the University of California v. Bakke." *United States Reports*
438 (1978): 265. Online. Mead Lexis. GENFED/US. 11 Aug. 1995.

<M204> "Robert E. Rubin, Secretary of the Treasury, Petitioner v. Coors Brewing
Company." Preliminary print. *United States Reports* (9 Apr. 1995): 29
pars. Case Western Reserve, Project Hermes. Available: ftp://ftp.cwru.
edu/hermes/ascii/93-1631.ZO.filt. 8 Aug. 1995.
> • Volume and paging for this item are not available for this pre-
> liminary print of *United States Reports*. This example gives the
> exact date the decision was issued to help identify the version.

<M205a> "Miller v. Johnson." *U.S. Lexis* (1995): 4462. Online. Mead Lexis. GEN
FED/US. 7 Aug. 1995.
> • See M205b and M205c for parallel citations to the *United States
> Supreme Court Reports, Lawyers' Edition*, and *U.S. Law Week*.

<M205b> "Miller v. Johnson." (1995, June 29). *United States Supreme Court, Lawyers' Edition, 2d* 132 (1995): 762. Online. Mead Lexis. GEN-FED/US. 7 Aug. 1995.

<M205c> "Miller v. Johnson." *U.S. Law Week* 63 (1995): 4726. Online. Mead Lexis. GENFED/US. 7 Aug. 1995.

F. House or Senate Reports

Basic Forms

United States. Cong. House or Senate. Committee. *Title of Report*. Number of report. Date. Medium. Supplier. Path (separate levels with forward slashes). Access date.

Sources Retrieved Using One of the Internet Protocols

United States. Cong. House or Senate. Committee. *Title of Report*. Number of report. Date. Medium. Supplier. Available (include protocol if relevant): Address or source/Path/File. Access date.

- The name of the committee responsible for the report should be included.

<M206> United States. Cong. House. Committee on Rules. *Providing for the Consideration of H.R. 1555, The Communications Act of 1995*. H. Rept. 104–223. 1 Aug. 1995. Online. Mead Lexis. GENFED/ CMTRPT. 8 Aug. 1995.

<M207> United States. Cong. Senate. Committee on Energy and Natural Resources. *To Transfer a Parcel of Land to the Pueblo Indians of New Mexico*. S. Rept. 104-85. 19 May 1995. Online. Mead Lexis. GEN-FED/CMTRPT. 8 Aug. 1995.

G. Laws, Statutes

1. United States Code

Basic Forms

"Title of section." Title number *Version of Code* Part (Pt.) number. Date. Medium. Supplier. Path. Access date.

Sources Retrieved Using One of the Internet Protocols

"Title of section." Title number *Version of Code* Part (Pt.) number. Date. Medium. Supplier. Available (include protocol if relevant): Address or source/Path/File. Access date.

<M208> "Abrogation of Treaties." Title 25 *United States Code* Pt. 72. N.d. Online. Cornell Law. Available: http://www.law.cornell.edu/uscode/ 25/72.html. 7 Aug. 1995.

<M209> "Bringing in and Harboring Certain Aliens." Title 8 *United States Code Service* Pt. 1324. 1994. Online. Mead Lexis. GENFED/USCODE. 7 Aug. 1995.

2. United States Statutes at Large

Basic Forms

"Title of Act." Public Law (Pub. L.) Number. *United States Statutes at Large* Volume (Date): paging or length of item. Medium. Supplier. Path. Access date.

Sources Retrieved Using One of the Internet Protocols

"Title of Act." Public Law (Pub. L.) Number. *United States Statutes at Large* Volume (Date): paging or length of item. Available (include protocol if relevant): Address or source/Path/File. Access date.

<M210> "Cancer Registries Amendment Act." Pub. L. 102–515. *United States Statutes at Large* 106 (1992): 3372+. Online. Mead Lexis. GENFED/ PUBLAW. 7 Aug. 1995.

  • In paging statement if length cannot easily be determined, follow the initial page with a plus sign (+) indicating that the item continues beyond that page, or give length in number of paragraphs, screens, lines, or words.

<M211> "Chinese Student Protection Act of 1992." Pub. L. 102–404. *United States Statutes at Large* 106 (1992): 1969+. Online. WESTLAW. US-PL. 15 Oct. 1992.

H. Patents

Basic Forms

"Name of the invention." By inventor's name. *Patent Number*. Date. Medium. Supplier. Path. Access date.

Sources Retrieved Using One of the Internet Protocols

"Name of the invention." By inventor's name. *Patent Number.* Issue date. Medium. Supplier. Available (include protocol, if relevant): Address or source/Path/File. Access date.

> • When citing patents, the most important element is the name of the invention, which is given first, followed by the inventor's name.

<M212> "Apple Tree 'Vermont Gold'." By William H. Luginbuhl. *United States Patent PP 7618* 13 Aug. 1991. Online. Mead Lexis. PATENT/PLANT. 8 Aug. 1995.

> • The date given is the issue date of the patent.

<M213> "Targeted Drug Delivery Via Phosphonate Derivatives." By Nicholas S. Bodor. *United States Patent 5177064* 5 Jan. 1993. Online. Center for Networked Information Discovery and Retrieval. Available: http://concord.cnidr.org/cgi-bin/agw?AIDSPAT+05177064+F. 8 Aug. 1995.

I. Periodicals

Basic Forms

Author. "Title." *Magazine* Date: paging or length. Medium. Supplier. Path. Access date.

Sources Retrieved Using One of the Internet Protocols

Author. "Title." *Magazine* Date: paging or length. Medium. Supplier. Available (include protocol if relevant): Address or source/Path/File. Access date.

<M214> Niles, Thomas M. T. "US Position and Proposed Actions Concerning the Yugoslav Crisis." *Department of State Dispatch* 17 Aug. 1992: 34 pars. Online. Mead Lexis. GENFED/DSTATE. 11 Aug. 1995.

J. Presidential Documents

Basic Forms for Documents in **Weekly Compilation:**

"Title." Nature of document, e.g., proclamation, speech. *Weekly Compilation of Presidential Documents* Volume (Date): paging or length. Medium. Supplier. Path. Access date.

Sources Retrieved Using One of the Internet Protocols

"Title." Nature of document, e.g., proclamation, speech. *Weekly Compilation of Presidential Documents* Volume (Date): paging or length. Medium. Supplier. Available (include protocol if relevant): Address or source/Path/File. Access date.

> • The name of the president, as author, is unnecessary because the date indicates the administration.

<M215> "Remarks on the 50th Anniversary of the United Nations Charter in San Francisco, California." Speech. *Weekly Compilation of Presidential Documents* 31 (26 June 1995):1121+. Online. Mead Lexis. GEN-FED/PRESDC. 8 Aug. 1995.

Documents Not Issued in the Weekly Compilation

Title. Nature of document, e.g., proclamation, speech. (Date of publication). Medium. Supplier. Available (include protocol if relevant): Address or source/Path/File. Access date.

<M216> *Statement by the President: I Strongly Support the Work First Bill.* Press release. 3 Aug. 1995. Texas A & M U. Available Gopher: gopher://info.tamu.edu:70/00/.data/politics/1995/welfare.0803. 8 Aug. 1995.

K. Rules, Regulations

1. Code of Federal Regulations

Basic Forms

"Title of section." Title number *Code of Federal Regulations* Part (Pt.). Date. Medium. Supplier. Path. Access date.

Items Retrieved Using One of the Internet Protocols

"Title of section." Title number *Code of Federal Regulations* Part (Pt.). Date. Medium. Supplier. Available (include protocol if relevant): Address or source/ Path/File. Access date.

<M217> "Dietary Supplements." Title 22 *Code of Federal Regulations* Pt. 71.12. 1993. Online. Mead Lexis. GENFED/CFR93. 7 Aug. 1995.

2. Federal Register

Basic Forms

"Title or Name of the Section." Agency report number if given. *Federal Register*
   Volume (Date): paging or length. Medium. Supplier. Path. Access date.

>   • If a CD-ROM version of the *Federal Register* is used, the
>   "Access Date" element does not need to be included.

Items Retrieved Using One of the Internet Protocols

"Title or Name of the Section." Agency report number if given. *Federal Register*
   Volume (Date): paging or length. Medium. Available (include protocol if relevant): Address or source/Path/File. Access date.

<M218> "Food Labeling: General Requirements for Nutrition Labeling of
        Dietary Supplements; General Requirements for Nutrient Content
        Claims for Dietary Supplements." *Federal Register* 60 (9 Feb. 1995):
        7711+. Online. Mead Lexis. GENFED/FEDREG. 7 Aug. 1995.

II. LEGAL SOURCES

Legal citation style varies significantly from MLA style. The accepted practice in
legal materials is to cite references in footnotes. The *MLA Handbook* (4th ed.) recommends that *The Bluebook: A Uniform System of Citation* (Cambridge: Harvard
Law Rev. Assn., 15th ed., 1991) be used as a guide when citing legal sources. This
section gives a few examples using the legal style of citation. Consult *The Bluebook*
for a complete elaboration of this approach.

A. Bills, Resolutions

Basic Form

Title, Bill, or resolution number, Congress, Session. (Date) (Electronic supplier,
   path).

<M219> Congressional Accountability Act of 1995 (Popular title: Contract with
        America), H.R. 1, 104th Cong., 1st Sess. (1995) (LOCIS, gopher://
        marvel.loc.gov/U.S. Congress/Online Legislative Databases at the
        Library of Congress/Connect to LOCIS/2/8/retrieve h.r. 1).

<M220> Return of Excess Amounts from Official Allowances of Members of the
        House of Representatives to the Treasury for deficit reduction, H.R.
        26, 104th Cong., 1st Sess. (1995) (LEXIS, Genfed, Bills).

<M221> Resolution Expressing the Sense of the Senate Regarding the Recent Announcement by the Republic of France That It Intends to Conduct a Series of Underground Nuclear Test Explosions Despite the Current International Moratorium on Nuclear Testing, S. Res. 149, 104th Cong., 1st Sess. (1995) (LEXIS, Legis, Bills).

B. Codes of Law, Statutes

Basic Form

Official or Popular Name (or both), Title number Source Section (\S\) number (Date) (Electronic supplier, path).

1. State Codes

Basic Form

The proper citation form for codes of law varies from state to state and with reporting service. A few examples are given below to show this variation. Consult *The Bluebook* for a complete guide to title abbreviations for each state service, and the style of capitalization (large and small capitals) for specific titles.

<M222> Application, Administration and Enforcement of Wildlife Laws: General Provisions, OR. REV. STAT. \S\ 496.004 (1991) (LEXIS, Codes, Orcode).

<M223> Vermont Water Resources Board: Duties and Powers, VT. STAT. ANN. tit. 10, \S\ 905 (1991) (LEXIS, Codes, Vtcode).

2. United States Code

<M224> Abrogation of Treaties, 25 U.S.C. \S\72 (No date) (Cornell Law, http://www.law.cornell.edu/uscode/25/72.html).

<M225> Bringing in and Harboring Certain Aliens, 8 U.S.C.S. \S\1324 *et seq.* (1994) (LEXIS, Genfed, UScode).
> • *Et. seq.* means "and following" and indicates that the item starts at 1324 but continues for subsequent sections.

3. United States Statutes at Large

Basic Form

Title of Act, Pub. L. No. Volume Stat. Page (Date) (Electronic supplier, path).

<M226a> Cancer Registries Amendment Act, Pub. L. No. 102–515, 106 Stat. 3372 (1992) (LEXIS, Genfed, Publaw).

<M226b> Cancer Registries Amendment Act, Pub. L. No. 102–515, \S\ 399H, 106 Stat. 3372 (1992) (LEXIS, Genfed, Publaw).
   • This example shows how to cite a particular section (\S\ 399H) in the act.

<M227>   Chinese Student Protection Act of 1992, Pub. L. No. 102-404, 106 Stat. 1969 (1992) (WESTLAW, US-Pl).

C. Court Decisions

1. State Courts

The proper citation form for citing court decisions varies from state to state. A few examples are given below to show this variation. Consult *The Bluebook* for guidance in citing these materials.

Basic Form

Name of case, Source(s) using legal citation style, (Date) (Electronic supplier, path).

<M228>   General Telephone Company of California v. Public Utilities Commission; City of Santa Monica, Real Party in Interest, 34 Cal. 3d 817, 670 P.2d 349, 195 Cal. Rptr. 695 (1983) (LEXIS, Cal, Cal).
   • The practice is to cite all of the decision-reporting services, whenever possible.

<M229>   Tina Labello, as Parent and Natural Guardian, Appellant v. Albany Medical Center Hospital, et al., Respondent, 1995 N.Y. Int. 128 (1995) (Cornell Law, http://www.law.cornell.edu/ny/ctap/085-0701.htm).

2. Federal Courts

Basic Form

Name of case. Volume Source Starting Page (Jurisdiction Date) (Electronic supplier, path).

   • Jurisdiction, district or circuit, is included in the date statement for District and Appeals court decisions respectively.

a. *U.S. District Courts*

<M230>   Johnson v. Miller, 864 F. Supp. 1354 (S.D. Ga 1995) (LEXIS, Genfed, Courts).

> • It is important to give the district in which the case was heard, in this instance Southern District, Georgia, which is abbreviated as "S.D. Ga."

b. *U.S. Court of Appeals*

\<M231\> Hetzel v. Bethlehem Steel Corp, 50 F.3d 360 (5th Cir. 1995) (LEXIS, Genfed, USApp).
> • Give circuit in which case is heard.

\<M232\> United States of America v. Daniel B. Hughes, a/k/a "Sonny", 716 F.2d 234 (4th Cir. 1983) (WESTLAW, Allfeds).

c. *Supreme Court of the United States*

\<M233\> Regents of the University of California v. Bakke, 438 U.S. 265, 98 S. Ct. 2733, 1978 U.S. LEXIS 5, 57 L.Ed. 2d 750, (1978) (LEXIS, Genfed, US).
> • This example shows citations for all of the major Supreme Court reporting services.

\<M234\> Robert E. Rubin, Secretary of the Treasury, Petitioner v. Coors Brewing Company, Preliminary print U.S. (Project Hermes) (1995) (Case Western Reserve, ftp://ftp.cwru/edu/hermes/ascii/93-1631.ZO.filt).
> • Volume and paging for this item are not available yet for this preliminary print of *United States Reports* (U.S.).

D. Periodicals

Basic Form

Author(s), *Title*, Volume Journal Page (Date) (Electronic supplier, path).

> • MLA style and legal citation style vary considerably here. For instance, legal citation gives the author's first *and then* last name, italicizes the article title, abbreviates journal titles, and puts journal titles in large and small capitals.

\<M235\> Donald E. Lively & Stephen Plass, *Equal Protection: The Jurisprudence of Denial and Evasion*, 40 AM. U.L. REV. 1307 (1991) (LEXIS, Lawrev, Allrev).
> • This is an example with more than one author.
> • Refer to *The Bluebook* for periodical abbreviations and form for capitalization of a particular title.

\<M236\> Christopher D. Stone, *Beyond Rio: "Insuring" Against Global Warming*, 86 A.J.I.L. 445 (1992) (LEXIS, Lawrev, Allrev).

E. Rules, Regulations

1. Code of Federal Regulations

Basic Form

Name of Section, Title number C.F.R. Part number (Date) (Electronic supplier, path).

<M237>   Dietary Supplements. 22 C.F.R. 71.12 (1993) (LEXIS, Genfed, CFR93).

2. Federal Register

Basic Form

Title or Name of the Section, Volume Fed. Reg. Page (Date) (to be codified at title C.F.R. part statement) (Electronic supplier, path).

<M238>   Food labeling: General requirements for nutrition labeling of dietary supplements; General requirements for nutrient content claims for dietary supplements, 60 Fed. Reg. 7711 (1995) (to be codified at 21 C.F.R. \S\ 101) (LEXIS, Genfed, Fedreg).

III. INTERNATIONAL AND FOREIGN GOVERNMENT DOCUMENTS

This section has a sampling of international agency and non-U.S. governmental documents. For a more comprehensive representation of citations for this area, see *A Complete Guide to Citing Government Information Resources: A Manual for Writers & Librarians* by Diane L. Garner and Diane H. Smith (Bethesda, MD: Congressional Information Service, 1993).

A. International Documents

1. North Atlantic Treaty Organization

Basic Form

Periodical Article

Author. "Article title." *Journal title* [Type of medium], volume.issue (date): paging or length. Medium. Available (include protocol if relevant): Address/Path/File. Access date.

<M239>   Ray, Robert. "Australia's Strategic Approach." *NATO Review* 43.3 (1995):
       25-30. Online. Available Gopher: gopher://marvin.stc.nato.int:70/00/
       natodata/NATOREVIEW/1995–1996/9503–5. 14 Aug. 1995.

2. United Nations

a. *Conferences*

Basic Form

United Nations. Conference on . . . , Location, Date of Conference. Title. Date.
   Medium. Supplier. Available (include protocol if relevant): Address/Path/File
   Access date.

<M240>   United Nations. Fourth World Conference on Women, Beijing, China,
       4–15, September 1995. Committee on the Elimination of Discrimi-
       nation Against Women. *Progress Achieved in the Implementation of
       The Convention on the Elimination of All Forms of Discrimination
       Against Women.* Report by the Committee. 21 June 1995. Online.
       United Nations Development Programme. Available: gopher://undp.
       org:70/00/unconfs/women/off/a-7.en. 14 Aug. 1995.
          • This item was prepared by a committee for the conference.

b. *Official Proceedings, Reports*

Basic Form

United Nations. Organ, Meeting number of Session. *Title.* Date. Medium. Supplier.
   Available (include protocol if relevant): Address/Path/File. Access date.

<M241>   United Nations. General Assembly, 50th Session. *Strengthening of the
       Coordination of Humanitarian and Disaster Relief Assistance of the
       United Nations, Including Special Economic Assistance: Special
       Economic Assistance to Individual Countries or Regions: Assistance
       to Yemen.* Report of the Secretary-General. 1995. Online. United
       Nations Development Programme. Available Gopher: gopher://undp.
       org:70/00/undocs/gad/A/50/95_08/301. 14 Aug. 1995.

c. *Item in a Collection*

Basic Form

United Nations. Organ, Meeting number of Session. "Title." *Source.* Date.
   Medium. Supplier. Available (include protocol if relevant): Address/Path/File.
   Access date.

d. *Resolutions*

Basic Form

United Nations. Organ. Subsidiary Body (if given), Meeting number or Session. *Resolution Number: Title* Date. Medium. Supplier. Available (include protocol if relevant): Address/Path/File. Access date.

<M242>   United Nations. General Assembly, 49th Session. *Resolution 215: Assistance in Mine Clearance.* 1995. Online. United Nations Development Programme. Available: gopher://undp.org:70/11/undocs/gad/RES/49/9576321E. 1 Aug. 1995.

<M243>   United Nations. Security Council, 2940th Meeting. *Resolution 667: [Recalling the Vienna Conventions on Diplomatic and Consular Relations of Which Iraq Was a Party].* 1990. Online. Wiretap Online Library. Available: http://wiretap.spies.com/ftp.items/GOV/UN/un-667.res. 11 Aug. 1995.

> • Some resolutions do not have titles; in such cases, supply a title that approximates content and place in brackets.

e. *Resolution in a Collection*

Basic Form

United Nations. Organ. Subsidiary Body (if given), Meeting number or Session. "Resolution Number: Title." *Source.* Date. Medium. Supplier. Available (include protocol if relevant): Address/Path/File. Access date.

f. *Treaties*

Basic Form

"Title of Treaty," Date—entered into force, Registry No. *Title of Compendium* volume (date): paging or length (paragraphs or lines). Medium. Supplier. Available (include protocol if relevant): Address/Path/File. Access date.

<M244>   "Protocol Additional to the Geneva Conventions of 12 August 1949, and Relating to the Protection of Victims on Non-International Armed Conflicts (Protocol II)," 7 Dec. 1978, No. 17513. *United Nations Treaty Series* 1125 (n.d.): 56 pars. Online. Wiretap Online Library. Available: http://wiretap.spies.com/ftp.items/GOV/Treaties/Geneva/protocol2. 15 Aug. 1995. This version gives information, as of April 1990, on parties ratifying the Protocols and year of ratification.

3. World Health Organization

Work by Title

Basic Form

Title. Date. Medium. Supplier. Available (include protocol if relevant): Address/
Path/File. Access date.

<M245>   *Country Profile for Burundi: UNDP/UNFPA/WHO/WORLD BANK*
Special Programme of Research, Development and Research Training
in Human Reproduction. 1993. Online. World Health Organization.
Available Gopher: who.org/WHO's Major Programmes/Human Repro-
duction Programme (HRP)/Country Profiles—1993/WHO/HRP
Country Profile for Burundi—1993. 15 Aug. 1995.
  • This publication was retrieved via a WHO Gopher, although it is
    produced by the combined efforts of several international agen-
    cies.

B. National Documents (Non-U.S.)

a. *Constitutions*

Basic Form

Title. Edition or Version. Date. Medium. Supplier. Available (include protocol if
relevant): Address/Path/File. Access date.

<M246>   *Constitution of the Republic of Macedonia*. 1992. Online. Wiretap
Online Library. Available: http://wiretap.spies.com:80/ftp.items/
GOV/World/macedonia.con. 14 Aug. 1995.

b. *Department or Agency Publications*

Basic Form

Nation. Department. *Title*. Series name and number, if part of a series. Date.
Medium. Supplier. Available (include protocol if relevant): Address/Path/File.
Access date.

<M247>   Canada. Environment Canada. *Water—Vulnerable to Climate Change*.
Freshwater Series. A-1. 1992. Online. Canadian Centre for Inland
Waters. Available: http://www.cciw.ca/glimr/data/water-fact-sheets/
facta9-e.html. 15 Aug. 1995.
  • This is an example of an item in a series. Series note follows
    immediately after title.

c. *Parliamentary Documents*

Basic Form

Nation. Parliament. House of Parliament. Committee name. "Title." *Source*. Date.
   Medium. Supplier. Available (include protocol if relevant): Address/Path/File.
   Access date.

<M248> Canada. Parliament. House of Commons. Standing Committee on
   Aboriginal Affairs and Northern Development. "Consideration of the
   Expenditure Plans and Priorities in Future Fiscal Years as Described
   in the Departmental Outlook." *Minutes of Evidence and Proceedings*.
   Meeting No. 50. 15 June 1995. Online. Parliament. Available: http://
   www.parl.gc.ca/committees/iand/iand-50-cover-e.html [and] http://
   www.parl.gc.ca/committees/iand/iand50_blk101.html. 15 Aug. 1995.
      • This item is a split file. To retrieve the whole document, both
      Uniform Resource Locators have to be used.

d. *Special Multilateral Governmental Reports*

Basic Form

Title. Date. Medium. Date. Available (include protocol if relevant): Address/Path/
   File. Access date.

<M249> *Consensus Report on the Constitution: Charlottetown, August 28, 1992*.
   1992. Online. Wiretap Online Library. Available: http//wiretap.spies.
   com/ftp.items/GOV/Canada/Charlottetown.acc. 15 Aug. 1995. Popular title: *Charlottetown Constitutional Accord*.

CHAPTER THIRTEEN

Other Sources

I. ENTIRE SERVICES

A. CD-ROM and Commercial Online Full-Text Databases

Basic Forms

Author/editor. *Title of Print Version of Database*. Place of publication: publisher, date. Medium. Information supplier. *Title of Electronic Database*. Database identifier or number. Access date.

Title of Print Version of Database. Place of publication: publisher, date. *Title of Electronic Database*. Medium. Information supplier. Database identifier or number. Access date.

> • If author or editor is not given, use the second basic form.
> • When a print and online version of a work exist, it is proper to cite both if information is easily available. The name of the database is either italicized or underlined.

<M250> *New York Times*. New York: New York Times Company, 1980–. Online. Mead Nexis. *New York Times*. NEWS/NYT. 10 Aug. 1995.

<M251> *Academic American Encyclopedia*. 1995. Online. Dow Jones News Retrieval Service. *Academic American Encyclopedia*. ENCYC. 27 May 1995.

> • It is not necessary to give place of publication and publisher when citing well-known reference sources.

Basic Forms When a Print Version Is Not Included in Reference

Author/editor. *Title of Electronic Database*. Edition statement (if given). Medium. Information supplier. Database identifier or number. Access date.

Title of Electronic Database. Edition statement (if given). Medium. Information supplier. Database identifier or number. Access date.

> • Access date is omitted in the case of citing a CD-ROM database. The proviso in MLA style is to cite a nonperiodical CD-ROM as you would a book, with the inclusion of the "medium" statement.

<M252> Sternberg, Martin L. A. *The American Sign Language Dictionary on CD-ROM*. Windows vers. CD-ROM. New York: HarperCollins, 1994.

B. Bibliographic Databases

Basic Forms

Author/editor. *Title of Print Version of Database* (if one exits). Place of publication: publisher, date. *Title of Electronic Database*. Medium. Information supplier. Database identifier or number. Access date. Bibliographic database.

Title of Print Version of Database (if one exits). Place of publication: publisher, date. *Title of Electronic Database*. Medium. Information supplier. Database identifier or number. Access date. Bibliographic database.

> • If author or editor is not given, use the second basic form.
> • When print and online versions of a work exist, it is proper to cite both. Note the name of the database is underlined. When only the online version of work exits, start the reference with the database title as the first element.

<M253> *Kompass Asia/Pacific*. 1995. Online. Dialog. 592. 28 May 1995. Bibliographic database.
> • This is a citation for an online database when a print version is not included in reference.

<M254> *Social Science Index*. Bronx: H.W. Wilson, Apr. 1974–. *Social Science Index*. CD-ROM. UMI. 1983–. 10 July 1995. Bibliographic database.
> • Start the reference with information about the print version, followed by information about the electronic version of a work.
> • Since this reference is serial in nature, give only the starting date, followed by a dash.

<M255> *AGRICOLA*. CD-ROM. Norwood, MA.: SilverPlatter, 1987–. Bibliographic database; current disc.
> • Access date is omitted in the case of citing a CD-ROM database.

C. FTP Sites

Basic Forms

Author/editor. *Title*. Date [last update]. Medium. Information supplier. Available FTP: FTP site. Access date.

Title. Date [last update]. Medium. Information supplier. Available FTP: FTP site. Access date.

- If author or editor is not given, use the second basic form.
- Give date of last update if this can be determined. Otherwise use "n.d." for no date.
- Treat FTP sites as edited or compiled works, nonserial in nature.

<M256a> *University of Virginia Electronic Text Center*. 18 June 1995 [last update]. Online. U of Virginia. Available FTP: etext.virginia.edu. 21 Aug. 1995.

<M256b> *University of Virginia Electronic Text Center*. 18 June 1995 [last update]. Online. U of Virginia. Available: ftp://etext.virginia.edu. 21 Aug. 1995.
- If the information is retrieved via the World Wide Web (WWW), write Uniform Resource Locator (URL) in the "available" statement.

D. Gopher Sites

Basic Forms

Author/editor. *Title*. Date [last update]. Medium. Information supplier. Available Gopher: Gopher site. Access date.

Title. Date [last update]. Medium. Information supplier. Available Gopher: Gopher site. Access date.

- If author or editor is not given, use the second basic form.
- Give date of last update if this can be determined. Otherwise use "n.d."
- Treat Gopher sites as edited or compiled works, nonserial in nature.

<M257a> *E-Text Archives Services*. 25 July 1995 [last update]. Online. CERT. Available Gopher: gopher.etext.org. 15 Aug. 1995.

<M257b> *E-Text Archives Services*. 25 July 1995 [last update]. Online. CERT. Available: gopher://gopher.etext.org:70/. 15 Aug. 1995.
- If the information is retrieved on the WWW, write the URL in the available statement.

E. Telnet Sites

Basic Forms

Author/editor. *Title*. Date [last update]. Information supplier. Medium. Available Telnet: domain/**login** (if required). Access date.

Title. Date [last update]. Information supplier. Medium. Available Telnet: domain/**login** (if required). Access date.

> • If author or editor is not given, use the second basic form.
> • Give date of last update if this can be determined. Otherwise use the copyright date.
> • Treat Telnet sites as edited or compiled works, nonserial in nature.

<M258>   *Sage: The Information Gateway for the UVM Libraries and Media Services*. 19 Aug. 1995 [last update]. Online. U of Vermont. Available Telnet: sageunix.uvm.edu/**login**: sage. [20 Aug. 1995].

F. WWW Homepages

Basic Forms

Author/editor. *Homepage Title*. Hp. Date [last update or copyright date]. Medium. Information supplier. Available: URL. Access date.

Homepage Title. Hp. Date [last update or copyright date]. Medium. Information supplier. Available: URL. Access date.

> • When author or editor is not given, use the second basic form.
> • Include "Hp." for homepage after title.
> • Indicate the date of the last update for the homepage if available; otherwise, use the copyright date.
> • Give the homepage site (domain) as the information supplier.
> • It is not necessary to repeat the protocol (HTTP) on the WWW after the "available" statement since it is stated in the URL.

<M259>   Altis, Kevin, and Nancy Tindle, eds. *City Net*. Hp. 14 Aug. 1995 [last update]. Online. City Net Express. Available: http://www.city.net/. 14 Aug. 1995.

<M260>   Mother Jones Interactive, ed. *MoJo Wire*. Hp. 1995 [copyright]. Online. Mother Jones Interactive. Available: http://www.mojones.com/. 14 Aug. 1995.

<M261> Wall Street Journal, ed. *Money & Investing Update*. Hp. 14 Aug. 1995
        [last update]. Dow Jones & Company. Available: http://update.wsj.
        com/. 14 Aug. 1995.

II. AUDIOVISUAL MATERIALS

A. Works of Art

Basic Forms

Author. *Title of Work*. Date (if given). Institution that houses the work (or the indi-
    vidual's private collection), City (or Country). Medium. Supplier. Database.
    File or accession number. Access date.

Author. *Title of Work*. Date (if given). Institution that houses the work (or the indi-
    vidual's private collection), City (or Country). Medium. Supplier. Available
    (include protocol if relevant): Address or source/path/file. Access date.

> • If an art work is retrieved from a commercial or CD-ROM data-
>   base, use the first basic form. The second form is used for art
>   work retrieved on the Internet.
> • Indicate, in a note, the kind of work being described (e.g., paint-
>   ing, illustration, photograph, computer image, cartoon).
> • Give the date when the electronic image is created.

<M262> Daniels, Michael. *Corinthian: Handle at Right*. 1991. Yale University
        Art Gallery, New Haven. CD-ROM. Perseus 1.0. Yale 1988.80.37. 19
        Aug. 1995. Photograph; date of electronic version given.
> • Note of explanation is given after the access date.

<M263> Sprangers, Hylke. *Untitled: Faces in the Crowd No. 1*. 1993. ArtVark
        Galler, Holland. Online. U of Amsterdam. Available: http://www.
        fwi.uva.nl/~boncz/artvark/faces/face1.jpg. 17 Aug. 1995. Image of oil
        painting.
> • Additional information is presented at the end of reference.

B. Film Clips

Basic Forms

"Clip Title." *Film Title*. Director. Distributor of original film, Distribution year.
    Type of medium. Supplier of electronic version of film. Database. File or
    accession number. Access date.

"Clip Title." *Film Title*. Director. Distributor of original film, Distribution year. Type of medium. Supplier of electronic version of film. Available (include protocol if relevant): address/path/file. Access date.

> • If the item is retrieved from a commercial or CD-ROM database, use the first basic form. The second form is used for item retrieved on the Internet.
> • All data that seems relevant to the film, such as leading performers, screen writers, and producers can be added between film title and film distributor.

<M264>   "Defied the World." *Braveheart*. Dir. Mel Gibson. Perf. Mel Gibson, Sophie Marceau, Patrick McGoohan, and Catherine McCormack. Paramount, 1995. Online. Paramount. Available: http://www.voyager. paramount.com/video/BHPRV02.mov. 25 Aug. 1995.

C. Sound Recordings

Basic Forms

Author. "Title of Work." *Title of Recording*. Original recording medium, if known. Artist or artists. Manufacturer, date. Medium. Electronic supplier. Database. File or accession number. Access date.

Author. "Title of Work." *Title of Recording*. Original recording medium, if known. Artist or artists. Manufacturer, date. Medium. Electronic supplier. Available (include protocol if relevant): address/path/file. Access date.

> • If the item is retrieved from a commercial or CD-ROM database, use the first basic form. The second form is used for item retrieved on the Internet.
> • The author, depending on the desired emphasis, can be composer, conductor or performer, etc.
> • For the artist or artists element include anybody who has made significant contribution to the recording.
> • Indicate the medium for the original recording, e.g., compact disc (CD), audiocassette, record (LP).
> • Include the supplier of the electronic recording in the reference.
> • It is not necessary to give the place of manufacture.
> • Indicate the medium for the electronic version of the recording (e.g., online, CD-ROM).
> • In the "available" statement, specify the protocol, domain (supplier address), path, and file if the piece is retrieved on the

Internet. If the piece is available from a commercial electronic supplier, indicate the database, search path, and file name.

<M265> Domingo, Placido. "Che Gelida Manina." *La Boheme* by Giacomo Puccini. *The Placido Domingo Album.* London Symphony Orch. Cond. Sir Georg Solti. CD. BMG, n.d. Online. On Ramp Inc. Available: http://classicalmus.com/av/domingo.mp2. 25 Aug. 1995.

> • Note about the particular piece follows directly after the song title.

D. Maps

Basic Forms

Title of map. Map, Scale: if known. *Source.* Location: Publisher, Publication date. Medium. Electronic supplier. Database. File. Access date.

Title of map. Map, Scale: if known. Location: Publisher, Publication date. Medium. Electronic supplier. Available (include protocol if relevant): address/path/file. Access date.

> • If the item is retrieved from a commercial or CD-ROM database, use the first basic form. The second form is used for an item retrieved on the Internet.
>
> • Give information on scale as follows: Map, Scale: 1:1,000,000.

<M266> "Turkey: Elevations" Map, Scale: 1:100 km. *Turkey.* Tempe, Ariz.: PC Globe, 1992. Diskette. PC Globe. Country, Turkey, Elevations.

> • "Country, Turkey, Elevations" represent the path taken to retrieve the specific graphical information displayed on the named map.
>
> • Access date is not relevant for this type of medium (diskette).

III. MEETING PROCEEDINGS AND SYMPOSIA

A. Paper in a Proceedings

Basic Forms

Author. "Paper Title." *Proceedings Title.* Editor of proceedings. Place of publication: Publisher, Date. Medium. Supplier. Database. File or accession number. Access date.

Author. "Paper Title." *Proceedings Title*. Editor of proceedings. Place of publication: Publisher, Date. Medium. Supplier. Available (include protocol if relevant): address/path/file. Access date.

> • If the item is retrieved from a commercial or CD-ROM database, use the first basic form. The second form is used for an item retrieved on the Internet.
> • Cite a paper in the proceedings like a work in a collection of pieces by different authors.

<M267> Silberberg, D. P., and R. D. Semmel. "The StarView Flexible Query Mechanism." *Astronomical Data Analysis Software and Systems III ASP Conference Series, Vol. 61, 1994*. Ed. Daniel Durand, Jeannette Barnes, and Dennis R. Crabtree. San Francisco: Astronomical Society of the Pacific, 1994. Online. Canadian Astronomy Data Centre. Available: http://cadcwww.dao.nrc.ca/ADASS/adass_proc/adass3/papers/silberbergd/silberbergd.html. 23 Aug. 1995.

> • Source gives only initials for authors' first names, which is reflected in the author element of this reference.
> • Italicize or underline meeting date, location, etc., as part of the title.

B. Entire Proceedings of a Conference

Basic Forms

Editor/author. *Proceedings Title*. Place of publication: Publisher, Date. Medium. Supplier. Database. File or accession number. Access date.

Editor/author. *Proceedings Title*. Place of publication: Publisher, Date. Medium. Supplier. Available (include protocol if relevant): address/path/file. Access date.

> • If the item is retrieved from a commercial or CD-ROM database, use the first basic form. The second form is used for an item retrieved on the Internet.

<M268> *Proceedings of the Third International World Wide Web Conference: Technology, Tools and Applications, April 10–14, Darmstadt, Germany*. Amsterdam, Netherlands: Elsevier Science B.V., 1995. Online. Fraunhofer Institute for Computer Graphics, Darmstadt. Available: http://www.igd.fhg.de/www/www95/proceedings/proceedings.html. 22 Aug. 1995.

> • Cite an entire conference proceedings like a book, with pertinent information about the conference when it is available.

IV. RADIO/TELEVISION TRANSCRIPTS AND WIRE SERVICE REPORTS

Basic Forms

Author/reporter/anchor/person interviewed. Interview with . . . (if any). "Title of the segment." *Title of program*. Name of the network. Call letters. Broadcast date. Medium. Supplier. Database. File or record number. Access date.

Author/reporter/anchor/person interviewed. Interview with . . . (if any). "Title of the segment." *Title of program*. Name of the network. Call letters. Broadcast date. Medium. Supplier. Available (include protocol if relevant): address/path/ file. Access date.

> • If the item is retrieved from a commercial or CD-ROM database, use the first basic form. The second form is used for an item retrieved on the Internet.
> • In the "available" statement, specify the protocol, domain (address), path, and file if the item is retrieved on the Internet. If the piece is available from a commercial electronic supplier, indicate the database, search path, and file name.

<M269> Dobbs, Lou. Interview with Mario Gabelli. "Wall Street Analyst Discusses Global Telecommunications." *Moneyline*. CNN. 18 Aug. 1995. Online. Mead Nexis. News/Script. 18 Aug. 1995. Television transcript.
> • Use a note to specify nature of document.

<M270> Worsnip, Patrick. "U.S. Assures Bosnia NATO Will Defend Gorazde." *BC Cycle*. Reuters North American Wire. 25 Aug. 1995. Online. Mead Nexis. News/Wires. 26 Aug. 1995. Wire service report.
> • Use a note to specify special nature of document.

V. THESES AND DISSERTATIONS

A. Section of a Thesis/Dissertation

Basic Forms

Author. "Section." *Thesis/Dissertation Title*. Diss. University, Year. Medium. Information supplier. Database. File or record number. Access date.

Author. "Section." *Thesis/Dissertation Title*. Diss. University, Year. Medium. Information supplier. Available (include protocol if relevant): address/path/file. Access date.

• If the item is retrieved from a commercial or CD-ROM database, use the first basic form. The second form is used for an item retrieved on the Internet.

\<M271\> Bierwagen, Paul. "Chapter III: Molecular Mechanics Investigations of Syndiospecific Zirconocene-based Ziegler-Natta Catalysis." *Computational Studies of Ziegler-natta Catalysis and Concurrent Resonance Computations*. Diss. California Institute of Technology, 1995. Online. Beckman Institute at CalTech. Available: http://www.wag. caltech.edu/theses/epb/Ch3.ps. 29 Aug. 1995.

B. Entire Thesis/Dissertation

Basic Forms

Author. *Thesis/Dissertation Title*. Diss. University, Year. Medium. Information supplier. Database. File or record number. Access date.

Author. *Thesis/Dissertation Title*. Diss. University, Year. Medium. Information supplier. Available (include protocol if relevant): address/path/file. Access date.

• If the item is retrieved from a commercial or CD-ROM database, use the first basic form. The second form is used for an item retrieved on the Internet.

\<M272\> Lim, Kian-Tat. *Mega-Molecular Dynamics on Highly Parallel Computer: Methods and Application*. Diss. California Institute of Technology, 1995. Online. Beckman Institute at CalTech. Available: http://www. wag.caltech.edu/theses/ktl/ToC.html. 18 Aug. 1995.

VI. ABSTRACTS

A. Monograph or Individual Work

Basic Forms

Author. Abstract of *Individual work*. Place of publication: Publisher, date. Medium. Information supplier. *Database name*. Database number (if given). Item number. Access date.

Author. Abstract of *Individual work*. Place of publication: Publisher, date. Medium. Information supplier. Available (include protocol if relevant): give sufficient information for retrieval. Access date.

• If the item is retrieved from a commercial or CD-ROM database, use the first basic form. The second form is used for an item retrieved on the Internet.

<M273> Kutner, Laurie A., and Rafael Mares. Abstract of *Environmental Discrimination*. CPL Bibliography 306. Chicago: Council of Planning Librarians, 1994. Online. OCLC FirstSearch. *PAIS Decade.* 94-1201535. 1 Sept. 1995.

> • Series title is provided after the individual work.

B. Journal Article

Basic Forms

Author. Abstract of "Article Title." *Journal, Volume* (Year): item number or paging information. Medium. Database. File or item number. Access date.

Author. Abstract of "Article Title." *Journal, Volume* (Year): item number or paging information. Medium. Available (include protocol if relevant): address/path/file. Access date.

> • If the item is retrieved from a commercial or CD-ROM database, use the first basic form. The second form is used for an item retrieved on the Internet.

<M274> Sengers, Phoebe. Abstract of "Madness and Automation: On Institutionalization." *Postmodern Culture* 5.Contents3 (1995): n. pag. Online. Available FTP: ftp.ncsu.edu/pub/ncsu/pmc/pmc-list/contents.595. 15 June 1995.

C. Magazine Article

Basic Forms

Author. Abstract of "Article Title." *Magazine.* Date: paging information. Medium. Supplier. Database. File or record number. Access date.

Author. Abstract of "Article Title." *Magazine.* Date: paging information. Medium. Information Supplier. Available (include protocol if relevant): give sufficient information for retrieval. Access date.

> • If the item is retrieved from a commercial or CD-ROM database, use the first basic form. The second form is used for an item retrieved on the Internet.

<M275> Ying, Tong. Abstract of "Singapore Airlines Moves into Intelligent Systems." *Computerworld.* 5 June 1995: 81+. Online. Dialog. *Magazine Database.* 47. 17344962. 20 Aug. 1995.

> • The elements in the path include: database name, database number, and item number.

D. Newspaper Article

Basic Forms

Author. Abstract of "Article Title." *Newspaper.* Date, edition: paging information. Medium. Supplier. Database. File or record number. Access date.

Author. Abstract of "Article Title." *Newspaper.* Date, edition: paging information. Medium. Supplier. Available (include protocol if relevant): give sufficient information for retrieval. Access date.

> • If an item is retrieved from a commercial or CD-ROM database, use the first basic form. The second form is used for an item retrieved on the Internet.

<M276> Purdum, Todd S. Abstract of "Hard Choice for White House on Hillary Clinton and China." *New York Times.* 17 Aug. 1995, late edition: A1. Online. Information Access. *Expanded Academic ASAP.* A17187821. 1 Sept. 1995.

Parenthetical Documentation, Endnotes, and Footnotes

I. PARENTHETICAL DOCUMENTATION

The system of parenthetical documentation recommended by the *MLA Handbook* (Gibaldi 183–202) directs readers to the source of a quotation or work under discussion in the alphabetically arranged list of works cited at the end of an article, chapter, book or dissertation. This chapter gives some of the more common examples of documentation in the text.

A. Work by a Single Author

Example 1: Merlan's work on Aboriginal narrative. . . .

> • If the whole work is being cited and there is only one work by this author in the list of Works Cited, mention of the author's name is sufficient attribution.

Example 2: Australia's Minister of Defense, Robert Ray, maintains that "In the next century a new pattern of strategic relationships will evolve in which the Asia-Pacific region will become more strategically self-contained" (25).

Example 3: "A philosopher is always someone for whom philosophy is not given, someone who in essence must question him or herself about the essence and destination of philosophy" (Derrida, par. 15).

Example 4: Holst's view of the move by the Norwegian Parliament to "ban" the national language is soon made clear: "The 1938 language reform bill served the heritage of the National Language the way Pol Pot served Cambodia; if the map and reality don't agree, then change reality" (par. 4).

• Examples 2, 3, and 4 each cite to a specific place in a work. Example 2 cites a page (25). In Examples 3 and 4, the references specify the location of the quotation in the document by giving the paragraph number.

• Note that in Example 3 a comma is needed to separate the author's name from the reference to a specific paragraph. A comparable page reference would not require punctuation.

B. Work by Two or More Authors

Example 1: Sikula and Costa used a large sample of college students to study the issue of gender and ethical values.

• Citing the authors of the study in the text is sufficient for locating the reference in the list of Works Cited.

Example 2: The study finds that ". . . among today's youth of normal college age, there are no significant differences between ethical values of male and female students" (Sikula and Costa 859).

• The authors' names are followed by the page on which the quote appeared; no punctuation is necessary.

Example 3: Mardeusz, Reit and Robertson report. . .

Example 3a: The findings in a recent study (Mardeusz, Reit, and Robertson) indicate. . .

Example 4: If a work being cited has more than three authors, give the first author's last name followed by et al. For example, a work by Barickman, Brew, Day, Kutner, Mardeusz, Reit, Robertson and Ross would be cited as: (Barickman et al.).

C. Work by a Corporate Author

Example 1: The United Nation's Fourth World Conference on Women will consider a report by the Committee on the Elimination of Discrimination Against Women (CEDAW) which suggests. . . .

Subsequent References

For corporate authors with lengthy names, subsequent references may be abbreviated as follows:

(U.N., 4th World Conf. Women, CEDAW).

Example 2: *Resolution 215* of the United Nations, General Assembly, 49th Session recognizes "the tremendous humanitarian problem caused by the presence of mines and other unexploded devices . . . to humanitarian aid operations . . ." (par. 3).

Subsequent References

(U.N., Gen. Assembly, 49th Sess., par. 12).

> • If there are other materials in the list of works cited from this session of the General Assembly, then part of the title of the work should be included to distinguish the item being cited from these other sources:

(U.N., Gen. Assembly, 49th Sess., *Resolution 215*, par. 12).

D. Works Listed by Title (No Author Given)

Example 1: In "Women of Anabaptist Traditions. . ." there is an interesting portrayal. . .

Example 2: In recent years, we have seen discussion of the landmark decision "Regents of the University of California v. Bakke" turn . . .

> • If a work is listed by title, it may be shortened, as in Example 1.

E. More Than One Work Cited Within the Parentheses

Example 1: An earlier study by Tsaikis and Oritz-Buonafini is at some variance with the findings of Sikula and Costa (509; 859).

> • In this case, the information in parentheses refers to page numbers where the study findings were summarized for each study. The semicolon separates the page citations.

Example 2: There are two recent studies that have relevance to this issue, but they present rather different findings (Tsaikis and Oritz-Buonafini 509; Sikula and Costa 859).

F. E-mail and Online Postings

E-mail messages include personal communications between individuals. Online postings include messages appearing on discussion lists and electronic bulletin boards.

Example 1: Martha Day finds the film *Bad Lieutenant* meets several criteria. . . (E-mail).

Example 2: RRECOME presents ten rules of film criticism in a recent message on the CINEMA-L (online posting).

- RRECOME represents the author's log-in name. The convention is to present that name in uppercase letters if the writer's name cannot be determined.

II. ENDNOTES AND FOOTNOTES

In some disciplines the practice is to use endnotes (numbered notes appearing at the end of the work), or footnotes (numbered notes appearing at the bottom of the page where the reference was made). The following sections give examples of this method of giving credit for work quoted. For much more detailed information on this procedure see Appendix B of the *MLA Handbook* (Gibaldi 242–256).

A. Work by a Single Author

[1] Francesca Merlan, "Narrative of Survival in the Post-Colonial North," *Oceania* 65.2 (1994) : 20, online, Information Access, *Expanded Academic ASAP*, A16878539, 12 June 1995.

[2] Robert Ray, "Australia's Strategic Approach," *NATO Review* 43.3 (1995) : 25, online, Available: gopher://marvin.stc.nato.int:70/00/natodata/NATOREVIEW/1995–1996/9503-5, 14 Aug. 1995.

[3] Jacques Derrida, "Of the Humanities and the Philosophical Discipline: The Right to Philosophy from the Cosmopolitical Point of View: The Example of an International Institution," trans. Thomas Dutoit, *Surfaces* 4.310 (1994) : par. 15, online, Available FTP: harfang.cc.umontreal.ca/Surfaces/Articles/Ascii/vol14/A_Derrida (ang) .ascii, 15 June 1995.

[4] Ingar Holst, "Language Reform 1907–1958," *How the Norwegian Parliament Banned the National Language*, (N.p: n.p., n.d.) par.4, online, Finnish University and Research Network, Available FTP: nic.funet.fi/pub/culture/text/ingar-holst/murder-of-norw-language, 11 June 1995.

B. Work by Two or More Authors

[5] Andrew Sikula, Sr. and Adelmiro D. Costa, "Are Women More Ethical Than Men?" *Journal of Business Ethics* 13.11 (1994): 859, online, Dialog, *ABI Inform*, 95-78695, 12 June 1995.

- If a work being cited has more than three authors, you can give only the first author's name followed by et al. For example, a work by Barickman, Brew, Day, Kutner, Mardeusz, Reit, Robertson and Ross would be cited as (Jake Barickman et al., "The Music of the Nineteenth. . ."). Or you could cite all of the authors, separating their names by commas.

C. Work by a Corporate Author

[6] United Nations, Fourth World Conference on Women, Beijing, China, 4–15, September 1995, Committee on the Elimination of Discrimination Against Women, *Progress Achieved in the Implementation of the Convention on the Elimination of All Forms of Discrimination Against Women,*

Report by the Committee (12 June 1995) par. 11, online, United Nations Development Programme, Available: gopher://undp.org:70/00/unconfs/women/off/a-7.en, 14 Aug. 1995.

Subsequent References

7 U.N., Fourth World...Women, *Progress*, par. 16.

> • Once a work has been fully documented, the practice is to give subsequent references in a much briefer (but recognizable) form.

8 United Nations, General Assembly, 49th Session, *Resolution 215: Assistance in Mine Clearance* (1995) par. 3, online, United Nations Development Programme, Available: gopher:// undp.org:70/11/undocs/gad/RES/49/9576321E, 1 Aug. 1995.

Subsequent References

9 U.N., Gen. Assem., 49th..., *Resolution 215*, par. 7.

D. Works Listed by Title (No Author Given)

10 "Women of Anabaptist Traditions in Historical Perspective," *Historian's Newsletter* 21 Mar. 1994: par. 6, online, Available E-mail: LISTSERV@ukanvm.cc.ukans.edu/Get histnews_2_9.txt, 21 July 1995.

11 "Regents of the University of California v Bakke," *United States Reports* 438 (1978): 268, online, Mead Lexis, GENFED/US, 11 Aug. 1995.

Subsequent References

12 "Women in Anabaptist... ," par. 4.

13 "Regents ... v Bakke" 269.

E. E-mail and Online Postings

E-mail messages include personal communications between individuals. Online postings include messages appearing on discussion lists and electronic bulletin boards.

14 Martha Day (MDAY@sage.uvm.edu), "Review of Film—*Bad Lieutenant*," E-mail to Xia Li, n. pag., Available E-mail: XLI@moose.uvm.edu, 30 July 1995.

> • No paging ("n. pag") is given for this note.

Subsequent References

15 Martha Day, n. pag.

16 RRECOME, "Top Ten Rules of Film Criticism," 1 Apr. 1995, pars. 2–4, online posting, Available E-mail: CINEMA-L@american.edu, 1 Apr. 1995.

> • RRECOME represents the author's log-in name. If the writer's name cannot be determined, the convention is to present that name in uppercase letters.
> • Several paragraphs (pars.) are being cited in this note.

WORKS CONSULTED

American Psychological Association. *Publication Manual of the American Psychological Association.* 4th ed. Washington, DC: APA, 1994.

Benson, Allen C. *The Complete Internet Companion for Librarians.* New York: Neal-Schuman, 1995.

The Bluebook: A Uniform System of Citation. 15th ed. Cambridge, MA: The Harvard Law Rev. Assn., 1991.

Boe, Tom, Cheryl B. Graubart, and Marge Cappo. *World Desk: A Student Handbook to Gopher and the World-Wide Web.* Santa Cruz, CA: Learning in Motion, 1995.

Directory of Electronic Journals, Newsletters and Academic Discussion Lists (4th ed.), Comp. by Lisabeth A. King and Diane Kovacs. Washington, DC: Assn. of Research Libraries, 1995.

ETEXTCTR. N.d. Online postings. Rutgers U. Available E-mail: LISTSERV@ RUTVM1.RUTGERS.EDU. Discussion list for electronic text centers.

Gale Directory of Databases. 2 vols. Detroit: Gale, Jan. 1995.

Gale Guide to Internet Databases. Detroit: Gale, 1995.

Garner, Diane L., Diane H. Smith, Deborah Cheney, and Helen Sheehy. *The Complete Guide to Citing Government Information Resources: A Manual for Writers & Librarians.* Rev. ed. Bethesda, MD: Congressional Information Service for the Govt. Documents Round Table, ALA, 1993.

Gibaldi, Joseph. *MLA Handbook for Writers of Research Papers.* 4th ed. New York: MLA, 1995.

Hahn, Harley. *The Internet Yellow Pages.* Berkeley, CA: Osborne-McGraw Hill, 1994.

International Organization for Standardization. Technical Committee 46. Subcommittee 9. *ISO/DIS 690-2: Information and Documentation—Bibliographic References—Electronic Documents or Parts Thereof.* Draft standards. Geneva: Intl. Organization for Standardization, 1995.

The Internet Directory. New York: Fawcett Columbine, 1994.

Internet World's on the Internet. Westport, CT: Mecklermedia, 1994.

Li, Xia, and Nancy B. Crane. *Electronic Style: A Guide to Citing Electronic Information.* Westport, CT: Mecklermedia, 1993.

PACS-L. N.d. Online postings. U of Houston Libraries. Available E-Mail: LISTSERV@UHUPVM1.UH.EDU. Public-Access Computer Systems Forum.

Patrias, Karen. "Electronic Information Formats." *National Library of Medicine Recommended Formats for Bibliographic Citation.* Bethesda, MD: Natl. Lib. of Medicine, 1991. 101–162.

Rosa, Alfred, and Paul Eschholz. *The Writer's Brief Handbook.* New York: Macmillan, 1994.

Stout, Neil R. *Getting the Most out of Your U.S. History Course: The History Student's Vade Mecum.* Lexington, MA: D.C. Heath, 1993.

Turabian, Kate L. *A Manual for Writers of Term Papers, Theses, and Dissertations.* Revised and enlarged by Bonnie Birtwistle. 5th ed. Chicago: U of Chicago P, 1987.

University of Chicago Press. *The Chicago Manual of Style.* 14th ed. Chicago: U of Chicago P, 1993.

Index

References are made to entry numbers. Entry numbers are preceded by an "A" for APA and "M" for MLA style citations. Index entries are limited to a reasonable number of examples, usually a maximum of 10 for each citation style.

Other Books of Interest from Information Today, Inc.

Key Guide to Electronic Resources: Health Sciences
Edited by Lee Hancock ($39.50/494pp/ISBN 1-57387-001-3)

Key Guide to Electronic Resources: Agriculture
Edited by Wilfred Drew ($39.50/124pp/ISBN 1-57387-000-5)

CD-ROM Finder, 6th Edition 1995
Kathleen Hogan and James Shelton, Editors ($69.50/520pp/ISBN 0-938734-86-5)

The Electronic Classroom: A Handbook for Education in the Electronic Environment
Edited by Erwin Boschmann ($42.50/240pp/ISBN 0-938734-89-X)

Document Delivery Services: Issues and Answers
By Eleanor Mitchell and Sheila Walters ($42.50/333pp/ISBN 1-57387-003-X)

Multimedia in Higher Education
By Helen Carlson and Dennis R. Falk ($42.50/176pp/ISBN 1-57387-002-1)

CD-ROM for Library Users: A Guide to Managing and Maintaining User Access
Paul Nicholls and Pat Ensor, Editors ($39.50/138 pp/ISBN 0-938734-95-4)

Electronic Image Communications: A Guide to Networking Image Files
By Richard J. Nees ($39.50/95pp/ISBN 0-938734-87-3)

Integated Library Systems for PCs and PC Networks
By Marshall Breeding ($42.50/464 pp/ISBN 1-57387-011-0)

Challenges in Indexing Electronic Text and Images
Raya Fidel, Trudi Bellardo Hahn, Edie Rasmussen, and Philip Smith, Editors
($39.50/316pp/ISBN 0-938734-76-8)

ASIS Thesaurus of Information Science and Librarianship
By Jessica L. Milstead ($34.95/150pp/ISBN 0-938734-80-6)

Directory of Library Automation Software, Systems, and Services
Edited by Pamela Cibbarelli ($69.00/450pp/ISBN 1-57387-021-8)

The Evolving Virtual Library
Edited by Laverna M. Saunders ($39.50/230pp/ ISBN 1-57387-013-7)

Essential Guide to the Library IBM PC: Volume 13
By Marshall Breeding ($34.95/200pp/ISBN 0-88736-188-9)

K-12 Networking: Breaking Down the Walls of the Learning Environment
Edited by Doris Epler ($39.50/190pp/ISBN 0-938734-94-6)

ProCite in Libraries
Edited by Deb Renee Biggs ($39.50/221pp/ISBN 0-938734-90-3)

INNOPAC: A Reference Guide to the System
By Terry Ballard ($39.50/216pp/ISBN 1-57387-015-3)

The Virtual Library: Visions and Realities
Edited by Laverna Saunders ($37.50/180pp/ISBN 0-88736-860-3)

Electronic Journal Literature: Implications for Scholars
By Jan Olsen ($25.00/100pp/ISBN 0-88736-925-1)

Information Management for the Intelligent Organization
By Chun Wei Choo ($39.50/250pp/ISBN 1-57387-018-8)

CD-ROM Book Index
Edited by Ann Niles ($39.50/207pp/ISBN 0-938734-98-9)

Proceedings of the 16th National Online Meeting, May 2-4, 1995
($55.00/448pp/ISBN 1-57387-004-8)

Annual Review of Information Science and Technology, Volume 30
Edited by Martha Williams ($98.50/525pp/ISBN 1-57387-019-6)

To order directly from the publisher, include $3.95 postage and handling for the first book ordered and $3.25 for each additional book. Catalogs also available upon request.

Information Today, Inc., 143 Old Marlton Pike, Medford, NJ 08055, (609)654-6266